HOLLYWOOD
ANDROGYNY

HOLLYWOOD ANDROGYNY

REBECCA BELL-METEREAU

NEW ENGLAND INSTITUTE
OF TECHNOLOGY
LEARNING RESOURCES CENTER

Second Edition

New York   COLUMBIA UNIVERSITY PRESS

Columbia University Press

New York   Chichester, Sussex

Copyright © 1993 Columbia University Press
All rights reserved

Library of Congress Cataloging-in-Publication Data

Bell-Metereau, Rebecca.
Hollywood androgyny
Rebecca Bell-Metereau.
—2d ed.

p.   cm.

Includes bibliographical references and index.

ISBN 0-231-08467-6

1. Female impersonators in motion pictures.
2. Male impersonators in motion pictures.
3. Sex role in motion pictures.
4. Motion pictures—United States—History.
I. Title.
PN1995.9.I43B45   1993
791.43'028—dc20
93-8321
CIP

p 10 9 8 7 6 5 4 3 2

Casebound editions of Columbia University Press
books are printed on permanent and durable acid-free
paper.

Printed in the United States of America

Thanks to
James Naremore and other friends
for advice and support
and to
Jean-Pierre Metereau for everything

Thanks to
James Naremore and other friends
for advice and support
and to
Jean-Pierre Metereau for everything

Contents

Preface to the Second Edition

The first edition of *Hollywood Androgyny* came out in 1985, when the society at large was beginning to develop an awareness of the issues of gender, sexuality, and sexual orientation. The AIDS epidemic was gaining public attention, and homosexual and other lifestyles began to enter public discourse for the first time in the history of the United States. Once the possibility of alternative gender roles impinged on the consciousness of mainstream culture, the film industry followed with an explosion of movies about gays, lesbians, masculine women, feminine men, and every nuance in between. In 1993, President Bill Clinton made history by calling for an end to the ban on homosexuals in the military. Such changes caused controversy and anxiety, part of which was displaced to the popular art forms of film and television. Regardless of viewers' attitudes toward the subject, everyone found something of interest in the play of new and startling images, reworking old stereotypes in a filmic exploration of repressed desires and suppressed anxieties. Films allow viewers to work through these impulses in the semidarkness of the movie theater, through vicarious role-playing that is seldom allowed in the course of daily life.

Dressing up and role playing constitute a major element of childhood play. The ludic aspect of watching and vicariously participating in such play is no doubt one of the film viewer's prime sources of pleasure in movies featuring cross-dressing. Attempts to be a different kind of person, to distinguish oneself from others, is fundamental to human nature. Everyone has experienced the negative aspects of being an outsider, as well as the private desire to be special—different in some positive way. Most clothing, language, and gestures, simultaneously fulfill both desires to be different and to bond with others. Society teaches children to speak and understand this code from birth, but along the way from infancy to adulthood, children quickly learn the seriousness of the games they play, as Marjorie Garber observes in *Vested Interests: Cross-Dressing and Cultural Anxiety:*

> Vestimentary codes, clothing as a system of signification, speak in a number of registers: class, gender, sexuality, erotic style. Part of the problem—and part of the pleasure and danger of decoding—is in determining which set of referents is in play in each scenario. For decoding itself is an erotics—in fact, one of the most powerful we know. But any erotics is also anxiety producing, and this kind of cultural and political anxiety often has real and adverse consequences for those who are testing the boundaries. The difficulty, the challenge, the interest posed by the complex interrelationship between transvestism and gay identity lie in simultaneously tracking the dissemination of the signifiers of sex and gender and in combating the oppressive effects of institutionalized binarity. For in political and social terms, in the lives of real people, male and female, straight and gay, there is no "free play of the signifier." There is play, plenty of play, but ultimately nothing—and especially not sexual life-styles—is free. [1]

The explosion of women's studies and gay and lesbian studies that occurred in the eighties and nineties produced books that problematized the "normal" or "natural" sense of gender identity as it had never been done before. Charlotte Brunsdon's *Films for Women*, Teresa de Lauretis' *Alice Doesn't: Feminism, Semiotics, Cinema*, Homer Dickens' *What a Drag: Men as Women and Women as Men in the Movies*, Lucy Fischer's *Shot Countershot*, Marjorie Garber's *Vested Interests: Cross-dressing and Cultural Anxiety*, Boze Hadley's *The Lavender Screen*, Annette Kuhn's *The Power of the Image: Essays on Representation and Sexuality*, Constance Penley's *The Future of an Illusion: Film, Feminism, and Psychoanalysis*, Vito Russo's revised work, *The Celluloid Closet: Homosexuality in the Movies*, Chris Straayer's *Deviant Spectators: Homosexual Discourse and Film/Video*, and Linda Williams' *Hard Core: Power, Pleasure and the Frenzy of the Visible*, are but a few of the works detailing role reversals and gender definitions, as portrayed in American and international films.

In looking at what constitutes "natural" differences between the sexes, one must also consider economic factors affecting behavior, as Katha Pollit observes in the *Nation:*

> In *The Mismeasure of Woman,* her trenchant and witty attack on contemporary theories of gender differences, Carol Tavris points out that much of what can be said about women applies as well to poor people, who also tend to focus more on family and relationships and less on work and self-advancement; to behave deferentially with those more socially powerful; and to appear to others more emotional and "intuitive" than rational and logical in their thinking.[2]

Tavris' work points to a natural common ground in the attitudes and interests of groups that have been traditionally disenfranchised, disempowered, or "disappeared" by the entertainment industry and the larger culture.

Changes in demographics and labor conditions affect the production of images, but often film presents reversals rather than one-to-one correlations between images and social realities. Film portrayals of "career women" offer an example of this phenomenon. The screen of the eighties and nineties features working women in such mainstream films as *Protocol* (1984), *Baby Boom* (1987), *Broadcast News* (1987), *Fatal Attraction* (1987), *Surrender* (1987), *Crossing Delancey* (1988), and *Working Girl* (1988). Through their plots and subtexts the vast majority of popular films encourage women to return to the home to have children, as in *Immediate Family* (1989) and *Parenthood* (1989). The contrasting images of battling domesticity or postdivorce bitterness in *Shoot the Moon* (1982), *The Good Father* (1987), *She-Devil* (1989), *Sea of Love* (1989), *The War of the Roses* (1989), *I Love You to Death* (1990), and *Sleeping with the Enemy* (1991) offer a nightmare alternative, with a woman often acting as the culprit, sacrificing home and her husband's happiness for her own "selfish" career ambitions.

Despite the push to traditionalize or marginalize nontraditional women, in what Susan Faludi terms a backlash against feminist gains, the film industry was, nevertheless, profoundly influenced by the demands of women, gays, lesbians, and people of color. Major companies like Walt Disney Studios found themselves rethinking their depiction of female animated characters in order to create an acceptably strong female and a sufficiently gentle male, thus acknowledging the growing popularity of androgyny in both sexes.[3] At the same time, however, when a film like *Thelma and Louise* (1991) featured two women shooting a rapist and going on a crime spree, the supposed reversal was so jarring that it caused a wave of unprecedented controversy.

The AIDS epidemic also had a profound effect on the entertainment industry, forcing more and more performers to address publicly their sexual orientation, beginning with Rock Hudson.[4] Movies tried to respond to the issue by portraying the tragic consequences of AIDS, not just among the homosexual and lesbian communities, but in the heterosexual population as well. A growing acceptance of AIDS sufferers and of gay and lesbian lifestyles in general coincided with the increase in films on the topic. A speech given by Shirley MacLaine at the Aids Project Los Angeles Benefit offers evidence of the entertainment world's growing acceptance of alterity: "Tonight was the first night of the end of the jive," declared Shirley MacLaine. "This party is for every man, every woman, and everyone who happily chooses to blur the distinction."[5] *Premiere* magazine notes that at the 1992 Academy Awards, Debra Chasnoff "didn't do any one-arm pushups, but the winner of the Academy Award for Best Documentary—Short Subject seems to have been the first Oscar winner ever to thank her 'life partner' (Kim Klausner) and to dance with her at the Governor's Ball."[6]

Any survey of recent literature in gender in film must acknowledge the explosion of gay and lesbian studies—a movement away from binary interpretations and paradigms—and continuing efforts to come to terms with violence in film, particularly in conjunction with women, homosexual, and lesbian figures, and the marginalization of women in film, a reaction thoroughly documented in the larger culture by Susan Faludi's *Backlash*. The decade also witnessed the simultaneous emergence of the female buddy film, particularly in the spectacular success of *Thelma and Louise,* along with a small but growing market in "women's pictures" such as *Fried Green Tomatoes* (1991) and *A League of Their Own* (1992). Feminist film scholarship has progressed in stages, first through the phase of documenting the marginalization and objectification of females in much of classic Hollywood cinema. These critics called for an alternative cinema, found among underground, gay, lesbian, and feminist filmmakers. The next phase of criticism encouraged rereading of mainstream film texts, against the grain, to posit a subtext that may be interpreted differently by marginalized groups, including women, gays, lesbians, cross-dressers, and a variety of ethnic or social minorities.

While an undertsanding of the "otherness" of these groups was instrumental in arriving at new ways of viewing mainstream films and valuing nontraditional film forms, critics soon realized that in taking on the category of otherness, one often continued to view the film text in terms of the dominant paradigm. For example, women in film who behaved in stereotypically masculine ways—active, brave, heroic, etc.—were valorized, because their actions fit the traditional model of a male hero. The alternative to this binary model became a third space, another nongendered norm which blurred the distinctions and celebrated the "slippage" of category terms. Characters who experience growth or transformation, or who demonstrate resoluteness, for example, offer normative nongendered behavior models that may include both ends of the gender spectrum and everything in between. Marjorie Garber encourages critics to reexamine the categories of gender that may have been taken for granted:

> But, as we will see, the distinction is not always an easy one to make; the borderline between gender and sexuality so important to much recent feminist and gender theory is one of the many boundaries tested and queried by the transvestite. The cultural effect of transvestism is to destabilize all such binaries: not only "male" and "female," but also "gay" and "straight," and "sex" and "gender." This is the sense—the radical sense—in which transvestism is a "third."[7]

Women have had a strong voice recognizing the "third" categories: Pauline Kael and Judith Crist and later Marjorie Rosen, Joan Mellen, Molly Haskell, Teresa de Lauretis, and Laura Mulvey,[8] to name only a few. Teresa de Lauretis identifies two strains of response among the critics who focus on gender: "one called for immediate documentation for purposes of political activism, consciousness-raising, self-expression or the search for 'positive images' of women; the other insisted on rigorous, formal work on the medium—or better, the cinematic apparatus, understood as a social technology—in order to analyse and disengage the ideological codes embedded in representation."[9] Regardless of their theoretical stance, all of these critics have focused on viewer identification and the depiction of gender as issues central to any discussion of film.

Answering the question of whether or not one likes a film often turns into a quesiotn of how much one likes the "self" one identifies with, as imaged on screen. Identification with that image is so deep, however, that viewers often forget that it is, after all, only a movie, at least in the sense that it is "made-up." In another sense, film is a dynamic, negotiated "reality" created by individual viewer and culture as well as by the filmmaker. Currently, feminists in film and other disciplines are, as Catherine E. Huchison puts it, "trying to come to grips with their own complicity with the very power they are trying to deconstruct,"[10] with the decentering process of self-critique at the slightly-off-center of that struggle.

Throughout its history, feminist film criticism has had two tempting yet unproductive roads to avoid. The first wanders through self-defeating and ultimately monotonous catalogues of ways in which movies exploit and portray the exploitation of women. The alternative path, although perhaps more soothing to the nerves and temper, yields little more than a comforting list of superheroines, seldom viewed avant-garde filmmakers, and reinterpretations of classic films with supposedly radical feminist subtexts. These two routes hold the similar virtue of being accessible to practically anyone, but they neglect basic questions of methodology. One of the most significant controversies to arise during the eighties was a division between "difference" feminists, such as Nancy Chodorow (*The Reproduction of Mothering*) and Carol Gilligan (*In a Different Voice*), on the left, to essentialists like Camille Paglia (*Sexual Personae: Art and Decadence from Nefertiti to Emily Dickenson*), on the right, and "equality" feminists, such as Susan Faludi (*Backlash*), Katha Pollitt ("Are Women Morally Superior to Men?"), and Carol Tavris (*The Mismeasure of Woman*), and mediators between the two, such as Jean Bethke Elshtain (*Meditations on Modern Political Thought: Masculine-Feminine Themes from Luther to Arendt*).

If we look beneath these apparently disparate foci at the mechanism operating in these responses, we find a similar structure. Viewers tend to dislike films that make them feel bad, and they tend to like those that make them feel good. Once this assumption is acknowledged, the more interesting questions lie in examining why and how a film makes particular viewers feel good. Understanding comes from looking at the mechanisms of this supposedly symbiotic relationship between product and consumer, at what economic, social, and class interests are served by peddling particular images contained within a given movie. Capitalist enterprise caters to women's and men's fantasies in their roles as consumers or, for a brief period, as subjects or objects of sexual desire. In film, this shows up as a heightening or glamorizing of those traits that contribute to vigorous economic activity—primarily buying the film, but also buying the makeup that gives women the heroine's looks or, for men, the cigarette that the leading man smokes, as well as the concessions that viewers munch on, the T-shirts that teenagers see in clothing stores, the mugs that housewives see in grocery stores, and the tie-in toys, games, books and breakfast cereals that children see advertised on television cartoons. Acknowledging the influence of market demands on film production, Pat Aufderheide observes, "In academe especially, it's easy to forget the concrete, and instead to sink into a morass of dense speculations on such abstract critical concepts as The Other, The Spectacle, resistance, empowerment and postmodern consciousness." Aufderheide goes on to suggest that "would-be analysts of popular culture tend to slight the most important shaping force behind commercial popular culture: the economics of entertainment businesses."[11] While this analysis includes a few Others and a nod to spectacle, empowerment, and postmodern fragmentation, the methodology is fairly simple, often including consideration of the commercial appeal and marketing of movies.

Filmmakers and producers attempt to attune their product to the needs of the individual and the marketplace. For example, a spate of films about twins, siblings, or parent-child confusion of identities (both male and female) answers not only personal fantasies of wishing to be two very different people at once—nurturing and ruthless, or carefree and responsible, or innocent and savvy—but also speaks to the dual demands of the labor pool for individuals who demonstrate practically mutually exclusive traits. Both women and men must be hard-nosed, productive workers on the job and compassionate, family-centered breeders of new consumers on the homefront. Viewers generally enjoy seeing images that validate what they experience in life, making them feel that the problems they suffer and the dreams they aspire to are more glamorous than they had thought. As Anthony Burgess and Stanley Kubrick's Alex notes in *A Clockwork Orange*, "It's funny how the colors of the like real world only seem really real when you viddy them on the screen." [12] The danger in this phenomenon is that viewers may begin to accept the images they view in film as being more "real" than the facts of daily life. Also, the sets of images are not coherent or consistent, from film to film, nor even within a single film. As Jackie Byars observes, "They are not simple texts; they are not ideologically coherent, nor are they monolithically repressive. They are participants in an ongoing ideological process; real ideological struggle goes on in theory as well." [13]

Indeed, many critics battle for changes in film content on the basis of their influence on perceptions of everyday life. Critics such as Lynn Spangler argue that positive images of women "have the power to make us feel good about ourselves and each other," [14] and are therefore good. Conversely, countless people, ranging from right-wing born-again Christians to left-wing radical feminists, call for elimination of filmic violence or images of women as sex objects and victims, with the same justification that films affect behavior and attitudes. The problem with such thinking is that it attributes magical properties to film, for it assumes that destroying the hated image or symbol will eradicate the evil itself. Christian Metz describes this phenomenon in "The Film and Its Spectator" as "reality confusion," or mistaking representations for perceptions. [15] Many of the "offensive" movies that angry, confused viewers wish to censor are made by the same filmmakers who try to highlight and denounce objectification and victimization of human beings.

Experts estimate that in the United States a woman is battered every eighteen seconds, and some would argue that films like *A Clockwork Orange* (1971), *Blue Velvet* (1986), or *Thelma and Louise* perpetuate these actions by spurring imitative behavior or by inuring people to violence.[16] Some fundamentalists fear that exposing their children to images of sex role reversal will encourage homosexuality or lesbianism. Viewer squeamishness about witnessing such scenes in the film world arises again from magical thinking—that acting on an imagistic or symbolic level produces concrete results in the mundane physical world. This belief comes from the same source as does their unwillingness to take concrete action to end violence against women. Their reactions stem from a sense of powerlessness, deeply ingrained in a culture that downplays the might of collective action.[17] Dazzling images of lone (usually male) heroes bombard the public, overshadowing or concealing the enormous influence of consumer opinion. Film images generally maximize the isolation of individuals and minimize the need to effect social change. The viewer's romance with the image must not be violated by disturbing emotions, connections to the outside world, or self-reflexive devices that call attention to the underpinnings of film as a fantasy creation rather than a mirror reflection of life.

Woman holds a special place in this schema, for she is both the consumer and the commodity. Film's connections with commerce are sometimes as obvious as a day's shooting being paid for by proper presentation of a Pepsi or Frigidaire logo for ten seconds in a corner of the screen. Because of the more elaborate sartorial coding involved in female dress, makeup, and hairstyle, producers and directors pay even greater attention to featuring the female in the center of the frame, presenting both products and self (another constructed product) in the most flattering way. The advantageous presentation of the female form and wardrobe therefore takes precedence over demands for realism, historicity, or anatomical verisimilitude. The female's position as a commodity affects her portrayal and placement in film in countless ways. As a product whose image is to be admired and emulated, a woman usually receives brighter, more filtered light. The woman is much less likely to be dirty or messy—unless she is attractively tousled. The female form is rarely subjected to violence (contrary to popular wisdom), and its notable absence in films (even those made long after Hays code strictures have vanished) has trained viewer to find the image shocking when it does occur. (Even the notorious "slasher" films usually have male victims or focus on the build-up to and aftermath of violence toward females, not on the act itself.)

If people did imitate the models presented in film to the extent that some suggest, we would have practically no abuse of women or children. Those instances in which the camera clearly shows a woman or child being struck are rarities that spark an outcry—*The Deer Hunter* (1978), *A Clockwork Orange, Blue Velvet*—and films in which women commit violence, such as *Extremities* (1986), *Fatal Attraction* (1987), or *Thelma and Louise,* arouse genuine fear and loathing in many of the viewers who watch them. Considering the actual rarity of physical violence against women in film (as compared to its frequency in everyday life), one should question not its presence on film, but its relative absence. Movies do portray males, on the other hand, as both victims and perpetrators on a massive scale, but these aggressive acts are usually sanitized and accepted as normal. Such scenes of physical aggression appear shocking if gender roles are reversed—when it is women delivering and being victimized by the blows, gashes, gunshots, kicks, stabs, and car crashes. If the victims, effects, and appearance of violence were played with anything approaching realism, viewers might be jolted out of their complacency and call for a halt to such behavior, both on- and off-screen.

Films do not often do this, of course, for they are products made for people who, for the most part, wish to make money selling an image that has been tested, negotiated, edited, revised, and reformulated to be as close as possible to what its creators think the greatest number of people want to see and be. If women feel powerless, they want to see themselves as protected and privileged. When movies like *Blue Velvet, A Clockwork Orange,* or *Thelma and Louise* violate the tacit code of consensus established by audiences and filmmakers, many viewers respond with outrage. Viewers do not wish to be made uncomfortable by films. Questions of gender often mask issues of power, class, and economics. This work attempts to analyze what films make viewers comfortable, what fantasies and fears speak to whom, and why certain exceptional films fascinate audiences with their ability to expand or even break the boundaries in ways that redefine what it means to be normal.

Instances of cross-dressing or sexual role reversal are particularly effective in demonstrating the murkiness of gender distinctions. Darrell Yates Rist, in replying to letters in the *Nation,* describes the fluidity of sexual categories:

> In the early ecstatic days of the 1970s and early 1980s, I knew countless men who would have told you that they were exclusively homosexual in both behavior and desire, who nonetheless found themselves in passionate relationships with women on the gay playground of Fire Island or in the balcony of the Saint, the old gay dance palace with corners for sex. I know men who are usually heterosexual who sometimes seek sex with men as long as their partner is *dressed* as a woman. And I know primarily heterosexual cross-dressers who, when they are in feminine dress, enjoy man-to-man sex, imagining it as a heterosexual. . . . And in my own once-liberal sexual play—when I was young—I experienced vast numbers of random men whose fantasies, during the very act, changed genders frequently, as did mine. Could it be that I am only acquainted with aberrations and am aberrant myself? And in all of this debate it would be wise to remember that masturbation, which only the fewest of human beings have not greedily practiced, is essentially a homosexual act." [18]

This kind of analysis makes many people distinctly uncomfortable, but then, any sort of change causes anxiety until people become accustomed to a new look or image for a particular category. The film or television image acts as one of the primary purveyors of such change, by making a particular new "look" acceptable or admirable (even though these do not carry the "magical power" discussed earlier). While films do not have the power to change behavior magically—overnight—images do play an important role in affecting attitudes, which may eventually influence behavior. Garber notes how styles, particularly those connected with gender identification, alter drastically over time, describing the female Stephen Gordon's hatred of her relatively boyish physical appearance:

> Yet re-read from the perspective of the 1990's, Stephen Gordon's anguished glance in the mirror offers an object lesson in histori-

cal relativism, for the monstrous body of 1928 is the ideal female body of the fitness generation. Cropped hair, menswear suits, thin flanks—these are not only the signature characteristics of "cross-dressed" entertainment figures like Annie Lennox or k.d. lang or Madonna, but also the high-style looks of the mainstream fashion magazines since the sixties. Stephen Gordon's tragic difference has crossed over into heterosexual style. [19]

She goes on to note a similar shift in what was once unacceptable for men, in the example of Quentin Crisp, who, in the 1920's and 1930's "wore makeup at a time when even on women eyeshadow was sinful," while in the nineties, "for example, even the most conservative straight politicians now wear makeup on camera—and sometimes off. Senator Strom Thurmond of South Carolina dyes his hair and applies eyeliner to his hairline; Senator John Warner of Virginia, the former spouse of Elizabeth Taylor, insists on doing his own makeup for television." [20] These examples offer but a few of the most striking proofs of the arbitrariness of particular types of dress or body configuration as a signifier of gender or sexual orientation.

One of the main questions in analyzing specific films is the extent to which the narrative, performances, and direction actually explore sexual variation and fathom the protean essence of androgyny. The approach to the films in this book is eclectic, for the films of different periods, styles, and intended audiences call for a variety of observations. In the discussion of men dressed as women before 1960, I have concentrated on the contrast between two key films, Howard Hawks' *I Was a Male War Bride* (1949) and Billy Wilder's *Some Like It Hot* (1959), two works at opposite ends of the spectrum in popular comedies before 1960. *Bride* reflects a paranoid, closed vision of role reversal, and *Hot* offers a refreshingly liberating, open vehicle for experimentation in sexual exchanges. The section on women dressed as men before 1960 analyzes representative films from a range of types, including the historical masculine heroine, the cowgirl, the career woman, the tomboy buddy, and the cabaret entertainer. The contrast between Katherine Hepburn and Marlene Dietrich highlights two points of origin for cross-dressing (for men as well as for women)—and Anglo-British type and the exotic, European (often Germanic) type. Although this appears to be a somewhat facile distinction, the vast majority of cross-dressing films presented to American audiences fall under one or the other category. Most light, comic films derive from the British dramatic, public school, and music hall traditions, while dark, often more threatening role reversals come out of smoke-filled cabarets—what many Americans see as the European dens of corruption and perversion.

The final three chapters on the last thirty years deal with male and female impersonation, examining in some detail a dramatic series of developments that have taken place over a relatively brief time span. This closing section of the second edition of *Hollywood Androgyny* explores the various types of female and male impersonation to develop with the easing of censorship, the growing AIDS epidemic, and the change in attitudes toward sex roles and sexuality in general.

1. Marjorie Garber, *Vested Interests: Cross-Dressing and Cultural Anxiety.* (New York: Routledge, 1992), p. 161.

2. Katha Pollitt, "Are Women Morally Superior to Men?" *Nation,* December 28, 1992, pp. 799–807.

3. Steve Daly, "Disney's Got a Brand-New Baghdad," *Entertainment Weekly,* December 4, 1992, pp. 14–20.

4. Boze Hadleigh, "Scared Straight," *American Film,* January–February 1987, pp. 47–51.

5. Malissa Thompson, "People Who Need People," *Premiere,* February 1993, p. 38.

6. "The Hits: *Premiere*'s 1992 Wrap Party," *Premiere,* Feburary 1993, p. 78.

7. Garber, *Vested,* p. 133.

8. "For Mulvey, women in narrative and film are the object of a fixation and obsession associated with male spectatorial desires, especially voyeurism and fetishism, and female spectators must oscillate between a passive feminine position and a regressive but active masculine position that allows them to engage with the film narrative. These positions results in an uncomfortable 'transvestism.' " Gorham A. Kindem, "Norway's New Generation of Women Directors: Anja Breien, Vibeke Lokkeberg, and Laila Mikkelsen," *The Journal of Film and Video* (Fall 1987), 39(4):34.

9. Teresa de Lauretis, "Aesthetic and Feminist Theory: Rethinking Women's Cinema," in E. Deidre Pribram, ed., *Female Spectators* (London: Verso, 1988), p. 175.

10. Christine Gledhill, "Recent Developments in Feminist Criticism," *Quarterly Review of Film Studies* (1978) no. 4, pp. 457–93.

11. Pat Aufderheide, "Pop Culture in Perspective," *In These Times,* January 29, 1993, p. 34.

12. Anthony Burgess, *A Clockwork Orange* (New York: Norton), p. 103.

13. Jackie Byars, "Gazes/Voices/Power: Expanding Psychoanalysis for Feminist Film and Television Theory," in E. Deidre Pribram, ed., *Female Spectators* (London: Verso, 1988), p. 112.

14. Gledhill, "Recent Developments."

15. Christian Metz, "The Film and Its Spectator," *Literature and Film Quarterly* (Fall 1987), 15-3:181–89.

16. M. Joyce Ewing and James Windell, *The Misunderstood Crime,* Minerva Press, 1986; Senate Hearings, 1987, 1990.

17. An exception to this tendency may be seen in fundamentalists' skill in organizing boycotts, demonstrations, or calling campaigns.

18. Darrell Yates Rist, "Rist Replies," *Nation,* January 25, 1993, p. 104.

19. Garber, *Vested,* p. 136.

20. Garber, *Vested,* p. 138.

CHAPTER ONE

AN OVERVIEW

"**D**ON'T YOU FIND it confusing being a woman in the '80s?" Jessica Lange asks Dustin Hoffman in *Tootsie,* one of the most popular films of 1982. Indeed, confusion is a key ingredient in films that explore sex role reversals, and audiences seem to delight in Hollywood's forays into the androgynous zone. A popular assumption in feminist film criticism is that American movie depictions of male and female roles restrict women to a small range of types while allowing male characters a full variety of dramatic possibilities. Defiance of society's gender definitions is comparatively rare, but films that feature role reversals and employ cross-dressing[1] violently contradict audience preconceptions about male and female identities; the identification of certain dress and behavior with sexual and social status is deep.

Cross-dressing might seem to be an oddity, but in fact more than two hundred films employ the motif either as a key feature in a crucial scene or as the pivotal element of the narrative. Cross-dressing may vary widely in function from film to film, but it invariably draws attention to the concepts of masculinity and femininity. As many critics have observed, males are usually the central force of the narrative, with their status an extension of this domination. In spite of, or perhaps because of, this standard male supremacy, the evidence shows that women are much freer than men to explore emotions and character types, from wilting flower to stoic martinet.

Role reversals and cross-dressing in films follow peaks that correspond to periods of greater experimentation in the society at large. During the pre–Hays Code era and the late sixties there seemed to be a general trend toward experimentation and toward rejection of confining sex roles. In contrast, in the era following World War II the motif was seen negatively, reflecting the society's attempt to regress to prewar conventions. Certainly the most dramatic change in cross-dressing films has occurred within the last twenty years because of the almost total lifting of censorship, a trend that may have begun to reverse itself. After Billy Wilder's innovative *Some Like It Hot* (1959) and Alfred Hitchcock's shocker *Psycho* (1960) female impersonation blossomed in an amazing variety of types ranging from the psychotic granny to the beautiful young siren. Male impersonation, on the other hand, almost dropped from the screen, its relative absence being, in part, a consequence of the fact that women now wear pants in everyday life. Indeed, many films that depict women in what had been traditionally male roles are no longer actual reversals; they are simply reflections of changing economic and social realities. Nevertheless, the critical response to a film like Ridley Scott's *Alien* (1979) indicates that these changes may not be so readily accepted as many would like to believe.

The shift in the status of women is mirrored in the change in depictions of female impersonation, the distortions in these images disclosing the anxiety with which changes have been greeted by many men. The objects of the sixties' and seventies' impersonators are no longer the sweet, harmless matrons of the thirties, forties, and fifties films. In the past two decades, male characters have generally impersonated female figures of power. The decrease in male impersonation and the increase in female impersonation coincide with an apparent rise in prestige for women within society. The nature of female impersonation has changed drastically, becoming much more explicit sexually and possibly more threatening. When censorship bans were lifted, previously covert connections between female impersonation and homosexuality suddenly became overt, populating the screen with all the varieties of impersonators that exist in real life. Male characters were no longer restricted to imitations of the dowdy, powerless little old ladies of *Charley's Aunt;* they could branch out into more aggressive, if often more frightening, versions of womankind.

Almost all cross-dressing films involve the relationship between authority and freedom—the extent to which the male is free to explore his female nature and the extent to which female characters are capable of establishing their own authority. These films also explore the individual's confrontation with "the Other." Imitation of the otherness of the female arouses curiosity, desire, fear, and even loathing in male characters within such films. When a film concentrates on the comic aspects, as did the majority of films before 1960, the ultimate movement is toward reconciling dichotomies between playful curiosity and obsessive fear. In the majority of films of the past twenty years, female impersonation has taken on the darker hue of psychosis. The imitation of male characteristics generally results in increased freedom, sexual appeal, power, or prestige for the woman, but if this change results in loss of status for the male, it is usually punished. This is particularly true of films of the fifties, in which tomboys and mannish women had to learn how to be feminine in order to be accepted by the society of the film world. The last twenty years have seen, along with a decline in male impersonation, a marked absence of female characters in comparison with earlier films. Many films of the past two decades that do include female characters are fraught with unprecedented violence and hostility toward women.

Here it is important to make a distinction often overlooked by feminist critics looking for sexist overtones in Hollywood films. A film that presents a likable yet powerless woman is no less sexist than a film that presents a despicable yet powerful woman; in fact, the latter film may carry a heavy misogynist message while implying superiority of females over males. The cross-dressing films of the sixties follow this pattern of misogyny and fear of the powerful female, but in the mid-seventies an interesting change occurs. For the first time, female impersonators become sympathetic characters—occasionally comic, yet no longer the figures of derision or harmless ridicule. In characters as dissimilar as Zaza of *La Cage aux folles* (1978) and Frank-N-Furter in *The Rocky Horror Picture Show* (1975) we find a common link in their ability to capture the affection of audiences through wit and a peculiar brand of bitchy charm.

The contrast between the likable drag queens of the seventies and matrons of the thirties, forties, and fifties points to two major categories of female impersonation, and to a vocabulary that serves as an excellent vehicle for analysis: the jargon of the homosexual and transvestite subcultures. This language is appropriate not because all cross-dressing necessarily indicates such impulses on the part of the directors, actors, or audiences, but because the terms work most effectively to describe cross-dressing in films. Just as we look to the Eskimo for refined terms describing snow or to Arabic for different qualities of sand, we may look to the homosexual and transvestite worlds for the specialized vocabulary of those who have reason to make fine distinctions in describing sexual impersonation. (It should be acknowledged that a not inconsiderable number of the directors and actors involved in cross-dressing films do have more than a passing interest in this social milieu.)

The distinction between the homosexual drag queen and the true transvestite is valuable even in a discussion of films that purport to feature "normal," circumstantially enforced cross-dressing for comic effect. Most transvestites deny any homosexual impulses, often avoiding the campy glamor that marks the drag queen. They claim to like women and relate to feminine concerns, a posture that explains the title of the transvestite journal *The Male Feminist*. Homosexual female impersonators are equally anxious to avoid association with heterosexual transvestism, and they frown on those who wear ladies' underwear or conservative feminine attire as being too much like ordinary women, whose status is low in comparison to the glamorous movie stars the drag queens imitate. In *Mother Camp* Esther Newton describes a stage situation that highlights this social differentiation:

> Another street-oriented boy, who was very much disliked by the other performers, and who had only been working for a few weeks, had outfitted himself largely with skirts and blouses. The emcee began to criticize this, saying his appearance was too transy. Soon the boy was in a state of some anxiety about it, and before he would go on stage he would nervously ask anyone who was standing around, "Does this look too transy?" to which they would always reply, "Yes." When I asked one of the older performers what this meant, he said it meant the boy's drag looked "too much like a real woman. It's not showy enough. No woman would go on stage looking like that."[2]

The homosexual impersonator's desire is to imitate a woman of power and prestige, a professional performer rather than a "real woman." The homosexual drag queen differs from the heterosexual transvestite not just in appearance but also in his attitude toward wearing the clothing, and in attitudes toward women in general. Transvestites often report liking the feel of feminine clothing, of being restricted, bound, and protected, often so much so that they wear women's underwear under their male clothing during the day. Homosexual female impersonators have as their main goal to be admired, but they generally report getting no thrill simply from wearing restrictive female clothing after their initial experiments. They are, rather, attracted to images of powerful, glamorous women or witty "bitches," following models of beauty and "camp."

In most films before 1959, men were imitating at least a caricature of the real woman of the society of that time—a sweet, rather sexless being who offered shelter from the aggressive competition of the male world. Billy Wilder's daring *Some Like It Hot,* in which the "women" are young and reasonably attractive, was a harbinger of change; Hitchcock then undermined the supposed harmlessness of the little old lady impersonator with *Psycho* in 1960. Impersonating a woman involves anxiety over loss of power, because it means that the male must identify with a typically lower-status figure. As one homosexual impersonator puts it:

> female impersonation is so involved with the transvestite thing that we all fear. Basically there is always that "I am a woman" or "I am my mother" thing. The first time I got in drag I must have jerked off five times with the feeling, "at last I have become mother."[3]

For the transvestite, identification with a woman is comforting rather than threatening because he does not have the accompanying hostility and fear of women that many homosexuals confess.

Although the identification with the mother may be stronger for the homosexual, it may be argued that the same kind of love/ hate relationship exists for so-called normal males. Leslie Fiedler argues that the counterculture of the late sixties and early seven-

ties placed a premium on the development of traditionally feminine characteristics in males:

> In a postindustrialist society the obsolescence of the dis-
> tinctively male functions—making things, making money, mak-
> ing war—had induced a radical metamorphosis of the Western
> male. Freed from the need to be Puritans, all around us, young
> males are beginning to retrieve for themselves the cavalier role
> once . . . surrendered to women: that of being beautiful and
> being loved. The source of alienation and therefore of the counter-
> culture, was the combination of emotional, dominating mothers
> with fathers who were seen as weak and uninterested. The coun-
> terculture, if this theory has any validity, may have drawn many
> of its recruits from the same psychological backgrounds that have
> classically produced homosexuals. . . .[4]

The hostility toward women then arises from the fact that in
female-dominated homes, it is actually the woman who is the
authority figure against whom the young man wishes to rebel.
Raymond Durgnat argues in a similar vein:

> The paradox of the American soul is that a strongly competitive,
> Puritan ethic, whose principles, for all the mitigating effects of a
> subsequent "fun morality" are, in their stern, simple imperatives,
> "masculine." Yet they are imposed by women, who thus become
> not so much the indulgent member of the family, as the taskmas-
> ter.[5]

The function of female impersonation in films changed as the
images of real women in society changed. What had served as
refuge from the male world, the protective mother figure, began
to turn into a domineering discipline figure soon after World War
II. By the beginning of the sixties, the point of view expressed in
most cross-dressing films was much closer to the anxiety-ridden
hostility described by Fiedler and Durgnat than to the fun-loving
stage impersonations of vaudeville, the British music hall, and
the public school and dramatic traditions. In order to understand
recent incidences of female impersonation in film, it may be most
profitable to regard them in terms of their appeal for gay audiences.

Female impersonations connected with or appreciated by the gay community are those that depict strong women. Their strength may come from their beauty, clothing, and pronounced feminine characteristics, or it may stem from their biting wit and verbal adeptness. In the seventies the screen became populated by a series of glamorous female impersonators whose way had been paved by the introduction of homosexuality to public art theaters in the sixties. *The Queen* (1968) featured a drag Miss America contest, and *Midnight Cowboy* (1969) introduced a naïve Jon Voigt and an unsuspecting audience to the realities of gay female impersonators. *Death in Venice* (1971) and Fellini's *Satyricon* (1971) featured beautiful boys, made up just enough to highlight their loveliness and enhance their homosexual allure. *Cabaret* (1972) includes a gay female impersonator passing as female to seduce a rich businessman, and in *Freebie and the Bean* (1974) the effectiveness of Christopher Morley in his impersonation of an attractive young woman is a key element in fooling characters within the film as well as the audience. Even as early as 1961, the entire plot of *Homicidal* relies on the completely undetectable female impersonation performed by Jean Arless; after the close of the film the audience is still left wondering whether Jean Arless is a man or a woman. In *The Rose* (1979), one of the relatively few joyful moments takes place in a bar where men are doing imitations of Elizabeth Taylor, Marlene Dietrich, Joan Crawford, and even Bette Midler.

In the seventies well-known actors tried their hand at female impersonation, adding a certain respectability to the routine, or a certain tarnish to their own images, depending on one's point of view. Marlon Brando's wearing of a granny dress and sunbonnet as the regulator in *Missouri Breaks* (1976) gave him another way to thumb his nose at the establishment, while establishing a chilling image of the gun-toting, puritanical matriarch of vengeance. Yul Brynner's rendition of "Mad About the Boy" in *The Magic Christian* (1970) is faultless, and after he pulls off his wig, a stuffy representative of the upper class moans "Oh no" as he almost faints from shock. Yul Brynner's drawled "Oh yes" creates a persona totally opposite to the macho types he played in many of his films. Although these themes treat female impersonation comically, the humor invites the audience to join in the joke, laughing at unsophisticated people who are shocked rather than amused at the impersonator. The films *Outrageous, The Rocky Horror Picture Show,* and *La Cage aux folles* all feature transvestites sympathetically as main characters, and the audience gains insight into three very different visions of the drag queen. These cult favorites will probably continue to attract audiences throughout the eighties, and the more recent *Cage II* has done excellent box office business in Paris and New York theaters.

Films that exemplify this imitation of glamor figures are not limited to the past twenty years. Indeed, well-known actors have done relatively competent drag acts in earlier films, such as Mickey Rooney's impersonation of Carmen Miranda in *Babes on Broadway* (1941) and Danny Kaye's version of Marlene Dietrich in *On the Double* (1961). These two figures, especially Dietrich, are still popular choices for impersonation because of their exaggerated glamor, aggressiveness, and cynicism. Early imitations differ from more recent ones in frequency and in intention and style; Rooney and Kaye's "women" are played strictly for laughs, and there are enough discordant male cues to undermine the impression and create a sense of removal rather than identification.

The matron was by far the most frequent object of imitation in earlier films such as *Kind Hearts and Coronets* (1950), *Charley's Aunt* (1925, 1930, 1941, 1952), *Devil Doll* (1936), and *The Mouse That Roared* (1959). Hitchcock's introduction of the psychopathic element in Anthony Perkins' little old lady of *Psycho* makes Bing Crosby's drag routine seem as dated and unsophisticated as the period dress he wears in *High Time* (1960) of the same year. In the sixties, even dowdy female impersonations move away from sweet little old ladies into younger, more sexually eligible figures. After *Some Like It Hot,* filmmakers saw that audiences were ready for younger impersonators and more sexual innuendo. *What Did You Do in the War, Daddy?* (1966) presents female impersonation as the traditional refuge from martial attack, while it also demonstrates the vulnerability of women to sexual assault. More daring is Dudley Moore's transformation into nun's habit in *Bedazzled* (1967). This variety signaled a breakdown of stereotypes in female impersonation, a trend that was to continue into an era in which true drag queens would make their popular screen debut. The shift toward imitation of stronger female types points to a drastic alteration of popular views on what constitutes masculinity and femininity.

Our culture identifies a variety of traits as gender related; some are biological and measurable, such as the relationship of shoulder to hip size, and others are cultural, time-bound, and more difficult to measure, such as aggressiveness in gestures or word choice. In the movies, it is not the society's actual beliefs and values surrounding gender that are at issue, but movie-makers' conceptions of these beliefs. In most commercial films of the last thirty years (during which advance screenings have become commonplace), cross-dressing has been presented in ways that filmmakers believe to be "popular" in the sense of profitable. "Within the limits of their tendencies to moral schematism," observes Raymond Durgnat, "American directors can calculate audience sympathies to the nth decimal place, with a finesse which, given the cultural diversity of their audience, is far from inconsiderable classicism."[6] Box office disasters would tend to undermine Durgnat's assertion, but it is correct to assume that most films represent an earnest attempt by filmmakers and producers to read the tastes of their public.

By their very nature, role reversal situations represent a discordant note, an exception to the rules. When we examine cross-dressing films we see those elements of dress and behavior that serve as paradigmatic gender cues to the film audience, regardless of whether such behaviors are in keeping with those of real men and women. Very few women in real life may assume the canting posture of the knee bent in, a sign of demureness and submission, futile protectiveness of the genital region. In film, this posture immediately indicates femininity or effeminateness, and it often has a comic effect precisely because it is an exaggeration rarely to be seen in everyday behavior. It is one of the many "approved typifications" that serve as "gestural externalizations of what can be taken to be inner response."[7] We all recognize such gender indicators when we see them being acted out by children or by adults in mock imitation of the opposite sex.

The number of sex-related gestures seems to be higher for women than for men because "masculine" behavior is typically characterized more by a lack of expressive gestures than by their presence. The "strong, silent" figure of the western is the American archetype of the masculine hero, a character who has set a frequently imitated standard for masculinity. From Japan to France to India, actors model themselves after John Wayne, whose monotone and deadpan expression are virtually synonymous with a particular brand of manliness. According to Naomi Weisstein, "in cross-sexed encounters in American society, women smile more, and more expansively, then men."[8] Women gesture more with the hands, face, and body, and exhibit a wider variety of gestures, a tendency that is underscored by the wide variety in clothing styles offered to contemporary women.

Erving Goffman observes that in advertising, the woman is more often presented covering the face with the hand(s), turning the gaze away, placing the hand or finger to the mouth, sucking or biting, using the fingers to touch someone or caress an object in a nonutilitarian way, or to touch or caress her own body.[9] Precisely these gestures are used in film to cue the audience to a male's attempt to imitate a woman, a woman's attempt to exercise self-consciously her feminine wiles, or a homosexual's inadvertent display of his true colors. Such gestures are not restricted solely to these characters, but when they are used elsewhere they nevertheless call the audience's attention to a gender-related feature of the character involved. When Charlie Chaplin wets his finger and arranges his eyebrows, it is in parodic imitation of the effete snob, the aristocrat, who is often associated with effeminacy, foppery, and vanity. When Harold Lloyd puts his fingers and thumbs together and shrugs his shoulders nervously, it is in imitation of the abashed child caught doing something he shouldn't. Such gestures are common to women and children, within this system of symbolic, ritualized movements. What they usually indicate is submission, attempts at appeasement, and acknowledgment of the superior power of the other character or characters in the film. Often the powerful figure is taller or looking down from some height, but if that is not the case, the humbled figure will lower his or her head and look up with the eyes to create the illusion of the "proper" physical subordination.

The evidence of cross-dressing films indicates a principle that may operate in a number of films without sexual reversals as such. Women, while suffering under the lower status of second-class characters, are allowed a wider range of expression and flexibility. Male comedians share in this freedom to deviate from a prescribed character type of societal expectation, and it is this sense of liberation that delights audiences. The extremely masculine hero is locked into a rigidly codified behavior pattern that allows only a minimum expression of emotion. He joins the ranks of the "manly" stoical heroes, and it is up to the audience to read emotion into his blank face. Cary Grant, Marlon Brando, Bing Crosby, Bob Hope, Tony Curtis, Jack Lemmon, James Dean, Danny Kaye, Peter Sellers, Jerry Lewis, and Charlie Chaplin all share in the chameleon-like ability to appear at times almost childlike, at other times almost feminine, through gesture or vocal expression. Actresses like Greta Garbo, Marlene Dietrich, Lauren Bacall, Katharine Hepburn, Joan Crawford, Bette Davis, Barbara Stanwyck, Rosalind Russell, Jane Russell, and Betty Hutton all have, in certain films, a masculine edge to their voices, physical features, or mannerisms. It is not surprising, then, that these actors and actresses find themselves in cross-dressing or sexual reversal roles at least once during their careers.

Although this book focuses on clothing, a number of other factors, including makeup, voice inflection, language, body postures, and gestures, all contribute significantly to the presentation of masculine and feminine images. Even choice of hobbies may determine the extent to which an audience will perceive a character as masculine or feminine. Peter Farb observes that what is considered "the effeminate voice has a wider pitch than normal for men; it uses glissando or sliding effects between stressed syllables, more 'breathiness' in voice quality, and an occasional switch to a higher register."[10] Thus, we can see that John Wayne is masculine not only in the roles he plays but also in the monotone quality of his voice. An actor like Bing Crosby is saved from accusations of effeminacy by the fact that he usually gets the girl at the end of his films. In more recent films, the homosexual drag queen is separated from the true female impersonator by the language he uses, which is likely to contain more vulgarity and direct reference to sex than a woman (or transvestite) might use. Many women avoid such language, speaking "in ways which more closely resemble the prestige way of talking," whereas, according to Farb, "males in most American and British speech communities unconsciously regard the roughness of working-class speech as displaying desirable masculine attributes."[11]

One female gender cue will break the illusion of masculinity, whereas a woman may carry a number of traditionally masculine gender cues, rarely undermining and at times even enhancing her feminine appeal. A female, who is often of lower status within the film, may imitate the male, but the male cannot lower his status by imitating a female. The difference goes even deeper, however. The ability to change roles, to adopt costumes, is in itself a trait that is valued in women more than in men. The function of costume for women, according to Goffman, is essentially different from what it is for men in our society: "Each guise seems to afford him something he is totally serious about, and deeply identified with, as though wearing a skin, not a costume,"[12] while women identify less closely with costumes, shifting readily from one mode to another. Males tend to be more restricted in the types of roles allowed in films for another significant social reason. In our society it is acceptable for females to be masculine as well as feminine:

> girls are not as "typed" in their preference or identifications as boys, because they identify with their fathers as well as their mothers. In the reality of the young child, "male" is equated with "big" and synonymous with "more powerful." Consequently, both boys and girls are likely to identify, to some extent, with their fathers and male things in general.[13]

An analysis of the cross-dressing roles of actresses in films before 1960 certainly supports this conclusion. Films offering male impersonation or imitation include a myriad of types: cowgirls, historical figures, mannish career women, tomboys, hoboes, soldiers, seductive cabaret or Broadway entertainers in tuxedoes, and covert or overt manhaters. Such characters may have been tamed by the end of the film, but images of independence, forcefulness, and nonconformity probably did more to excite and incite women to rebel than the endings did to convince them of the safety and desirability of a domesticated life. Actresses like Dietrich, Garbo, Hepburn, Crawford, and Davis offered female models of glamor and strength, sexual allure that cloaked an iron will.

The relationship between film representations of social realities and the actual conditions is not a simple one. A particular subculture may have developed a certain style long before it is featured in films, but the films then act to popularize or co-opt these styles, making them part of a new trend in the larger society. Anne Hollander notes that certain stylized ways of dressing and behaving in early films became part of a cinematic code of meaning:

> Messages could be exchanged through clothing, based on common cinematic experience. The same became true of gestures—ways of smoking, crossing the legs, shrugging the shoulders, and kissing. Both men and women began to dress and behave and respond to each other as they saw the people in the movies dressing and behaving, who were in turn purporting to represent reality.[14]

Although clothing may seem to be a superficial part of social reality, its influence is not merely cosmetic. Role reversals in film reflect and even promote changes in the roles of men and women in society. When pants for women became acceptable attire—in large part because of the popularizing force of film—women were gradually freed to pursue hobbies, sports, and careers without having to concern themselves with the restrictive clothing that had inhibited their ability to function in a wide variety of roles. The change in men's roles in movies of recent decades reflects anxiety over status. Although the rise of the anti-hero offers a certain emotional liberation from the demands of saving face, it carries with it a loss of prestige, power, and authority. Male characters become siphons for the anxieties of an age that no longer dictates that men must "act" in order to be men. "Men may then feel themselves doubly threatened: not only dislocated and possibly emasculated, but also 'seen through' in their weaknesses more clearly than ever before by women whom they can no longer dominate and to whom they feel distinctly inferior."[15]

One response of many popular films to this change in the status of women and men was to eliminate male/female relationships almost altogether, substituting the male buddy teams. When one sex is excluded from a film, often a character will take on its attributes. In Wilder's *Stalag 17* (1953), Animal and Harry form the male equivalent of a married couple, and in one scene Animal dances with and then declares his love to Harry while he hallucinates that he is holding Betty Grable. In *Thunderbolt and*

Lightfoot (1974), which has a minimum of women, Jeff Bridges first takes on the female role in a symbolic fashion, behaving in a supportive, submissive fashion, and later putting on women's clothes to help his friends in their scheme. Here, again, it is useful to turn to the distinctions made by the homosexual subculture to gain clearer insight into single-sex teams:

> At any given homosexual party, there will be two competing, yet often complementary people around whom interest and activity swirl: the "most beautiful," most sexually desirable man there, and the "campiest," most dramatic, most verbally entertaining queen. The complementary nature of the two roles is made clearest when, as often happens, the queen is holding the attention of his audience by actually commenting (by no means always favorably) on the "beauty" and on the strategies employed by those who are trying to win the "beauty's" favors for the night.[16]

Comedy teams like Bing Crosby and Bob Hope, Dean Martin and Jerry Lewis, and Tony Curtis and Jack Lemmon all demonstrate this same pattern, with Crosby, Martin, and Curtis being the "beauties" who get the girls while the "campies" get the laughs. What distinguishes these earlier film teams from more recent ones, aside from the sophistication of the impersonation, is the fact that the early teams were after women, whereas the later buddies are very little concerned with women other than an occasional prostitute.

Although the most dramatic changes in male and female impersonation have occurred over the last twenty years, films of the teens, twenties, and early thirties demonstrate a remarkable freedom and variety in their treatment of both male and female crossdressing. Charlie Chaplin plays the sexpot and the battleaxe with equal ease, and comedians as disparate as Buster Keaton and Fatty Arbuckle find themselves in women's clothes. Edna Purviance, dressed as a boy, is caught kissing Charlie Chaplin in *Behind the Screen* (1916), and Charlie's boss is ready to fire him for being a homosexual. Julian Eltinge, one of the most famous stage impersonators, made the transition to film in the teens and played a wide variety of roles, from blushing bride to grandmother. As late as 1936, Tod Browning's *Devil Doll* presents Lionel Barrymore as an old lady who gets vengeance on the three men

responsible for his/her undeserved prison sentence; this disturbing character echoes the evil old lady of Browning's earlier *The
Unholy Three* (1925, 1930). The self-imposed Hays code of 1934,
with its stricture against any hint of perversion or sexuality, put a
damper on Hollywood's treatment of female impersonation,
which for about twenty years was limited to farcical comedies
featuring stereotyped matron roles. Male impersonation was
marked by a much greater range of types, and it occurred in
serious contexts as well as comedies.

A number of older films, such as *Sylvia Scarlett* (1935), *Morocco*
(1930), *Queen Christina* (1933), and almost any Mae West, Joan
Crawford, or Bette Davis film, became favorites for a homosexual
subculture during the sixties and seventies. More recent films
that deal with the issue of masculinity and femininity have become popular, and with the arrival of *The Rocky Horror Picture
Show*, audiences flocked to repeated viewings to participate in the
rituals appropriate to the film. Movies had long carried connotations of religion, with the vocabulary of film suggesting the
movie house as a place of worship where "fans" (fanatics) adored
the latest movie "idols." Many followers of *Rocky Horror* have
memorized the entire screenplay, so often have they seen the film
and chanted the responses created for the original stageplay.
What began as a popular ground for "cruising," looking for homosexual partners, soon became the scene for high school crowds
looking for a sense of group solidarity and rebellion against
stodgy elders. One teenager, who attends weekly shows dressed in
the black garters and hose of Frank-N-Furter, the central transvestite character of the film, comments on the appeal of this
ritual:

> There's no other role I could play. It's the one that's closest to me.
> Frank N. Furter is vicious and likes to be on top. The first time I
> walked down the stairs to show my mom my transvestite outfit,
> she was a little upset. . . . It's fun to see people freak out at
> something that's not that weird.[17]

In the exhibitionistic and somewhat hostile elements described,
the pleasure gained from such participation seems much closer to
the motivation of the drag queen than it does to the true transvestite, who wishes desperately to "pass" and to avoid making

people "freak out." The teenagers who have made *Rocky Horror* passé for the more sophisticated homosexual crowd may not have the same sexual preferences; they do, however, have some of the same feelings of sexual ambivalence prompting them to reject society's rigid standards of behavior.

Just as telling as this subculture rejection is the general audience's acceptance of alternative modes of behavior, as shown by the popularity of a film like *La Cage aux folles*. That gay or rebellious youth audiences should flock to films depicting deviation from the sexual norm is hardly surprising, because attendance at showings promotes a strong sense of community. The content of such films also offers a pleasurable identification with the characters on screen, who are appealing, strong figures, even though their sexual habits differ from standard practices. When viewers from a wider spectrum of society appreciate a film that celebrates cross-dressing, this indicates not only that the film has an intrinsic emotional appeal, but that the general audience is ripe for the message of sexual variation and tolerance.

The whole issue of identification is key to any discussion of cross-dressing films, for they call on the audience to identify in some way with the opposite rather than the same sex. The film that successfully depicts sexual role reversal leads the viewer to explore the hidden "other" within and, in so doing, makes us realize that many of the boundaries are arbitrarily imposed. Films that advocate role reversal are akin to what Leo Braudy has described as open vehicles, for they allow references and identification that go beyond the particular milieu presented by the film. Such open treatments of the theme are rare in comparison with the closed vehicle, the cross-dressing film that discourages variation from the sexual norms and dress codes of the period in which the film was made.

A thematic analysis and overview of a significant number of films from the silent period to the present day reveal clearly identifiable patterns that distinguish the functions of male and female impersonation and past images from more recent depictions of role reversals. The changes that have taken place, particularly in female impersonation, point to an alteration in our perception of women's role and status. When women had lower prestige, impersonating a woman was necessarily ludicrous because it presented belittlement of a comic character. As sex role definitions began to change in the years after World War II, role exchanges were depicted as comic but often with a strong underlying current of threat. In the sixties the threat became overt, and role reversals were often featured as psychotic, with the female figures gaining menace as they gained in power. Screen portrayals of female impersonation began to open up, flooding theaters with an enormous variety of images, many of them frightening, some absurd, some pathetic. By the beginning of the seventies, filmmakers had come to see something rather ridiculous in all this anguish, and parodies spiced with sex and violence came into vogue. In the mid- and later seventies, female impersonation manifested itself in characters that were human, believable, and appealing to the mass audience. American audiences eagerly responded to imports like *La Cage aux folles,* which set the U.S. record by grossing $40 million, more than any previous foreign language film.[19] Male impersonation and imitation have always been on the screen in a wide variety of forms, but in the past two decades the emphasis has shifted from disguise to costume, with women entering male realms as a natural extension of their ability to take on new roles.

Cross-dressing in film often reflects and highlights the changes in society, but regardless of its particular manifestations over time, the device is distinctively suited to the film medium. Norman Holland argues that "all movies take us back to childhood. They give us a child's pleasure in looking at things, which we, as film critics, respond to in our demand that the film be true to its medium, that it be visual."[20] Few cinematic experiences appeal more to our sense of delight in viewing the fantasies of childhood than does cross-dressing. We are allowed forbidden glimpses of what was once a very real confusion over sexual identity—visions that call back a long-buried fascination with adult costumes of gender. The childhood thrill of experimenting with the father's tuxedo or the mother's lingerie reemerges when we witness actors and actresses playing with sexual identity through clothing reversals.

Paul Rotha suggests that a thorough understanding of mise-en-scene "means paying just as much attention to make-up, lighting, decor, costumes, gesture, and other 'technical stylistic' details of a film as to dialogue and plot—noticing them not for their own sakes, but for their emotional meaning, their psychological impact."[21] The cross-dressing film draws the attention of the audience to the otherwise neglected elements of makeup, costume, voice, and gestures because these features emphasize the disjuncture between fact and the sensuous illusion on screen. Unlike magic or sleight of hand, which often do not translate well onto the screen, impersonation—a kind of magic—is enhanced in many ways by film's ability to alter physical proportions through camera angling, eliminate discordant gender cues by editing out or soft-focusing them, or emphasize the incongruities between gender and costume through lighting, camera angle, or close-ups.

The film exploration of cross-dressing has as many different manifestations and functions as transvestism has had historically in various societies and periods. The transvestitic shaman has been considered a source of renewal, vitality, and magical unity in tribal societies. The transvestite has also been considered a threat to social, political, and religious order, particularly in Western countries with a strong biblical tradition of censuring clothing exchange and sexual variety. Sexually neutral clothing prevailed before the refinement of tailoring, but once fitted clothing became prevalent, regulation of clothing along gender lines became more and more pervasive. One of the marks of a conservative trend in the society at large is the increase in strictures placed on gender- and status-related clothing. An example of this pattern may be found in the dress code imposed on the White House staff by the Reagan administration: Men were directed to wear coats and ties, women to wear dresses, and absolutely no one was to wear denim.[22] The denim outfit of the blue collar worker carries a number of connotations that are antithetical to the fixed hierarchy of conservative establishments. Such clothing costs less and is therefore easily attainable by anyone of any status; it allows greater freedom of movement, and it is less governed by the gender-based dictates of cut and style. The popularity of these apparently harmless, functional clothes is threatening to the conservative world order not only because it undermines distinctions between classes and sexes, but because the unisex costume of the laborer is often associated with radical revolutionaries and communist calls for a classless society.

In his analysis of ritual behavior, Max Gluckmann proposes that the ritual channels serves as a means of coping with conflict within the society.[23] Wearing clothes is not a ritual in itself; but the switch from one mode of dress to another may be an integral part of the passage from one role to another in society, a change that necessitates a kind of ritual formula to preserve order. When a segment of society takes on a new role, such as the shift from homemaker to business executive, an accompanying change in clothing signals social recognition of that change. Countless articles appear in women's magazines on how to dress for a job interview, an issue that has particular significance for women, who do not yet have a uniform so clearly identified with rank and status as the three-piece suit of the male executive.

Just as the attempt to conform to a socially recognized uniform represents a desire for cohesion, social order, and unity, the opposite behavior of deliberately defying dress codes marks a demand for departure from the old order, the anarchic assertion of individual freedom. Both impulses have their appeal for various segments of the population at different periods of individual and social development. In looking at individual films that offer role reversal, cross-dressing, and exchanges in costumes, we can examine our attitudes about male and female images as well as the appeal of androgyny for our past and present society. The androgyne has long been the mythic symbol of wisdom and self-sufficiency—a figure whose in-between status inspires fascination, dread, and reverence. In our own culture, priests and nuns have historically striven for angelic wisdom by denying their sexuality and forfeiting participation in the gender-related rituals of mating and procreating. Cross-dressing in film is as much an artifact of our culture's superstitions and beliefs about androgyny as are the bisexual costumes of the shaman or the statues of Hermaphrodite or Rajshahi. Movies are the mirrors of our popular culture, often broken shards or funhouse distortions of the realities we experience, but occasionally devastatingly lifelike reflections that let us see how we really behave, how we really picture our fellow human beings. And films that depict sexual role reversals give us that peculiarly telling image of the double mirror, echoing into the infinite curves of past and future, that highlights the shapes of our recurrent fears and desires. At the same time, the movies shape our ideas of what we ought to be and what we can be if we dare.

CHAPTER TWO

FEMALE IMPERSONATION
BEFORE 1960

BEFORE 1960 FILM COMEDIES that present men dressed as women fall into two broad categories: the open treatment that expands our sense of possibilities, creating more questions than answers; and the closed vehicle that establishes identifiable boundaries and resolves ambiguity.[1] Movies that derive their humor from the humiliation of the man dressed as a woman present exaggerated farcical imitations that would fool no one in real life. The cross-dressing in these films often functions as an expression of hostility and anxiety. By the end of the story it is clear that any haziness in sexual identity is unthinkable and must be purged from our imaginations by ridicule. The audience response of laughter releases tension about an area of sexuality that makes many people uncomfortable. Such a film defines the rules by which we are to respond, "teaching its audience how to watch its particular world."[2] By ridiculing the man who dresses as a woman, the closed film affirms the majority of the audience's supposedly normal status and confirms the sense of clearcut boundaries between genders.

The "open vehicle" offers much more convincing impersonations, and the humor is more subtle, complex, and ambiguous. In reacting to films in this category, our urge to laugh is, in part,

a natural outgrowth of our own confusion, our inability to reconcile the apparent femaleness of the character with our knowledge
that he is in fact a man. At the same time, inside knowledge
gives the audience an advantage over the characters in the film; as
we take part in the impersonator's conspiracy our response is one
of satisfied laughter at the superiority of our position. A film that
presents a convincing female impersonation must preserve a fragile balance to be effective for the mass audience. It must excite
our desire to imagine ourselves the mysterious "other," to venture
into a shadowy realm that defies our sense of what reality can be.
But the film cannot challenge the viewer's sense of propriety too
greatly or he or she will reject the portrayal as tasteless and,
consequently, not very funny.

Within these two large categories there are several recurring
situations that may either subvert or reaffirm social norms. A
common one is that of males cross-dressing to seek refuge rather
than stand and fight. Male characters who do this sometimes
begin to think of themselves as women, so serious is their emotional and physical investment in the disguise. The experience
teaches the man some of the benefits of being female, with the
amount of enlightenment depending on the extent to which he
allows himself to actually feel, behave, and react as he imagines
the opposite sex would. Even though this character learns of the
advantages of being female, he may be more struck by the problems he encounters. This may take the form of a simple observation that high heels and restrictive clothing require coordination,
endurance, and a high tolerance for discomfort. In some cases the
educational process may include exposure to unsolicited attention
from "wolves." The lessons to be learned are often ambiguous.
We may either assume that all men should, like the orthodox
Jew, begin each day with a prayer of thanks for not being born
female, or we may interpret the depiction as the filmmaker's
attempt at reform.

Whether a film opens up new possibilities or returns to an
affirmation of old sexual standards depends in large part on the
filmmaker's depiction of gender-related behavior. If the film reveals "normal" male or female behavior to be at least as ridiculous
as a man dressing as a woman, then it may subvert social conventions by making us laugh at both. In films of this type our

identification with the man is fairly strong, and we tend to view the other characters in the film as one-dimensional, locked into a stereotyped version of manhood or womanhood. Billy Wilder's *Some Like It Hot* (1959) is an excellent example of a film that does not merely reflect the spirit of the times, but also undermines standards by mocking convention and "good taste."

In films that maintain the status quo, the man dressed as a woman is the central object of ridicule. He is always the butt of the joke, and the audience laughs at him, not with him. In such films a woman's image suffers as well, for female dress and behavior are frequently shown as frivolous and superficial. Even worse than a feminine woman, though, is one who attempts to be like a man. She may be taught a lesson and shown that this is impossible, or she may succeed, thus guaranteeing a life of misery for the man in the role of a helpless Dagwood Bumstead, forever ruled by his wife. Howard Hawks' *I Was a Male War Bride* (1949) is one of the grimmest comedic visions of this kind, for when the woman is in charge (as she is throughout the film) it means nothing but problems for the man. Films like *Bride* depict the man as extremely uncomfortable and unduly humiliated by the necessity for female disguise; the impersonator almost never seems to experience any identification with female concerns.

One of the most common cross-dressing formats is some variation on the buddy motif. Two men find themselves in a situation that demands that one or both of them dress as women. The covert homosexual element in such a relationship is often simultaneously emphasized and masked by the fact that both men are after the same woman. Teams like Bing Crosby and Bob Hope, Tony Curtis and Jack Lemmon, Dean Martin and Jerry Lewis, and Jeff Bridges and Clint Eastwood exhibit behavior similar to that of a male-female couple. The straight man is often the handsome, macho member of the couple, the one who will eventually get the girl, the one who gets fewer laughs, and the one who usually convinces the other partner to dress as a woman for one reason or another. The clownish member of the team is the more feminine, often more childlike, carefree, and trusting. Although he may balk at the notion of dressing as a woman, he soon enters into the game with all the enthusiasm of a child dressing in Mommy's clothes. He sometimes takes the nagging, cautious role of wife and mother, especially when confronted with too much daring on the part of his friend. The audience laughs at the campy clown, but the ridicule is not necessarily cruel; the audience may actually identify with this character more than with his straight partner. The cross-dressing situation in a film like *Some Like It Hot* is much less embarrassing for the man than it is in a film like *I Was a Male War Bride,* because the character is able to accept his female role without feeling degraded. In identifying with the cross-dressing comic male, the viewer enters once again into the pre-heterosexual phase in which distinctions between the sexes are relatively insignificant. A film that allows the audience to do this subverts stereotypes by making adult sex roles seem restrictive or irrelevant.

A film may play on one or on several of these basic themes simultaneously. It may explore male and female sex roles by allowing the man to learn what it is like to be a woman. A movie may establish a strong covert homosexual bond between a straight man and his comic "female" counterpart, and it may also ridicule the societal strictures placed on both sexes. *Some Like It Hot* operates on several levels, offering subliminal suggestions of breaking taboos and at the same time shielding the average audience from any blatantly transvestite or homosexual implications. An audience more attuned to such hints may view them as intimations of creeping moral decay. In commenting on the increase in sexual innuendo in recent films, Judith Crist remarks:

> it is in *Some Like It Hot,* made in 1959, that the smut starts to show. Seen it lately? All pretty cute and jazzy, with Marilyn Monroe a delight and lots of comedy kick-ups with Tony Curtis and Jack Lemmon masquerading as a couple of girl musicians in a twenties setting. Look at it closely again and you start to notice how for every raucous and/or ribald masquerade joke there is another that involves a transvestite leer, a homosexual "in" joke or a perverse gag. Here is the prurience, the perversion, the sexual sickness that is obsessing the characters and plots of our films.[3]

Crist's puritanical bias is evident, but her basic observation on the trends in recent movie themes is sound. In contrast to her condemnation of the phenomenon, critics like Parker Tyler see this as a positive cinematic contribution to the struggle against social restrictions and repressive sexual stereotypes.[4] *Some Like It Hot* is indeed a pivotal film, for unlike many of its predecessors, it seems to alter rather than merely bolster existing attitudes toward sex roles. *Some Like It Hot* and *Male War Bride* represent opposite ends of the spectrum in attitudes toward cross-dressing and the broader issues of sexual identity and possibilities for individual freedom.

Before and After the Production Code

Because of the strong influence of censorship on the handling of female impersonation, open treatments of the theme in the period before 1960 follow a fairly distinct pattern. In the silent film era the emphasis on purely visual entertainment, the relative lack of censorship, and the ludic quality of a newborn art form all combined to create imaginative, relatively open cross-dressing films. Many of the routines were standard types like Old Mother Riley, but along with stereotyped grandmothers there sometimes occurred truly innovative versions of male-as-female. In *Our Hospitality* (1923), we even see the parasoled, full-skirted rear end of a horse as Buster Keaton's female disguise for escape from a feuding clan. Many such films have been lost, but from the films that remain of Chaplin, Keaton, Laurel, Julian Eltinge, and Wallace Beery we can see that female impersonation received a full range of treatments. Individual actors and directors had more freedom to experiment with themes that intrigued them during a period when improvisation and cooperative efforts were common production methods.

Charlie Chaplin was willing to exploit the full potential of sexual innuendo and allusions to homosexuality without dictating judgments to the audience. In *The Masquerader* (1914), Charlie is fired from his job as an actor and then disguises himself as a beautiful woman in order to get his job back, a routine that involves flirting outrageously with all the men on the movie set. Chaplin's imitations of women are extremely convincing because of his small stature and the delicacy and beauty of his features.

More important, though, is the fact that he is willing to become a woman to the best of his considerable ability. He does not hesitate to adopt feminine mannerisms, to wear makeup, or to flirt with men as enthusiastically as a true coquette would do. The audience becomes implicated in the cross-dressing situation as Chaplin allows us to witness every part of his metamorphosis from male to female, his attitude toward this role exchange apparently one of playful experimentation.

In *A Woman* (1915), the most subtle of his impersonations, we see his transformation as he wiggles into a skirt, stuffing a large pincushion for breasts under his jacket. When the daughter of the family sees him, she delightedly tells him that if he removes his moustache and wears a pair of her shoes, he'll "be perfect." The disguise is so complete that Chaplin looks as if he might be his own twin sister. His dark eyes are even more heavily made up than usual, and his almost luxurious lips are accentuated by dark lipstick. His mannerisms are coy, subtly demure. This feminine manner is sharply contrasted to the way he behaves when he drops the role, for example, in delivering a roundhouse that floors the father, 250-pound Billy Armstrong. His flirtation with Armstrong is as devastating as his punch, and the frequent jokes on the pincushion breasts include Armstrong getting a pin in the elbow when he tries to rub against what he assumes to be Chaplin's breasts. The underlying homosexual element of this man-to-man romance is underscored by Chaplin's trick of offering his cheeks to the father and his friend, and then ducking out at the last moment, leaving the two men kissing each other.

The discovery that Charlie is really a man takes place when the father pulls down Charlie's skirt and sees the striped underwear and man's legs underneath. In a temporary happy ending, Charlie gets the father to shake his hand, but then as soon as Charlie kisses the daughter, Father kicks him out of the house. It appears that Charlie's transvestite behavior is less objectionable to the father than his heterosexual gesture of kissing the daughter. As is typical of Chaplin films, the tale ends on a slightly melancholy note, yet with the suggestion of infinite possibility, ever-new departures.

Charlie Chaplin's delicate features and large eyes make him an ideal female impersonator in *A Woman* (1915, Essanay Films).

Louise Brooks and Richard Arlen share a boxcar together in William Wellman's *Beggars of Life* (1928, Paramount Famous Lasky Corp., cour tesy of The Museum of Modern Art/Film Stills Archive)

Lon Chaney's criminal granny (Echo) in Tod Browning's *The Unholy Three* (1925) and Jack Conway's sound remake (1930, shown here), was one of the last dangerous matrons to appear until the psychotic "mother" of Alfred Hitchcock's *Psycho* in 1960. This sound version was Chaney's first and last talking picture, after which he died of throat cancer. (Metro-Goldwyn-Mayer, courtesy of Cinemabilia)

Greta Garbo (center) wished to make her male disguise more authentic and less glamorous than her director, Rouben Mamoulian, chose to do in *Queen Christina* (1933). John Gilbert appears at the right. (Courtesy of The Museum of Modern Art/Film Stills Archive)

Katharine Hepburn plays a courageous aviatrix in Dorothy Arzner's *Christopher Strong* (1933). In George Cukor's *Sylvia Scarlett* (1935) she becomes a truly androgynous figure, pictured here with Brian Aherne. (Courtesy of The Museum of Modern Art/Film Stills Archive)

These four versions of *Charley's Aunt* all feature the matron, the most popular figure for female impersonation until after 1960. Ethel Shannon and Sydney Chaplin appear in the 1925 production; Hugh Williams (top left), Roddy McLennon, June Collyer, Charles Ruggles (as Charley's Aunt), and Flora Sheffield play in the 1930 version; Jack Benny appears in the 1944 version and Ray Bolger in the 1952 musical rendition entitled *Where's Charley?* (Courtesy of The Museum of Modern Art/Film Stills Archive)

Mickey Rooney does a relatively authentic imitation of Carmen Miranda, a popular choice for impersonation, in Busby Berkeley's *Babes on Broadway* (1941, courtesy of Metro Goldwyn Mayer)

In Charles Vidor's *A Song to Remember* (1945) Merle Oberon plays a glamorous, wicked George Sand, quite unlike the real personality on which the film is loosely based. (Courtesy of Columbia Pictures)

According to Josef von Sternberg, Marlene Dietrich often chose to wear male attire in her personal life as well as for her stage persona. (Courtesy of Cinemabilia)

Judy Garland (as Jane Falbury) displays definitely feminine legs beneath an abbreviated man's suit in a musical number from *Summer Stock* (1950), directed by Charles Walters. (Courtesy of Metro-Goldwyn-Mayer)

Vienna (Joan Crawford, center), shown here with Ben Cooper (left) and Scott Brady (far right), dresses as a man in Nicholas Ray's *Johnny Guitar* (1954). (Courtesy of Cinemabilia)

In Orson Welles' *Touch of Evil* (1957, U-I), Mercedes McCambridge (far right) makes an unbilled guest appearance as a tough character reminiscent of her role as Crawford's rival in *Johnny Guitar*. (Courtesy of Cinemabilia)

Historical films glamorized their subjects almost beyond recognition, as evidenced by a comparison of the real Calamity Jane with Cecil B. De Mille's Jane (played by Jean Arthur) in *The Plainsman* (1936, Paramount) or Jane Russell pictured rescuing Roy Rogers and Bob Hope in Frank Tashlin's *Son of Paleface* (1952, Paramount). Doris Day's characterization in the 1953 *Calamity Jane* turns her into the girl next door. (Courtesy of The Museum of Modern Art/Film Stills Archive)

In a publicity photo for Billy Wilder's *Some Like It Hot* (1959), Jack Lemmon (center standing) manages to blend in with the other women. (Courtesy of Cinemabilia)

Ingrid Thulin (right) dresses as Aman, the male assistant to the magician, in Ingmar Bergman's *The Magician* (1959). Pictured with Tgivo Pawlo as Starbeck and Ulla Sjoblom as his wife. (Courtesy of Cinemabilia)

While Chaplin boldly explored the comic potential of female impersonation, Tod Browning was to investigate the darker possibilities of sexual disguise. Browning's films stand out as works that transcend the influences of particular decades. His haunting silent and the subsequent sound version of *The Unholy Three* (1925, 1930) feature Lon Chaney as Mr. Echo, a ventriloquist working with a midget and a slightly retarded strong man to rob the rich. Chaney impersonates an old lady, and the midget impersonates a baby—a deceptively harmless duo that gains access to wealthy people's homes in order to steal from them. The pattern of the sinister character hidden behind skirts is repeated in the falsely condemned central character of *Devil Doll* (1936), another film that fascinates audiences with the morally ambiguous sympathetic portrayal of the outcast criminal. Browning's unconventional treatment of the transvestite theme was indeed an exception to the majority of cross-dressing films, particularly after the close of the silent era. With the arrival of sound, experimental views of female impersonation began to disappear, and film artists were no longer so free to explore their potential as *artistes*.

The new industry toy of sound for a time distracted filmmakers from many of the purely visual possibilities of cross-dressing. Film treatment grew more repressive in that it would not allow serious female impersonation even in comedy. The Production Code of 1934 made explicit the self-censorship trend already developing, spelling out features of popular taste and morals. Films would no longer carry any hints of sexual perversion. Consequently, female impersonators who were young, convincing, or who obviously relished such imitations became increasingly rare, eliminating a whole range of potential jokes and comic situations from cross-dressing films. Works that did present female impersonation could offer only the blandest varieties of matronly characters, clearly maintaining masculine identity and heterosexual orientation throughout.

Directors and producers nevertheless recognized the continued popular appeal of such routines, and they relied on the traditional favorites as their source of material. The fact that the play version of *Charley's Aunt* had earned more than $25,000,000 in royalties for Brandon Thomas and his heirs did not escape the notice of the film industry, for Hollywood made five different movie versions.[5] The exaggerated, farcical treatment of the theme in Archie Mayo's 1941 version is typical of cross-dressing films of the period from about 1929 to 1959. Masculine cues like cigars and strong language make it clear that the man who dresses as a woman is really quite manly and doesn't enjoy his female role in the slightest. The stigma of female impersonation is lifted by the fact that Jack Benny plays an *old* woman, and in our culture old women have a peculiarly sexless status. Also, as Billy Wilder once pointed out, placing characters in period costumes makes everyone appear a bit odd, taking the edge off the drag costume. In farcical imitations, it is the incongruity that delights audiences, particularly children, whose sense of the gender distinctions is often shakier than adult conceptions. Children are obviously thrown off balance, surprised, and delighted by the blatant contradictions of a man dressed as a woman. In a review of the 1941 *Charley's Aunt,* Philip Hartung notes the enthusiasm of the younger portion of the audience:

> The large number of youngsters in the audience shrieked with glee during the antics and were positively beside themselves every time Jack Benny, wrapped in petticoats, fichue and other antiquated woman's garb, hoisted his skirts to expose his trousers underneath, or smoked a cigar, or tippled, or was almost caught shaving or doing any masculine gestures that accentuated the absurdity of his disguise.[6]

More subtle incongruities appealed to other kinds of audiences, those who found little humor in the broad slapstick of films like *Charley's Aunt.* During the period of the Hays Code influence, a number of covertly homosexual types appeared as butlers, timid bachelors, or in traditionally feminine supportive positions, often wearing an apron to indicate the housewife's role. This character type had been established in earlier films, and audiences intuitively recognized its comic functions. In his analysis of Robert Florey's *Murders in the Rue Morgue* (1932), Robin Wood points out how the "plump and effeminate" friend of Pierre (the central character) is the archetypal asexual homosexual. "His relationship with Pierre (they share an apartment, he wears an apron, cooks the dinner, and fusses) is a parody of bourgeois marriage."[7] Similar characters later took center stage, becoming more domineering and sophisticated. Certain misogynist, aristocratic types such as Clifton Webb were typecast as characters that suggested unacknowledged homosexual tendencies. In *Sitting Pretty* (1948), Webb becomes a more efficient wife and mother than the real wife, and he exhibits no sexual interest in women, a pattern that continued through subsequent Belvedere movies. In *Dreamboat* (1952), he literally fights off the advances of the aggressive old-maid character played by Elsa Lanchester. Although Webb ("Dreamboat") has a daughter (played by a very severe Anne Francis) as proof of his one-time virility, he appears to have no desire for women. His daughter seems to have inherited his confusion over gender identification, as she wears a mannish woman's suit and tie and a persistent scholarly scowl through much of the film. Clifton Webb is but one of the many actors who found himself frequently cast in roles that hinted at androgyny. Following an established film tradition, Webb's waspish urbanity and erudition carried connotations of asexuality, effeminacy, and even repressed homosexuality.

Within the limits created by the Production Code, other comedians milked as much humor as possible from totally unconvincing, absurdly funny costumes. Bob Hope makes brief appearances in a sarong in *The Road to Singapore* (1940), a harem girl's outfit in *The Road to Zanzibar* (1941), a lady's bathing suit in *They Got Me Covered* (1942), and an imitation Carmen Miranda outfit in *The Road to Rio* (1948). The brevity of these cross-dressing scenes and the exaggerated, farcical quality of the imitations save them from censorship. Although such impersonations present no sexual threat, the very absurdity of the portrayals is a minor tribute to the comic spirit of anarchy. Cross-dressing films of the forties and fifties often suggested rebellion against social, military, or economic order, but by the end of the film the discord would usually be resolved and bundled into the conventional wisdom of the day. These works are closed vehicles in that they tidily pigeonhole each character and provide standardized, pat conclusions.

Male-as-female comedies made in the thirties, forties, and early fifties tend to support the status quo and reinforce already existing prejudices. Judith Crist argues that "films, much like literature and drama, come out of our society and mirror it, and that beyond matters of clothing and interior decoration, movies reflect and do not set patterns."[8] This proposition is debatable, but even if we grant that only clothing and interior decoration are affected by movies, then a significant element of daily life is directly influenced by films. Robert Sklar maintains that "Hollywood's sexual behavior was the most publicized frontier of a new morality—or lack of one—during the 1920's, and there is reason to believe that the Aquarians of Hollywood were a vanguard of the increasingly larger role sexual openness has played in American public behavior during the past half-century."[9] During the thirties, pressure on the movie industry which forced the self-regulation of the Production Code made movies a conservative force in terms of sexual mores:

> So in 1933–34, spurred by the changes in national mood brought about by the New Deal and prodded by the Legion of Decency, Hollywood directed its enormous powers of persuasion to preserving the basic moral, social and economic tenets of traditional American culture. This inaugurated a period of peace that was to last, by force of circumstances, until the end of World War II.[10]

The postwar years saw treatment of relatively controversial subjects in such films as *The Best Years of Our Lives, Gentleman's Agreement,* and *Johnny Belinda.* Nevertheless, the general trend remained conservative, and became somewhat more so as an atmosphere of paranoia swept the movie industry and the nation as a whole. Sklar notes the effect of anti-Communism in the late forties and early fifties:

> Movies were always less courageous than some organs of information and entertainment, but they were more iconoclastic than most, offering a version of American behavior and values more risqué, violent, comic and fantastic than the standard interpretation of traditional cultural elites. It was this trait that gave movies their popularity and their myth-making power. And it was this trait that the anti-Communist crusade destroyed.[11]

The response of many filmmakers to financial and political uncertainty was to create innocuous pictures like *Francis the Talking*

Mule and *On the Town*. Brooding, inward-directed psychological studies like *The Snake Pit, White Heat,* and *Sunset Boulevard* treated more controversial subjects, but even these ventures were not so risky as they seemed because they featured relatively well-known stars, directed by canny, strong box-office filmmakers who had a feel for audience appetites.

The topic of female impersonation was far too hot to handle in a serious way in the postwar decade. In the male-as-female comedies that cluster around the year 1950, a high degree of covert hostility is apparent, and it is clear that the topic of sex roles is of paramount interest to audiences. The comedy in many of these movies is directed against females and feminine men; women are often associated with restrictions that victimize men. *I Was a Male War Bride,* which grossed $4,100,000 and was advertised in *Variety* as "the happiest pick-up in box office history," is the supreme representative of the anxiety-ridden, paranoid rendering of the theme of sexual role reversal.[12]

Behind the Screen in 1949

To see how the film expresses concerns of the day, it is necessary to consider a number of factors that influenced public attitudes in 1949. The last year of the decade witnessed the nadir of movie popularity and, most critics feel, general quality. This slump was largely a consequence of the new popularity of television, although critics attributed the decline to a variety of factors, including the theory that movie producers had simply lost touch with their audience. W. R. Wilkerson of the *Hollywood Reporter* argued that Hollywood was "committing artistic suicide" by constantly feeding audiences grim settings and stories. In 1949 the filmmaking industry had not yet responded to television by creating more sexually sophisticated entertainment. On the contrary, Hollywood's initial response was to assume as harmless an exterior as possible. The conservatism is explainable in political terms as a response to growing anti-Communist suspicion, or it might be viewed in purely financial terms:

These uncertainties made bankers retreat. To win their approval a picture had to have proven box-office stars and traditionally effective stories or formulas, and there is no question that the emphasis on these helped make Hollywood's product more timid, trite and conventional.[13]

During the period from 1945 to 1950 the general mood of the nation had seemed to shift subtly from innocent optimism to defensiveness, vague disillusionment, and anti-red hostility. There was relatively high unemployment among returned veterans, and these men expressed an intense resentment of the women who had recently taken on traditionally masculine jobs and social functions. The term "Momism" came into vogue at this time, and the hollowness of victory for many called into question the whole American myth of man's control over his own happiness. Joseph Degler notes the connection between the ethos of individualism and the fear of being dependent:

> American culture may, in a special way, have a particular sensitivity to "Momism" precisely because it has long emphasized an opposite myth of absolute individualism—that of the child's eventual capacity to achieve total independence from its parents (and from everyone else)—and this sensitivity makes us the first to seek out "Momism" in our midst.[14]

Women, as portrayed in advertising, movies, short stories, and popular psychology, were predatory creatures whose apparent softness was a ruse to cover their huntress impulses. The description of a story in a 1949 *Saturday Evening Post* poses this question: "Is she pliant, submissive, eager to please? Then watch out—the lady's about to get her own way."[15] The 1948 Cary Grant film, *Every Girl Should Be Married* is featured in *Variety* as the story of "the female of the species on the prowl."[16] Despite the frequent attempts to portray women as ruthlessly pursuing entrapment of the male, there was also a growing awareness of women's desire to escape the confines of the housewife role. In a 1949 article entitled "What *Do* Women Want, Anyway?" Robert Yoder reports on a recent opinion survey: "Home, in spite of John Howard Payne's famous claim that it outdoes pleasures and palaces, showed up clearly as man's castle, woman's Alcatraz."[17] At this time, men seemed more interested than ever in determining what women wanted, and yet they vacillated between viewing them as doggedly fighting to become housewives or desperately wishing to become bachelor career women.

The castration anxiety and hostility suggested by these radically opposing views of women is clearly identifiable in cross-dressing films of the period. Many filmmakers, perhaps influenced by Freudian imagery popular at the time, present men forced to dress as women through entrapping situations. Often they are frightened, angry victims unable to control their own destiny. Hatred of authority and red tape is often aligned with resentment of women: because women were in charge at home during the war, they were blamed for the humiliating bureaucratic requirements that faced the returning veteran. Although men had created the regulations, women were often the enforcers. *I Was a Male War Bride* exemplifies the feelings of masculine powerlessness and chaotic reversals by presenting a woman who behaves like a man and a man who is forced to behave like a woman. Ann Sheridan as an efficient WAC comes to represent the army itself. Through condensation and displacement, women become the keepers of authoritarian rules, promoters of what was once a strictly masculine domain—the military world. But it is now a military realm robbed of its glamor, camaraderie, and glory. War and the military community, in the tarnished light of 1949 disillusionment, become petty, constricting, womanly pursuits rather than liberating adventures. Masculine women are the scapegoats, taking the blame for everything from unemployment to the housing shortage, from dehumanizing regulations to bureaucratic inadequacies.

The Closed World: A Closeup of *I Was a Male War Bride*

I Was a Male War Bride gives a sense of ever-increasing confinement—man gradually restricted until he can no longer move. The film opens with some European location footage, establishing a minor conflict between two Germans who cannot decide on directions. Cary Grant (as a Frenchman) asks an American for directions and then confidently informs his cabbie that he knows how to get to his destination. At the beginning of the film we see Grant as a take-charge, capable man, but this bravado does not last long once he encounters Ann Sheridan's mannish, matter-of-fact control of the situation. We soon learn that Grant (Henri Rochard) has worked with Sheridan (Lieutenant Catherine Gates) before, and when he discovers that he has a new army assignment with her he tells her, "Keep your mouth shut and do as I tell you." She remains unimpressed by his manly instructions and laughs at him when she learns that he still wears traces of the blue dye that she pushed him into on their previous assignment together. She threatens to bring a knife and a revolver with her, signs of her intentions to defend her honor, to dominate, and eventually to symbolically castrate him. His disgusted reply, "American women," could sum up one of the major themes of the film: the weary resignation, bewilderment, and resentment that the male feels toward female powerhouses like the one played by Ann Sheridan.

Without the color, sparkle, and sex appeal of a Katharine Hepburn or even a younger Ann Sheridan, the bones of Hawks' message glare through the film. The American woman is a ball-breaker, and mating is a joyless battle destined to destroy man's self-esteem. Toward the beginning, Ann Sheridan describes Grant as "Jack the Ripper" to a cute Southern girl that she thinks is going with him on the mission. Grant, as a Frenchman, doesn't know who Jack the Ripper was. Just as Sheridan and Grant are leaving, the girl begins to say, "Jack the Ripper was a famous. . . ," but she is allowed neither by time nor by the still influential Code to finish her statement. We soon see the irony in the notion of Grant raping a woman who can not only take care of herself, but manage also to run the whole operation, turning the man into a helpless victim. As the female commander says to Grant, referring to Sheridan, "She's your man all right."

We know from the title that Grant will be a "male war bride" of some sort, but the first clothing reversal is when Ann Sheridan emerges in a uniform with pants and drives the side-car motorcycle that is to take them to Bad Nauheim. When she drives off, leaving Grant sitting paralyzed in a side car with no engine, it is just the beginning of a series of peripeties in which Grant gets the short end of the stick—or no stick at all. Ann Sheridan has the deep voice of a woman in her early forties, and, dressed in a jump suit, goggles, and protective motoring cap, she makes a much more passable male than Grant eventually does a female. Her mannerisms are brusque, commanding, and efficient. The uniform conceals any breasts and the padded shoulders and baggy pants make her look virtually like a man. The only example of stereotypical femininity comes in the form of Sheridan's occasional paroxysms of laughter, always as a result of Grant's repeated humiliations.

As the truly masculine member of the duo, Catherine takes the initiative through much of the film. When they encounter a road block, she suggests that they drive into a boat and sail to Bad Nauheim. As they float downstream they dispute about whether the roar they hear is a C47 or a C54. She is the first to realize that it is a waterfall, and she manages to catch a rope thrown to them from a bridge, saving their lives. As they crawl to shore, Henri gets in one of the few licks the script allows him when he tells her, "You're subnormal." When Lieutenant Gates is not doing a better job than Henri at something masculine like lifesaving, she is making him do things that result in embarrassing accidents. Henri is suspended upside down on a train-stop gate while trying to retrieve her lipstick, and later he gets covered with wet paint while climbing a pole at her request.

The pace of the film picks up considerably when humiliation and entrapment combine in a scene of enforced intimacy. Henri rubs Catherine's back until she falls asleep, and then as he attempts an honorable exit from her room, the door handle falls off, leaving him trapped. The next morning, Catherine is at first outraged at his presence, but eventually she softens and believes that he didn't stay overnight on purpose. Then Grant becomes the victim of yet another female, as the concierge beats him out of the second story window with a mop. Once they arrive in Bad Nauheim the lieutenant cynically exercises her female charms to complete their assignment. Henri is trapped, this time by the police, and Catherine betrays him by telling them she doesn't know him. This puts him in jail until she can accomplish her final triumph, showing up with the man they were to contact in order to complete their mission.

As long as the two characters are enemies, Henri is fighting a losing battle. However, once a tie of affection is established, tenuous as it may be, he is even more victimized. Though her putting him through his paces is relatively well-intentioned, he is to face ultimate humiliation in his simple quest to consummate their union. As Henri is dozing while Catherine seeks directions, their motorbike is set in motion by some local children. In perhaps the funniest line of the movie, the almost sleeping Henri tells the absent Catherine, "In fact, I'd miss you if you weren't here," as the bike plows toward a haystack. Once more confined, this time in the interior of a haystack, he is found by Catherine and they practice kissing "the French way." This is the only sexually suggestive scene in the entire film; in fact, it is the only scene in which there is some suggestion of the female lieutenant's vulnerability or susceptibility to physical desire, and it is the only moment in the film that allows Henri to be on top both literally and figuratively. This brief moment of passion seals his doom for the rest of the film.

From the moment Henri is sexually entrapped, he becomes the property of the bureaucracy. In a subtle way, the film implies that women are responsible for the routines, procedures, and forms of postindustrial society. One is reminded of the song in *Guys and Dolls* that lists a series of ridiculous things one sees men doing, always ending with the phrase, "You can bet that he's doing it for some doll." So with Henri Rochard, who must undergo everything, including the marriage ceremony, in triplicate. The wedding scenes in this film are one of the most deromanticized depictions of matrimony in the American cinema. Only if a shotgun had been included would the process have looked more unpleasant for all involved. As Henri points out, in China (where the women are under control), "the bride and groom just drink out of the same bowl." Many U.S. filmmakers before World War II offered marriage as the standard happy ending, whereas Hawks almost never showed his couples getting married. In this exceptional case, each of the three marriage ceremonies Hawks depicts is a tedious nightmare. Numerous films of the postwar era began to follow this pattern of deromanticizing matrimony by featuring women as power-hungry and possessive, seeking control of the man.

In *Bride* the bureaucracy indirectly turns the man into a woman, both on paper and in appearance. Henri is powerless against the demanding rituals of the army. As he answers questions for the war bride form, we see him getting into his new role, even professing to be pregnant for twenty months and suffering from female trouble. As he waits in a room full of wives and mothers, he listens to the stateside fashion report. In the most subtle situation of the film we see Grant reacting to the descriptions of the latest in fashion, responding as if he were a woman sincerely interested in the news. When the voice informs the women that the new breastline is smooth, with no lumps or pockets, Grant almost absentmindedly removes his wallet from his breast pocket. After having held a baby he dubs "Niagara," he comments to Sheridan, "I'm learning what it is to be a soldier's wife." This effective scene is actually the exception to the major part of the film, for in general Henri refuses to give in and learn anything about being a woman. He usually simply suffers, if not stoically, at least without breaking down and crying.

After interminable shuffling from men's quarters to dependent females' quarters and back again, Henri eventually spends a sleepless night holding yarn for a female guard—yet another instance of male servitude to female activities. The lesson seems to be that he cannot be both a man and a dependent. He is stuck with the worst of both worlds, for he doesn't even get to sleep, unlike women, who "always get a place to sleep." After spending one night in a bathtub Henri observes that of course women really are the stronger sex because they get enough sleep.

In the scene of final degradation, Rochard must don a woman's uniform to get on board ship with his wife. She assures him that once he gets on the ship, everything will be over, and he will "be a man forever." The makeshift horsetail wig, the suggestion that he wear lipstick, and the whistle from a passing sailor as Henri adjusts his garter—all make his symbolic castration complete. Throughout this scene Rochard is the unwilling victim, sour-faced yet helplessly resigned to being manipulated, prodded, poked, coiffed, and dressed by his new bride.

The eventual happy ending is charged with irony. Rochard is finally allowed to consummate his marriage in the ship's brig. He locks himself in the tiny confines with his wife and tosses the key out the porthole, vowing not to come out until they have to break the door down. The Freudian implications of the last shot of the Statue of Liberty through a porthole suggest sexual intercourse and liberation, but even this supposedly masculine triumph is subtly undercut by the very fact that the phallic statue is, after all, a woman. The home that should be man's castle has shrunk to a prison cell, the largest domain the male figure can successfully command.

Making Connections

In 1949 the United States as a whole was exhibiting what in an individual might be diagnosed as mild paranoid schizophrenic symptoms, complete with delusions of grandeur and persecution. In many respects, postwar America was experiencing an unprecedented boom; things were better than ever, with the United States one of the few nations in history to profit so enormously from war. Nevertheless, between the years 1945 and 1950 developments were such that this statement by Joe McCarthy struck a chord in many Americans: "The reason why we find ourselves in a position of impotency is not because our only powerful potential enemy has sent men to invade our shores but, rather, because of the traitorous actions of those who have been treated so well by this nation. . . ."[18]

The feeling of "impotency" extended to more than foreign policy, for fundamental changes had taken place in the American marriage and family structure as a result of the war. In 1945 "thousands upon unhappy thousands of men returned 'home' to discover that it had not survived their absence; that their marriage no longer existed, in emotion or in reality. The mobility of warfare shook the institution of marriage to its core."[19] The United States had the highest industrial production in 1945 of any nation, but it also had "the highest divorce rate in the world—thirty-one divorces for every 100 marriages."[20] Although it would be inaccurate to paint a picture of millions of housewives across the nation suddenly burning their aprons, one of the reasons for the astoundingly high divorce rate was the fact that women had learned they could make it on their own. "For the first time in her history American woman learned she could find and hold a job, drive and maintain the family car, keep the checkbook in balance—without the help of a man."[21] American women had worked in factories, offices, and high-level positions not previously held by women. Unlike the temporary increase in women's employment during World War I, this trend continued after the war; "between 1949 and 1959 . . . over four million married women entered the labor force, some 60 per cent of *all* additions, male and female."[22]

Despite the fact that things were better than ever in terms of production, the standard of living, and world prestige and power, the war had left an aftermath of disappointments that, unlike the depression or the First World War, served to alienate men from women. Returning veterans looked forward to high-paying jobs and a comfortable life in the suburbs, a situation made even more appealing by dreams of a grateful, admiring wife. What they faced, in fact, was a "housing shortage of unparalleled magnitude," according to a government study.[23] Veterans had also envisioned high wages that failed to materialize, while the loans provided by the G.I. Bill of Rights would only allow them the minimum of housing, if they were lucky. Houses provided in quickly constructed suburbs were horrors of workmanship, and they also failed to provide the community comforts, shopping facilities, and neighborhood gathering places found in older communities. As a consequence, many women were either locked into an association with others who shared similar complaints or left isolated, "trying to cope with the monotony of their children and housework. The husband may drive off to the city each day, but for the women, there is no escape."[24] Because the average new community no longer offered the same kinds of satisfaction and escapes for housewives, more and more married women were turning to careers and/or divorce as a solution to their general sense of malaise.

Veterans who were not married seemed to have similar problems with women who failed to meet their expectations, creating an enmity that was just as little understood by the women as by the men:

> when the *New York Times* published an article by a veteran comparing American girls unfavorably with Europeans ("Being nice is almost a lost art among American women") the storm of protesting mail was so immense that the *Times* self-defensively devoted two full pages to the females' rebuttal.[25]

When veterans complained of the immaturity, aggressiveness, and unappreciative attitude of American women, the women automatically assumed that the men meant that American women refused to give sexual favors as freely as their sophisticated European counterparts. No doubt jealousy and resentment over imagined (or not-so-imagined) overseas liaisons made it that much easier for American women to defend their chastity. Relations between men and women had never been described so accurately as the "battle of the sexes" as during the post–World War II years in the United States.

All of these concerns are directly expressed in *I Was a Male War Bride,* even though the touchiness of the subject is buffered by making the male protagonist a Frenchman and the story take place in Europe a couple of years before the film's release. The housing shortage is transferred to the isolated case of Henri Rochard, who cannot find a place to sleep, a situation that makes what American veterans experienced appear relatively insignificant. The army bureaucracy in the film no doubt reminded many people of the Veterans Administration, "a horror house of red tape and inefficiency," that left thousands of veterans with "neither money nor care for months on end."[26] It is apparent that the character played by Ann Sheridan is convinced that Henri is as lecherous as anything chaste American womanhood could project for the returning veteran. It is equally apparent that his actions, if not his intentions, are honorable, and that he is much more victim than victimizer.

That the film reflects many of the anxieties of the day is clear, but it is not so clear why male audiences would take any pleasure in identifying with Cary Grant's position in the movie. Many women may have vicariously enjoyed taking the role of the capable woman played by Ann Sheridan, but men could hardly be comfortable imagining themselves in the role of Henri—homeless, powerless, humiliated, and trapped. One possibility is that if a man like Cary Grant, the ultimate in urbane manliness, can survive the situation, perhaps the condition of the average male in the audience will appear happy by comparison. This explanation is plausible enough, but a more encompassing phenomenon may better account for audience identification with losers and victims. The film historian Robert Thom notes that during the late forties and early fifties "in a small but significant number of pictures Hollywood dropped its traditional the-good-guy-wins attitude toward America."[27] As Joseph Goulden points out, "it was a time of 'losing winners,' when people fantasized with the loser. There was a revulsion with success—perhaps because the artistic people who conceived of movies, and dominated the industry briefly, saw that the 'success' of winning the war was being compromised and tarnished with what happened after peace."[28] Many contemporary critics viewed this trend toward bleak films and suffering heroes as a self-destructive impulse on the part of a movie industry that had already faced a series of financial catastrophes in the postwar television era. W. R. Wilkerson comments: "Audiences are yearning for some good belly-laugh comedies and pleading for those great love stories of yesterday. . . ."[29]

Yet the directors like Howard Hawks, who were once able to produce just such material, find themselves in 1949 producing comedies like *I Was a Male War Bride,* which has a dismal, quiet desperation lurking beneath the slapstick veneer. *Bride* features the Hawksian fear of sexual humiliation noted by Peter Wollen and other critics, but the grim tenor of the film seems to derive at least as much from the times as from Hawks' private vision. Nowhere does *Bride* offer the comforting "man's world" of the Hawks dramas, nor does it include the elevating relationship that he professes to have used in a number of films—"a love story between two men."[30] In other films the masculine elements of Hawksian women are less threatening, because it is the isolated woman who "has to win her place in this closed group *as a man* (or asexual human being, if you prefer), proving that she is as honest and courageous and loyal as any of them."[31] In *Bride* the dream turns ugly, for the woman is already at ease in the man's world, having taken it over and feminized it to the point where it is the man who must put on skirts in order to be accepted.

The character of Henri Rochard is not, like many of Hawks' earlier male protagonists, "woman-shy, living in a male world where he is comfortable with his relationships."[32] Henri is supposedly a thwarted wolf, and the world he operates in is hardly, as Barbara Bernstein describes Hawks' settings, "a fourth-grade classroom where the boys wouldn't be caught dead talking to the girls, and the girls keep trying to trick them into it."[33] The Hawksian characters have grown up by 1949, for it is the man who aggressively pursues the woman and the woman who flees from the "wolf." The comparatively idyllic men's society of *The Dawn Patrol* (1930), *Sergeant York* (1941), and *To Have and Have Not* (1944) has given way to an alienated and alienating nightmare in which the woman is not only at home in men's territory but bests the man at every turn. The vision is only one step away from a paranoid delusion, and yet to audiences of the day, it looked like good clean fun. An examination of the contrasting *Some Like It Hot* will show just how far *Male War Bride* is from being a truly lighthearted, liberating comedy.

An Open Vision: *Some Like It Hot*

In *Big Bad Wolves* Joan Mellen touches on the topic of transvestism, arguing that in neither *Some Like It Hot* "nor in the 1949 *I Was a Male War Bride* is the theme of transvestism treated seriously."[34] But *Some Like It Hot* is hardly, as Mellen calls it, the "typical fifties film." She condemns both films as being everything that earlier cross-dressing films often were:

> The transvestism serves to bestow contempt upon women, since the men imitate female behavior with mincing steps, high voices, narcissism, and self-indulgence, a grotesque caricature of the sex. Instead of emasculating these males or challenging macho stereotypes, the drag enforces old values by pointing up the supposed absurdity of being female. These disguises thus work to disparage both women and effeminate men who do not live up to the womanizing, leering role Curtis and Lemmon assume when they are not wearing women's clothes.[35]

One wonders whether she ever saw the film. In fact, Lemmon's Daphne actually begins to think of himself as a woman; he begins to think about marrying Osgood (Joe E. Brown). Josephine (Curtis), who remains heterosexually devoted to Sugar Kane (Marilyn Monroe), nevertheless learns a great deal as the result of his sojourn in the land of women. Far from demonstrating self-indulgence, the Curtis character reveals the selflessness and generosity he has gained from his experience. When, toward the end of the film, he marches up to the heartbroken Sugar, kisses her, and says, "Forget it, Sugar, no man is worth it," he is finally proving that he really is worthy of her love, even though his past is filled with the deception and thoughtless exploitation of vulnerable women that had made him unworthy of anyone's love.

In a perceptive analysis of *Some Like It Hot,* Brandon French argues that it "can be perceived in part as a good-natured dream of sexuality as a sliding scale from male to female, from straight to gay, from potent to impotent, on which every human being dances an endlessly variable jig."[36] Curtis, who maintains his heterosexual orientation beneath the drag exterior, becomes more sympathetic, sincere, and loving as a direct result of his experience as a woman. As he gets to know Sugar "woman to woman," he "must confront the consequences of his own cavalier behavior: the fear, the sadness, the drinking, the self-denigration."[37]

In his discussion Douglas Brode observes that the key difference between earlier screen comedies' use of drag and Wilder's treatment rests in the attitude toward wearing women's clothes. In previous films the men are generally uncomfortable, but "in *Some Like It Hot,* Curtis and Lemmon very quickly take to the idea of being dressed up as Josephine and Daphne. . . . If drag was not new to movies, the attitude toward drag was."[38] Billy Wilder was very much aware that he was treading on thin ice in treating the theme of transvestism. "Well, I know that transvestites are cases for Krafft-Ebing," Wilder comments, "but to me they are terribly funny."[39] Wilder set the story in the twenties and he chose to shoot it in black-and-white in order to lessen the vulgarity and possible censorship problems of filming it in color. Marilyn Monroe wanted him to use color to highlight her own beauty, but when she had seen the color tests of Lemmon and Curtis in drag, Tom Wood notes, "even she was appalled by the gruesome, unwholesome results, and she gave in—though not with good grace."[40] Despite the fact that Wilder makes such attempts to avoid shock, the main thrust of the film is to go beyond barriers of popular taste and undermine prudish attitudes about men dressing as women and about sexuality in general.

The daring quality of the film is not so much in the basic plot, but in the treatment of that plot and the degree of the men's identification with female concerns. As in Shakespearian comedies and a number of silent film treatments of the motif, qualities of gentleness, pacifism, and distaste for violence are favorably presented as reasonable feminine alternatives to the masculine values of aggression and combativeness. *Hot* sets up two realms— the frightening, masculine underworld of the city, and the comforting, feminine refuge of the all-girl band—and it is clear that any sane person would choose the latter. The film opens with Joe (Tony Curtis) and Jerry (Jack Lemmon), two relatively innocent musicians, accidentally witnessing the St. Valentine's Day Massacre. The gangsters are after them, and they are desperate for any means of escape. They disguise themselves as women in order to join an all-girl band on its way to Florida. The minute Joe/ Josephine sees Sugar Kane (Marilyn Monroe), he falls in love with her, at first romancing her quite cynically, but eventually becoming sincere. He takes on yet another disguise as an impotent millionaire with a remarkable resemblance to Cary Grant. Meanwhile, Jerry/Daphne becomes engaged to a real millionaire, Osgood, played by Joe E. Brown. When the gangsters arrive and catch on to their scheme, the film comes to a hectic climax, complete with fast cutting on chase scenes and novel shots of our hero/heroines dangling from balconies, hiding under tables, and trying to pass as a bellboy wearing high heels. Sugar Kane is now convinced that her millionaire has abandoned her, and as she sings "I'm through with love," she begins to cry. Joe/Josephine, still in full drag, witnesses this scene and goes up to her on stage, kisses her on the lips, telling her that no man is worth it. Monroe, with a look of wide-eyed wonder, breathily squeaks out "Josephine," and Curtis pulls off his wig, causing a ripple of shock through the nightclub audience. In their final escape from the gangsters, who manage to gun each other down, Joe reveals his true identity to Sugar and Jerry reveals his true identity and gender to Osgood. Both Sugar and Osgood accept the real selves of Joe and Jerry as the two couples race off into the sunset in a speedboat.

What is exceptional about the film is the thoroughness of the transformation from male to female. Wilder is willing to explore the reversal not only in its superficial aspects but also at the level of its transvestite and homosexual implications, distinctly touchy areas for the average audience of 1959. The first scene to give some indication of what the two men are learning takes place at the train station in the beginning of the film. Joe and Jerry are struggling with the problems of female clothing, commenting on the draftiness, the feeling of vulnerability, and the difficulty of even walking in high heels. Just at this point, they see Sugar Kane; as she walks past, Daphne/Jerry comments that the way she walks is like "Jell-O on springs." Their admiration can be taken as the drooling of lecherous males, fulfilling the sexual stereotype, or it can be viewed as utterly worshipful appreciation of pure female essence. The latter interpretation takes on added authority as we see Josephine and Daphne try to emulate their female ideal in the way they walk and eventually in the way they talk about men and life in general. It is almost as if they admire femaleness to such an extent that they are eager to do as good a job as they can at actually becoming female. As in a number of other cross-dressing films, the disguised men's safety depends on their success at imitating women, but these two characters throw themselves into the venture with real enthusiasm and considerable skill.

The thoroughness of the disguise provides an interesting contrast to *I Was a Male War Bride.* Lemmon and Curtis initiate the disguise themselves, and they go all out, unlike Grant, who does not have the idea in the first place and only reluctantly agrees to any part of it. When Ann Sheridan suggests that Grant try a little makeup he refuses, saying that he is more the natural outdoors girl. In other words, if he is going to agree to be a woman at all, it will be a tomboy, the closest thing possible to a man. Lemmon and Curtis do the full transvestite routine, wearing nylons, stiletto heels, lipstick, and eye makeup; even in their private lives they do "feminine" things like wonder which dress to wear or luxuriate in a bubble bath. Grant's distaste for the drag routine grows out of anxiety over his own masculinity and fear of female dominance, whereas the willingness of Curtis and Lemmon to participate fully in female impersonation creates a strong sense of identification with and sympathy for women's concerns.

Hot offers a number of subtle role reversals and exchanges of dominance in addition to the obvious clothing disguise. Curtis masquerades as a millionaire, but even in this ploy to attract a woman there is an interesting element of passivity; he pretends to be impotent, and it is therefore up to Sugar Kane to take the initiative. Although this is an idea that many men may have toyed with, few are actually willing to sacrifice their pride to the extent of going through with it. By so doing, the character of Joe relinquishes the traditional masculine control over the situation. One of the main reasons he can do this without fear of ridicule is that Sugar is totally nonthreatening, sympathetic, and warm, and Joe knows this as a result of his woman-to-woman contact with her. One can hardly imagine any man with an ego strong enough to confess impotence, even as a ploy, to a woman like the hard-bitten character played by Ann Sheridan in *Male War Bride.* Two reversals are evident in Joe's situation, for as a woman he takes on the traditionally masculine role of protector and adviser to Sugar. Then when he is playing the man, it is Sugar who must aggressively lead, arouse, and seduce him. It is also interesting to note that Curtis, the "beauty" of the duo, makes a more subtle and attractive woman than does the already rather effeminate Lemmon. Lemmon is the campy transvestite, slightly dowdy, whereas Curtis is the glamor drag queen, exercising dominance over Sugar and Daphne/Jerry.

Jerry's behavior goes even further into the realm of unmanliness than does Joe's. In a scene deliberately filled with maracas in order to allow for laugh time, Jerry (still dressed as Daphne) dances around the room describing how he has become engaged to Osgood. Through this scene, except for those moments when he is reminded of his real gender, Jerry describes his experience with all the exuberance of a young girl who has just been asked to her first prom. Although Jerry is impressed by Osgood's money, it is not altogether clear that this is the only attraction. We also get the sense that Jerry is flattered by Osgood's attentions and amused by his company, especially since he has lost the companionship of Joe, who spends all his spare time romancing Sugar. As the "female" part of the couple, Jerry can be more assertive with Osgood than he can be in his relationship with Joe, to whom he must cater and eventually submit. When Jerry/Daphne dances with Osgood, it is clear that he relishes this chance to lead; he also appreciates the worshipful admiration he receives as Osgood's loved one. It is ironic that as a woman Jerry can play the man, whereas in his supposedly normal man-to-man relationship with Joe he is the cajoling, submissive female.

The final sequence is one of liberation from a variety of restrictions, and it is here that the film really establishes itself as an open vehicle. Joe voluntarily reveals that he has been masquerading as a woman, and his unselfish advice to Sugar demonstrates that he has learned how to love in a more complete, mature way than he ever had before. Because Spats has been eliminated, Joe and Jerry are freed from him and his gang (even though they may have acquired yet another pack of pursuers). In the last getaway scene we see a heterosexual couple and an ambiguous two-male couple flying across the open water in a speedboat. Osgood's final line, a classic in movie finishes, demonstrates his total acceptance of Jerry/Daphne. When Jerry reveals that he is not a woman, Osgood replies with a broad smile and perfect aplomb, "Nobody's perfect," leaving the audience to speculate on the future of the odd couple.

The carefree final scene of *Some Like It Hot* makes the ending of *Male War Bride* look like a condemned man's last supper. Both films close with the protagonists sailing off in a boat, but the freedom represented by the open speedboat peopled by two unconventionally happy couples is a far cry from the claustrophobic, cramped atmosphere of an army ship's locked prison cabin. The future for the two couples in *Some Like It Hot* is replete with possibility, but the future of a French immigrant newly arrived in postwar, high-unemployment America is grim. Despite his wife's assurances that after this is over he can "be a man forever," in reality such a person would probably be a househusband or idle for quite some time after his arrival in the States.

Gerald Mast comments on the fact that the bureaucracy in *Bride* makes no allowances for any deviations from its rules:

> The horrifying thing about a bureaucracy is that it is totally unprepared to handle the unusual and the exceptional. Hawks subjects Henri to this comic horror—without explicit moralizing, without sentimentality . . . , and without commenting that this is a loony comedy played with breathtaking pace against the background of a country in postwar rubble.[41]

The lack of comment is exactly what gives the film its air of hopeless resignation to an unchangeable situation. In the end Henri is anything but free in any sense, despite the ironic presence of the Statue of Liberty outside the porthole. On the other hand, the two couples in *Some Like It Hot* have achieved freedom at several levels, perhaps the most important being their personal freedom from the need to pretend to be what they are not. They defy society's code for what is proper, most obviously in the suggestion of two men getting married, but also in the fact that Joe and Sugar take off together unmarried without even mentioning the subject. The joyous spontaneity of their mating is the exact opposite of the regulation-bound marriage in triplicate of the couple in *Bride*. The clothing and role reversals of *Male War Bride* may be funny in a painful way, but by the end of the film, Henri seems just as beaten and weary as the war-torn countryside of Europe.

Although there are vast differences between the two films in terms of the effectiveness of the disguise, the degree of difference between "drag" and "straight" behavior, and the final results of the reversals, critical reception of the two films focused on basically the same issues in each film. The reviewers were concerned with "taste," that elusive quality that varies from individual to individual and from decade to decade. The consensus on both films seems to be that they skirt the borders of good taste but rarely go beyond them in their treatment of a potentially risqué subject. *Life* commended Hawks for keeping the "broad humor" of the film "sparkling without letting it get offensive."[42] The *Newsweek* review commented that "although some of the proceedings may try the Legion of Decency's patience, they are handled too delightfully by both Grant and Miss Sheridan to offend any but the most squeamish."[43] Bosley Crowther suggested that "maybe the boys have loaded it on him [Grant] a little heavily in the end, when they force him to dress up like a woman, with a horse's tail for a wig."[44] He was one of the few critics to observe that the character is stuck in a "cheerless situation" with an "unmerciful helpmate." It is as if the majority of reviewers took the grimness of postwar life and an unsympathetic, almost sadistic wife as part of the normal course of events, the material for "convulsingly zany" comedy.

The critical response to *Some Like It Hot* also focused primarily on whether or not the film is in good taste. *Newsweek* had this comment: "Some of this is really quite amusing, especially the slapstick showing the boys struggling with feminine garb; and some of the jokes, both visual and verbal, are pretty vulgar."[45] The *New York Times* film review noted that "a viewer might question the taste of a few of the lines, situations and the prolonged masquerade, but Mr. Wilder and his associates generally make their points with explosive effect."[46] The review does not go into detail on those points: the undermining of sexual stereotypes, the unglamorous side of the underworld, and the possibility of unconventional bliss. Many of the objections arise from Wilder's treatment of Monroe rather than his handling of cross-dressing:

> Female impersonation is a risky enough comedy subject; attempting to make the St. Valentine's Day massacre seem funny is even riskier. Co-author-director Billy Wilder, however, succeeds so well in some instances with his difficult, self-imposed assignment that the picture's subsequent lapses from taste and common decency (mostly involving leading lady Marilyn Monroe) can be presumed to be deliberate rather than the result of ineptness.[47]

The key concept here is the notion that Wilder is intentional in his lapses from conventional good taste. It is precisely this fact that distinguishes Wilder's 1959 film from the 1949 Hawks production. Most films both reflect and affect popular culture to varying degrees, but certainly *Male War Bride* was more a mirror of its society than *Some Like It Hot,* which went as far as a successful mass market film could go toward shocking, disorienting, and reversing the expectations of the audience. Although it is not necessary to assess the artistic merit of a work in order to appreciate how the film reflects or moves popular taste, it is nevertheless apparent that *Hot* succeeds partly because it is a liberating comedy, one that simultaneously exploits conventions and establishes new ways of viewing them. Wilder has little fear of offending, as long as he makes a reasonable profit on his films. For his own personal satisfaction, Wilder makes his themes quite intentionally skirt and sometimes cross over the boundaries of popular opinion and social standards.

If Wilder has always been a director who aims to offend while he entertains, Hawks has always been a director with his finger on the pulse of public attitudes. One need only look at the contrast between *Male War Bride* and Hawks' 1938 film, *Bringing Up Baby*, to see a darkening of what is essentially the same vision of the relationship between men and women. Cary Grant plays a backward, retiring scientist who is engaged to a bookish co-worker. His inexperience and lack of interest in women make him similar to other Hawks heroes, and the aggressive, madcap character played by Katharine Hepburn is the Hawksian woman par excellence. Unlike Grant's stodgy fiancée, she is ready to do anything, and in many ways she thinks more like an adventurous man than like a passive, stereotypical heroine. Despite her masculine qualities, she is a far cry from the mannish, threatening figure of Lieutenant Gates in *Bride*. Hepburn's character is appealing because of her supposedly masculine traits of daring and drive. Her rival has more in common with the character played by Sheridan in *Bride*. She wears mannish clothing, does a man's job, and exudes an air of stolid competence and lack of emotion.

Cary Grant's wearing of female clothing is far less humiliating in *Baby* than it is in *Bride*. In *Bringing Up Baby* he finds himself wearing Hepburn's negligee because his own clothes have been soaked. He meets Hepburn's aunt in this attire, but because she is a bit of an eccentric, his appearance is not alarming or ridiculous to her. The transformation in *Bride,* on the other hand, is embarrassing and complete, although somewhat crude. More important than this is the fact that his cross-dressing in *Bride* is in the context of the much more repressive military environment in which discovery is ground for imprisonment. He wears the negligee with much more of a casual air, and at times even seems completely relaxed in his new attire. The woman's army uniform, on the other hand, seems to make him wince with every step, just as he winces at each new humiliation.

In 1938 the bubble of gentle fantasies had not yet burst. The rich could still be viewed as a set of harmless eccentrics with good hearts. Scientists might be foolish bookworms who spent years putting together useless skeletons, but they were not the creators of the bomb. And women who resembled men were still attractive to Hawks and his contemporaries, a sentiment that shines through in his treatment of Hepburn in *Bringing Up Baby*. The specter of equality and feminist career demands did not loom large enough to threaten male audiences or male directors. A decade and a world war later, the American public was as much more suspicious as it was more prosperous, and even women who remained in their traditional roles were viewed by many men with new anxiety and hostility.

In 1959, whether or not audiences were ready to accept something different, Billy Wilder was going to deliver it to them. The thrill of *Some Like It Hot* grows out of the fact that it legitimates transvestite behavior by having two well-known male stars dress as women. They experience no embarrassing moment of discovery, and no chagrin over the way they appear in their drag clothing. In this film, what is bad about possible discovery is not shame but the fact that being found out means death for the two central characters. Wilder's depiction of the male world reverberates with the black humor which was to surface later in such films as *Myra Breckenridge* (1970) and *The Rocky Horror Picture Show*. In *Some Like It Hot* the satire is aimed specifically at masculine behavior; the two female impersonators appear wholesome and eminently reasonable in comparison with Spats and the other gangsters. The "real men" in the film carry death and random destruction, and even the slim glimpses of their domain reveal the absurd violence of all of it, from the machine-gunning to the bootleg liquor that offers deceptive solace to a vulnerable, insecure woman like Sugar Kane.

The realm of women is saturated with perfumes, silky clothing, softness, and giggles, and because Curtis and Lemmon are in a very special situation, they are allowed to luxuriate in these without loss of prestige. This glorifying of feminine interests, this reveling in the rich emotional warmth of women, provides a return-to-the-womb fantasy with any castration anxiety displaced to the male world of Spats and his gangsters. In *Bride* there is unrelieved anxiety, for the male world disappears and woman is the castrator; she is neither a nourishing mother figure nor is she the billowy, childishly appealing fount of sexuality offered by Marilyn Monroe. The contrast between Monroe in a diaphanous, sequined dress, her breasts pendulous, practically exposed, her voice a soft whisper, and Sheridan in a jumpsuit and goggles, with her deep abrasive voice and abrupt gestures, reveals how one film allays anxieties and the other confirms them. It may be argued that these images are simply two sides of the same coin, for neither one offers a representative portrait of womankind. Nevertheless, *Hot* comes much closer to offering a multidimensional figure because it allows us to catch a glimpse of the sadness and cynical wisdom behind the sex goddess exterior.

Some Like It Hot marks the beginning of a trend toward more open sexuality in movie cross-dressing. One of the main reasons it appeals to popular audiences is that even while it shows us fairly authentic female impersonation—a taboo circumstance that may make many people uneasy—it offers the comforting antidote of Monroe, soft as a Persian kitten, warm and loving as everyone's fantasy of the perfect mother. On the one hand, the film attempts to shock us out of our complacent, drab view of sexual possibilities. On the other, it reassures the audience by presenting cross-dressing as a necessary survival mechanism, an escape from physical danger and not a perversion. The film also follows the tradition of female impersonation as just another disguise, much like the Alec Guinness and Peter Sellers films in which they play multiple roles. Since Tony Curtis does a passable Cary Grant imitation while pretending to be a millionaire, the feline quality of his female persona may be viewed as simply another facet of his ability to assume vastly different roles. What distinguishes *Hot* from the British and American products of the previous twenty-odd years, however, is the fact that Lemmon and Curtis (in particular) make rather attractive women who are obviously young and available. This peculiar situation of having male characters with feminine appeal offers a singular threat to heterosexual male audience members, but the theme has nevertheless struck a responsive chord. After this somewhat shocking introduction of drag to popular audiences, the female impersonator went on to become a recurrent image in films of the sixties and seventies.

The vast majority of female impersonation films produced during the era of the Production Code offered exaggerated, farcical, flat depictions in the context of narratives that encouraged eventual suppression of any aberration from the norm. Although the comedy in such films had occasional elements of anarchic wit, the humiliation of the cross-dressing character and the ultimate resolutions of conflict subtly encouraged conformity to rigid standards of manhood and womanhood. These images both grew out of and promoted stultifying attitudes toward sexual roles. Like the film that incites racial prejudice by showing blacks raping white women, the caricaturized cross-dressing film makes men feel threatened enough to consider themselves justified in clinging to their ideal of male superiority. Just as film images of blacks, with rare exceptions, have tended to offer only two basic stereotypes—the evil, no-good Negro and the good-hearted Uncle Tom or nanny—movie depictions of female impersonation during the Code era fall into similarly constrained categories. Men are seldom allowed to take on feminine clothing or roles without being punished for betraying their sex. Films that give the female impersonator any power or dignity are the fascinating exceptions to the rule. They usually say more about the director or individual actor's daring than they do about public attitudes. On the other hand, negative renditions of the androgynous vision are usually wrapped up in the concerns of the day, forced to take on the dreary cast of contemporaneous anxieties. A film that defies society's codes of dress and sex roles implies that we can be liberated from superficial restrictions and sexual limitations, for in truly exploring androgyny the work taps the most profound psychological and mythic sources of art—the genderless human psyche.

CHAPTER THREE

MALE IMPERSONATION
BEFORE 1960

IN DISTINCT CONTRAST to the relative rarity and negative
connotations of female impersonation before 1960, females
dressed in male clothing appear frequently in American film.
Molly Haskell argues that women "who emulate men will continue to be aggrandized by their efforts, just as male impersonation operates on a principle of aggrandizement (and is therefore
not funny), while the adoption of female characteristics, and
female impersonation, resting as they do on the principle of
belittlement, will continue to be comical."[1] This is not always
the case. Indeed, it appears that the key element in both male
and female imitation is whether or not it is willingly performed
and sympathetically accepted by the social group within the film.
The woman who is like a man but wants to be like a woman may
be comic or tragic; she is not necessarily aggrandized simply by
the possession of male attributes. The film approach toward female impersonation has also changed drastically over the last two
decades, thus undermining the notion that female impersonation
"will continue to be comical."

There are definite differences in the film treatment of male and
female impersonation. Rigidity and codification characterize
most films treating female impersonation, whereas myriad plots,

ranging from semihistorical and western films to musicals and fantasies, depict a wide variety of female-as-male characters. In the latter group of films there is no distinct line between comic and serious plot and character. Also, the attitude toward masculine women implicit in the film's treatment of the theme is often ambiguous. Despite the range of treatments, certain structures are discernible, particularly within such genres as the historical film or the western. The majority of these films define the character of the woman in terms of her relationship to a man, but often she is also set in contrast to a woman who represents opposing values. The key element in distinguishing films that support the status quo from those that offer alternatives is whether the masculine woman is allowed to survive as such. Will she be killed by a society that doesn't understand her, as in *Joan of Arc* (1948)? Will she be ridiculed into becoming a "real woman," as in *Calamity Jane* (1953)? Or will she, as in *Queen Christina,* be doomed to a life of exile for being neither masculine nor feminine, neither sovereign nor subject? It is the rare film, like *Sylvia Scarlett* (1936), that allows the heroine/gamine to have a man and still maintain her androgynous behavior and clothing in the end.

Male imitation in a film may be used to support the status quo by depicting the masculine woman as a kind of freak who threatens the natural social order, or the film may present her as exceptional and superior to the society. If she is a villain of the early thirties, a destructive temptress, her sexual powers will far surpass the appeal of the conventional good woman, and her aggressiveness will conquer the uninterested bachelor and the Casanova alike. In later films this same figure becomes comic or tragic as censorship, political pressures, and audience tastes combine to diminish the serious appeal of the vamp and her cross-dressing doppelgänger. The film that shows the masculine woman as a freak and one that depicts her as exceptional in a positive sense are not necessarily at opposite extremes. The crucial distinction is, rather, between films that allow her to exist as one of the normal verities in nature and those that view her as unnatural (whether in a positive or negative sense) and unable to survive within the world of the film. More often than not, the female-as-male situation is a hybrid rather than an extreme, and these ambiguous, neither black nor white depictions come closest to being believable characters with whom the audience can identify.

The film image of the masculine woman or the woman dressed as a man follows the course of the nation's military, economic, and censorship activities, vacillating between idolizing masculine women and ridiculing or pitying them. Before, during and right after World War I, women were the most popular stars in the serials, and "in the early serials, the heroine saved the hero's life nearly as many times as he rescued her."[2] Women were expected to perform stunts as an integral part of their acting, and the plots often required that they wear men's clothing, doing everything from scaling buildings and piloting planes to riding horses and leaping on locomotives. Pearl White saves the Panama Canal in *Pearl of the Army* (1916), and Ruth Roland leaps on a train from a rope ladder suspended from a plane in *White Eagle* (1922) and hangs from a rope over a cliff in *The Timber Queen* (1922)—all typical activities for the serial queens. At this time the masculine woman was admired, but in the twenties we see the rise of the flapper, who could do everything a man could do and still wear the short skirts that revealed her girlish legs. The flapper was an ambiguous figure who, like masculine women of the fifties, proved to be tough on the outside, but often flighty and secretly in need of the reform brought about by attachment to a man.

The change from wholesome heroine to jaded flapper was a gradual one; it moved through the athletic, boyish character to the more worldly woman who maintained the flat chest and slimness of the tomboy but took on the cabaret habits of dancing, smoking, and drinking. She was attractive because of her daring, but also she was often destined to pay for her wild ways. This ambiguous figure replaced the capable, rough-and-tumble heroines of the teens. Perhaps because she was somewhat threatening in her duplicity, the flapper made the naïve male impersonator a relic of the past age of relative sexual innocence. In Allan Dwan's 1924 *Manhandled*, the girl played by Gloria Swanson is ridiculed by her supposedly sophisticated friends for doing a Charlie Chaplin imitation. The character's willingness to do the impersonation is part of what makes the audience like her, and yet it also is intended to reveal her lack of social savvy. During the twenties, with a move toward censorship of any form of violence against women, females became less important as leads, serving more often as the traditional love interest to be rescued and pampered.[3]

The next rise in the appearance of women dressed as men occurred from 1930 to 1934. After the stock market crash, female possession of certain masculine attributes and imitation of masculine behavior became acceptable once again. In 1933 the attributing of masculine traits to a woman was a compliment, and comments like the following on Marie Dressler's performance as Tugboat Annie were commonplace: "'Actor' is the only word to describe Marie Dressler. She shouldn't be called an 'actress.'"[4] In assessing Greta Garbo's performance in *Anna Christie* (1930), the reviewer speaks flatteringly of her voice: "Her speaking voice is low and guttural, almost masculine in quality and utterly in keeping with her singluar power."[5] Many women were forced to go to work at this time and films presented images of strong, masculine women as positive role models. Perhaps film directors and critics celebrated the masculine aspect of woman in an unconscious attempt to reconcile audiences to the economic realities of the day, when an increasing number of women were usurping the role of provider for the family. This is not to suggest a causal relationship in either direction, but the prevalence of masculine heroines during this period of economic crisis points to the way in which film addresses contemporary conflicts at the same time that it creates, codifies, and promotes "solutions" to these conflicts.

Whereas the majority of films would explore the positive elements of the androgynous woman, Josef von Sternberg, with his darkly romantic European imagination, would concentrate on the somewhat fearful image of woman as omnipotent, unfathomable destroyer and man as eternal victim to her mysterious power. Sternberg's private fantasy of the androgynous woman, capable of encompassing all characters, male and female, could only find free expression during an era of experimentation and transition. In 1934 censorship put a cover on the sexual aspect of the female-as-male, and the sultry opposite, the sex siren, disappeared almost altogether for a time. The femme fatale of Marlene Dietrich is one of the last serious screen portrayals of the vamp. After her such women were no longer fatal; they became comic, occasionally tragic, or they were the transmogrified buddy, the masculine-feminine career woman.

The sexually charged figures of the early thirties were replaced by the less erotic (and less threatening) buddy, who was willing to make the first move toward a cynical, disillusioned hero. This situation satisfied the censor, for the unwilling male would not take up the female's suggested invitation—at least not until after the end of the film. With the U.S. entry into World War II, interest in the masculine woman increased once again, and at this time the career woman became the most popular type of buddy. She wasn't the kind of heroine who would turn down the hero because she never even got asked. She would either be too busy trying to get the hero to respond to her (as in *To Have and Have Not*) or, if she was a career woman, she would be too busy with work to give the man (or the censors) any innuendos to worry about (as in *His Girl Friday*). Many of these films of the early forties end with the woman relinquishing her masculine role and settling down in happy subordination to a man, but most of those still popular today allow her to have a man and maintain her autonomy. After World War II, the foreign import takes on such forms as the thoroughly wicked, probably lesbian spy played by Signe Hasso in *The House on 92nd Street* (1945). In this tedious propaganda film, praised at the time as a revealing semidocumentary on spy techniques, the mysterious Mr. Anthony, leader of a German spy ring, is in the end a woman in disguise. The treachery of woman, whether in a comic or serious setting, becomes a common theme in the postwar years.

After the war and through the fifties, American film reveals an almost schizophrenic obsession with the role of the masculine woman, portraying her in some films as the wholesome, harmless tomboy-next-door and in others as the castrating, deceptive, covertly controlling Mom of the male's most humiliating fantasies. As Molly Haskell observes, "In the comedies of the later forties, the underside—the bitterness, the sense of victimization of one partner by the other (usually husband by wife)—begin to show through."[6] It is during the fifties that people become increasingly aware of the fact that there are no clear-cut boundaries between masculine and feminine behavior. With the move to the suburbs, the American family witnessed the growing importance of the mother as the real authority in the family, the one who disciplines the children while the father is either absent or too tired to care.

The fifties' screen offers some of the most ludicrous, unflattering portrayals of the woman-as-man in film history, either as manipulative controlling agents or as bungling tomboys who just haven't figured out how to be "real" women. Very few complex female characters appear in fifties films; the schizophrenic view of woman as fiendishly capable or unbelievably sweet is the popular theme. The wholesome Doris Day, Debbie Reynolds, Betty Hutton, or June Allyson is the natural antidote to the driving neurotic woman portrayed by actresses like Crawford or Davis in earlier films. The kid-next-door also offers a nonthreatening alternative to the Jayne Mansfield and Marilyn Monroe sex kittens, who, despite their obvious appeal, may be too much for some men even to fantasize about. The very flatness of these tomboy buddies is, paradoxically, the source of their sexual appeal for both the men and the women of an audience longing for lost purity.

Even during the periods of film censorship and apparently defeminized women, sex doesn't leave the screen; it simply goes underground, turning the vamps into little girls like Shirley Temple, who do cute Mae West or tuxedoed gentlemen impersonations, and putting older women into men's roles that force a different kind of intimate contact betwen the sexes. Often the masculinization of the woman plays on the covert homosexual fantasies engendered by the wartime spirit, which places a high emotional premium on masculine virtues. This notion of the sexual appeal of men for each other is beautifully expressed in Renoir's *La Grande illusion* (1937), as the camera pans along the expressions of men witnessing a young soldier's impersonation of a chorus girl. "Ça fait drôle, n'est-ce-pas?" he asks, but the look of desire on the faces of these men, deprived of real female companionship, is anything but humorous.

In the United States, with its strict censorship of sexuality, when directors could not make a woman sexy by accentuating her feminine characteristics, they increased her sex appeal by making her more masculine. Although the war movie, the career story, or the buddy film all appear antithetical to eroticism, they simply offer a different brand of sexual expression that the popular audience and censors could view as wholesome. By taking lovers out of the boudoir and placing them in the battlefield or the business

office, directors were still able to create scenes of enforced intimacy and a sense of that battle between the sexes which is really
no battle at all. Many people brought up in the tradition of the
sexual allure of the forbidden, the unknown, and the covert, find
these films more erotic than the more explicit films of the last
fifteen or twenty years. Just as the woman adorned with traditionally feminine clothing and makeup is never without sexual
overtones, so the woman outfitted in male attire is suggestive
simply because the reversal also calls attention to gender distinctions.

Regardless of the decade, the majority of films involving
women dressed as men are attempts to reconcile the masculine
woman to her role in society. The strong woman is acceptable as
long as she does not use her abilities to undermine men, but she
is sure to suffer if she attempts to maintain permanently her
independence, indifference, or dislike toward men. The image of
the lone cowgirl riding happily off into the sunset simply has not
existed in American cinema until very recent years. Usually films
show the woman sacrificing social duty or career to her domestic
interests. Hollywood's penchant for domesticating women is particularly apparent in the historical film, in which it is often
necessary to twist the facts in order to create a man-oriented
masculine heroine. Films like *A Song to Remember* (1945) portray
the woman as jealous and possessive, ignoring the man's commitment to his political duty. In *The Plainsman* (1937) Calamity Jane
betrays the army by saving the man she loves at their expense.
Queen Christina (1933) shows the Swedish queen abdicating not
for the historically accurate religious reasons but for the love of a
man. All these stories run counter to fact but with the current of
popular taste, maintaining the image of woman as essentially
emotional, domestic, and without outside political or ethical
concerns.

The Historical Figure

Hollywood's treatment of the historical female figure almost
never lets us know what the real person was like in any sense, but
its portrayals of masculine heroines tell us a great deal about what
audiences wished or feared about women of the day. For the most

part, film depictions of history's female cross-dressers are simply intended to highlight the attributes of a particular star, using readily obtainable material with the built-in exotic appeal of the past. Certain otherwise suggestive scenes could be justified on the basis of their educational value. Despite the occasional good intentions of certain stars and directors, or the studio's justification of a film on its instructional merits, most historical films of the thirties, forties, and fifties came no closer to revealing the past than science fiction films did to predicting the future.

Rouben Mamoulian's 1933 treatment of Queen Christina of Sweden provides a typical model of the two-way influence of the star on the role and vice versa. Mamoulian was well aware that it was Garbo's appeal, not the historical figure's charisma, that would draw audiences to the film. At the same time, Garbo's playing of the role adds masculine resonances to her image. Charles Affron comments that "the actress hovers in that area between male and female, leaning into her identity as a woman, to be sure, but not abandoning the richness of her compound being."[7] She alone carries a picture, at least as far as her fans are concerned, and for this reason she must remain Garbo rather than become a homely Swedish queen.

Mamoulian's version of Queen Christina would have been much less glamorous had Garbo had her way. Garbo wished to sacrifice her star image to the demands of realism, but Garbo's wishes were largely overruled by her director and her studio. "Garbo wished to appear with a large nose and massive, masculine eyebrows. She said that Sweden would expect a real portrayal of Christina."[8] Naturally, Mamoulian ignored the expectations of the Swedish people, following the financial expectations of his producer. Like the Spaniard in the film, Mamoulian decides it best to "disguise the elemental with the glamorous."

Despite the studio's insistence on conventional makeup, Garbo's portrayal is distinctly androgynous, primarily because of her movements, voice, and manner. The opening sequence establishes the circumstances of Christina's childhood reign, in which she is reared as a boy, her personality molded in the image of her late father. The next scene shows what appears to be two men riding furiously through the open countryside and into the castle courtyard. One dismounts and runs up the stairs, accompanied by two dogs. A widebrimmed hat conceals the face of the wearer until it is removed, revealing Garbo's face, no less beautiful for the severity of expression and hairstyle. Throughout this scene Garbo maintains the large stride and bold gestures of a man. Her face, usually quivering with expression, is comparatively stony, without the mobility we see in *Grand Hotel* (1932) or *Mata Hari* (1931).

The emphasis throughout the first scenes is on the masculine elements of Christina's personality. In keeping with her upbringing, Christina has a manservant who helps her on with her pants and boots and combs her hair as she reads Molière. When her adviser tells her she cannot die an old maid, she quickly replies, "I shall die a bachelor!" Her clothing is masculine through the first third of the film, and her relationship with a court lady named Eva is very much that of lover and mistress. She kisses her on the lips, dismisses her from the boring business of politics, and even gets jealous when she learns that Eva is planning to marry. All these elements are written into the script, but the rest of Garbo's masculinity resides in herself—in the brusqueness of her movements, the long stride, the forceful hand gestures, the tone of her voice, and the angularity and big-boned quality of her frame.

Christina never loses her androgynous quality, but the rest of the film shows her transformation from a sort of feminine male to a masculine female. She eventually begins wearing dresses, and yet the shift in manners takes place not because of any outside force, but by her own decision to soften and reveal herself. The turning point in Christina's metamorphosis is the inn sequence, in which she, disguised as a man, decides to give up her disguise and stay with the Spanish ambassador, Antonio. Until this point the character of Christina has "all the virile qualities" that Antonio admires in Sweden. As Christina decides to spend the night with him (while he believes her to be a man), she lightly touches her hand to her breast, with a musing tilt of her head. At first she makes a show of masculine movement, tossing her hat off with abandon. It is then in repose, not in movement, that she first reveals to Antonio that obvious outline of her breast beneath her thin shirt. She is still dressed as a man, but there is gentleness of expression—her head lowered and her body angled at three-quar-

ters profile, one knee demurely bent in, in the classic pose combining feminine modesty and seductiveness. Always a rather
heavy-handed director, Mamoulian creates the rather obvious
symbolism of passion by having a roaring fire burning in the
fireplace behind Garbo. This moment is the real turning point in
the film, for here Christina becomes very feminine before our
eyes, simply by the posturing of her body.

> In the inn sequence, Garbo progresses through various stages of
> sexual ambiguity and leads an audience to a new level of percep-
> tion. . . . Until this point in the film, the fun and high spirits of
> Garbo's androgynous tomboy radically tamper with her glamour-
> girl image.[9]

After the seduction—engineered by the female rather than the
male—Garbo wanders through the room, caressing various objects, almost making love to them, so as to remember the room.
This action typifies Christina's androgynous character, for it may
be considered masculine in its initiative, feminine in its tenderness and luxuriant softness.

With Christina's return to the court, she loses a certain appeal,
appearing in dresses that she wears with little grace, and making
decisions that reveal her loss of devotion to duty and to her
people. Until this point in the film, Christina is admirable in her
no-nonsense determination, her ability to cut through the emotional pleas for war and see the needs of her people. Then she
abandons her sense of duty in favor of following her man to Spain.
Love makes her turn inward, taking on some of the negative
qualities of the stereotyped feminine woman. Even though
Christina is being governed by the new woman born of love,
however, she maintains the duality of her nature. She now dresses
in the elaborate gowns of a queen, but she still gestures with the
abruptness and walks with the stride of a man. She forgets her
duty and plays with her new lover, and yet she has the bravery and
self-assurance to confront her people as they storm the castle in
attempted revolt; she turns them back with a stare and a few
words. By abandoning her role as queen, Christina relinquishes
her claim to greatness, and by placing her emotional desires
above the needs of society, she joins the ranks of Hollywood's
typical heroines, eager to sacrifice principle to love, society's
needs to private needs.

The transformation is not at all simple or one-sided, though, and what makes the film emotionally affecting is the very fact that Christina maintains conflicting impulses, creating real tension within a single character. Garbo carries the film in a number of senses, for it is not just her face, her words, and her gestures that enrapture us; all the dramatic conflict of the plot also takes place within her character. Christina expresses the desire to simply love and be loved as a woman, not a great queen. Nevertheless, her greatness shines through as she stoically delivers her abdication speech. She sticks by her decision not to marry Charles, the man chosen for her by her father, and she manages to remain almost impassive as her people cry and clutch after her as she leaves the court. At this point, she still has the thought of her love to bolster her decision, but her true bravery reveals itself when she arrives at the boat and discovers that he is dead. The camera captures Garbo's stoic expression, the tear-glazed eyes, as it zooms into its final shot, a full closeup of her standing at the ship's helm, a woman left with nothing—no kingdom and no future but the hopeless pilgrimage to the land of her lost love.

Historical films like *Queen Christina* are problematic, for they posit that women such as Christina do exist but do not survive as such. The masculine woman who is truly brave, gifted, and iron-willed is beyond the comprehension of society or any one man. Therefore, she is not allowed to live happily ever after, a situation which is often quite true to life. The agonized lives of women like Joan of Arc or Queen Christina may not be used in film merely as a lesson to all women, but such films do emphasize the suffering of these women at least as much as they highlight their heroic qualities.

Film renditions of the lives of masculine women almost invariably "disguise the elemental with the glamorous." Ingrid Bergman's saintly religiosity in *Joan of Arc* (1948) is sensual simply because the camera focuses on her fresh-faced beauty, her passionate expression. In *A Song to Remember* (1945) Merle Oberon, one of the screen's most beautiful actresses, is a far cry from the real-life George Sand, who was as plain as she was brilliant. The point of all this is not to bemoan the fact that Hollywood distorts history. Rather, it is to underscore the notion that star vehicles are exactly that. The studios deliberately pick historical figures that will add a particular flavor to the mystique of their stars, and vice versa.

Always, though, the choices made must brighten the image of the actress. Molly Haskell, in *From Reverence to Rape*, remarks on this process: "Dietrich in white tie and white tails, Garbo as the lesbian Queen Christina (although with a 'cover' romance), Eleanor Powell in top hat and tails for her tap numbers, and Katharine Hepburn as the Peter Pan–like Sylvia Scarlett; all introduced tantalizing notes of sexual ambiguity that became permanent accretions to their screen identities."[10] By association with a great historical figure, the star will take on the exceptional attributes of honesty, courage, intelligence, passion, religious fervor, purity, or what have you. As much as stars like Bette Davis battled against being typecast, the studios encouraged typecasting because they saw it as a distinct advantage in most cases. Rather than depend solely on the script and acting to provide adequate characterization, the director could rely on all the associations that attached themselves to a particular actress as a result of previous roles.

Films may also be used to legitimate or explain the star to the public. Garbo's famous "I want to be alone" both reinforced and explained her solitary life, her refusal to marry. A film like *Queen Christina* explains her androgynous qualities to the public, showing that beneath the masculine exterior, she is what the audience can view as a real woman. In the end she is alone, but this is acceptable because she once loved a man.

The historical films of the thirties idealized, glamorized, and sexualized the masculine female, but with the self-imposed Hays Code the sexual aspect was suppressed. Between 1933 and 1934 the Legion of Decency launched an effective campaign to clean up the movies.[11] Scenes of enforced intimacy continued, but the acknowledgment of the sexual element disappeared, thus making the kind of focal seduction sequence found in *Queen Christina* impossible after 1934. The whitewashed historical figures of the late thirties and early forties were even more inaccurate than a glamorized figure like Queen Christina, because they had no sexuality whatsoever. If a woman were sexually active outside marriage, she had to be portrayed as almost totally without merit, as in *A Song to Remember* (1945). The reviewer in *Commonweal* commented:

> Lavishly costumed Merle Oberon hardly looks like the woman who has been referred to as a dumpy sibyl. Her George Sand

selfishly appropriates Chopin for her own whim but suggests neither the witty, cigar-smoking novelist of the 1840's nor the motherly nurse who administered to the frail victim of tuberculosis. [12]

The pacifist vision is shown to be a female whim, and any attempt to argue against warfare is paralleled with domineering women trying to manipulate men, keeping them from their higher duties.

The pure in heart and body receive much better treatment, as we see in the 1948 Ingrid Bergman version of *Joan of Arc,* one of the most expensive and well-publicized films of the day, featuring a seventy-foot plastic figure of Bergman in white armor to overlook the film's opening. In spite of all the publicity, reviewers generally felt that Bergman was appropriately pure for the part, giving it the "unlipsticked dignity and the spiritual conviction that the story demands."[13] But just as the 1945 portrayal of Sand as a possessive, unpolitical witch was replete with political and social connotations, Joan's 1948 message of moral justification for warfare was not without significance. The review in *Harper's* points to the military appeal of her closing speech:

> To finish it off, Miss Bergman delivers at one point a short speech to the effect that the peace we have is not really peace, for our enemies are arming against us and everywhere we are dissipating our own strength. I trust no one is under the impression that little items like these get into many-million-dollar movies by mistake. [14]

Even a maiden who appears to serve purely political or religious purposes also has her Hollywood quota of covert sexual appeal. Those reviewers who see only Bergman's purity are obviously blind to the sadomasochistic potential of a giant screen filled with a shot of Bergman in chains, crisscrossing her breasts, her expression a cross between agony and sexual bliss.

If Queen Christina served MGM's purpose of justifying the exotic aloofness of their shy star, films like *Joan of Arc* and *A Song to Remember* justified and sentimentalized our nation's military and political stance. Every film about a historical masculine heroine has its own purposes, but studios almost invariably exploit both the historical figure and the actress to deliver a strong message concerning politics, economics, or sexual roles. The very existence of a strong female historical figure in a story reduces the escapist quality of the film and gives the work an added element of social relevance to be manipulated at the movie-maker's will. The appeal to precedent gives the chosen message a ring of authenticity.

The Western Heroine

In American film, the most popular tales of historical figures are subsumed into the category of the western, a genre dominated by masculine virtues. In the classical western, women are traditionally aligned with civilization, fences, and pacifism, making woman the opposite of almost everything appealing about the Old West—its recklessness, rugged individuality, and violence. And yet the fragile prairie flower is not the only representative of women. Indeed, the genre provides some of the most fertile ground for sexual reversals, and screenwriters and directors have continually incorporated the cowgirl and the masculine heroine into their works, modifying her through the decades according to the tastes of their audiences.

During the silent era the cowgirl is represented in a number of films, usually as one of the plucky pioneers who wishes to tame the land rather than leave it open to cattle herds and outlaws. In *The Fighting Shepherdess* (1920) Anita Stewart, in fringed gaucho pants, broad-brimmed hat, and boots, is the experienced westerner, in distinct contrast to Wallace McDonald, who wears the woolen suit of the city slicker from the east. Colleen Moore, in King Vidor's *The Sky Pilot* (1921), wears a similar practical outfit as she displays her skill as a horsewoman. Ruth Mix, daughter of the famous Tom Mix, starred in a number of minor westerns in the late twenties and early thirties. These skilled riders and stuntwomen were a significant force in westerns of the twenties, although they were outnumbered by soft, frail figures like the one depicted by Lillian Gish in Victor Seastrom's *The Wind* (1928).

Many 1920s cowgirls were the serial queens of the teens who had remained popular into the twenties; they were superwomen

like Pearl White or Ruth Roland, who were stars as much for
their ability to do stunts as for their acting. Little attempt was
made at realism, with these women conquering insurmountable
obstacles and demoniacally persistent villains in film after film,
fulfilling the audience's need for escape and adventure. These
films could appeal equally to male and female audiences because
there was constant action as well as the usual love interest. The
serial queens and later cowgirls were not so much women as they
were wonders of nature, required by their incredible adventures
to put on clothing suited to their missions. One could hardly
chase a speeding locomotive in crinolines, and the choice of male
attire was therefore a necessity rather than a self-conscious attempt to defy the norm. A woman in dire circumstances is forced
to become a man in a sense, simply to survive. At the end of the
twenties the western was at its least popular in the history of the
genre. At the same time that depression audiences wanted glamor
and relief from reality, the film industry was presenting some of
its grittiest products. Probably the most true-to-life film depiction of Calamity Jane ever offered was that of Louise Dresser in
Paramount's 1931 *Caught*. The talkiness and lack of gloss and
action in such westerns undercut their popularity with audiences
clamoring for escape.

By the mid- to late thirties, Hollywood had realized the importance of the well-groomed good guy, and men and women
alike were wearing cowboy gear more suited to a rodeo show than
to a cattle drive. In *Black Bandit* (1938) Marjorie Reynolds wears
the dapper pants, shirt, bandana, and boots that would be standard attire for the cowgirl on into the fifties. In *Arizona Legion*
(1939) Laraine Johnson adds a snappy bolero and flirtatiously
cocked cowboy hat. Even Jeanette MacDonald, the most ladylike
of heroines, wears gaucho pants, bolero, and hat in the 1938 *Girl
of the Golden West,* although this hardly qualifies her as a full-time
cowgirl. In the earlier *Rose Marie* (1936) her masculine attire
accentuates her highly feminine features rather than increases her
male attributes; the contrast between her delicate beauty and the
bulkiness of Nelson Eddy's army coat emphasizes her vulnerability, her need for masculine protection. This same enhance-
ment principle operates in any situation in which the frail,
defenseless female puts on the huge overcoat, pajamas, or shirt of
the powerful male.

Hollywood had quickly picked up on the public's desire for glamorous cowgirls. Sex had not yet become a blatant feature of the western, but the cowgirls had undergone a real before-and-after beautification process. One need only contrast Louise Dresser's fat and aging 1931 Calamity Jane with Jean Arthur's slim, neatly coiffed version in De Mille's *The Plainsman* (1937) to see the trend toward glamorizing historical figures until they were practically unrecognizable. The Calamity Jane played by Jean Arthur is thoroughly representative of the industry's standard treatment of the masculine heroine of the thirties—a mixture of tomboy features and stereotypically feminine attributes. Gary Cooper, as Wild Bill Hickok, inarticulately sums up the problem central to most female cross-dressing films when he is unable to provide an adequate definition of woman. He ends his explanation of the facts of life by stuttering, "Well, a woman is . . . well, you never know what she'll do."

De Mille's treatment of Calamity Jane rests precisely between the poles of defending and offending the status quo of society. Although Jane does a number of things that women don't ordinarily do, whenever she is attacked or defended, it is on the grounds that she is a woman. In contrast with Bill Cody's wife, Jane is strong, confident, and brave. Just as in the 1953 Doris Day musical, *Calamity Jane,* she is juxtaposed with a "lady," and she is proven awkward and ignorant of the household and fashion secrets that all women supposedly know. Jane becomes the masculine member of the household as soon as the men leave, comforting Cody's wife and saving her life by sending her off when the Indians come. Jane offers the Indians some women's hats as trinkets, and for a minute we see the cabin filled with Indians wearing feathered hats. (This incident prefigures a more serious situation in *The Searchers* [1956], in which a buck wears the blue dress of the little girl they have captured.) When the chief sees himself in a mirror he decides the hats are no good, and when they hear Bill's wife riding off, the Indians become incensed and take Jane with them by force. The portrayal of Indians as savage and ignorant is underscored by having them put on women's hats and wear them with delight. Jane is just as ridiculous for not wearing such finery as the Indians are for thinking they can wear it, and as soon as Jane meets a real lady, she senses her own inferiority. All Jane's masculine attributes—her skill with a whip, her mannish stride, and her buckskin clothing—are explained by her circumstances; it is never suggested that Jane does any of this out of choice.

If Jane isn't accepted in men's clothing, her situation is even worse when she is in women's clothing. As soon as she puts on a dress, she is captured by the Indians, kept under bondage, and forced either to reveal the destination of the cavalry or to see Wild Bill burned alive. When she gives in and tells the Indians, Wild Bill has nothing but disdain for her, disgustedly calling her "a woman." Later, when she is harassed by the townspeople, Wild Bill defends her against being strung up on a rail by saying, "She's a woman, isn't she? And sometimes women talk when they shouldn't." Even though Jane is exceptional in comparison with other women, she requires the defense of a man. It is ironic that she saves Wild Bill's life not through masculine daring but through her supposedly feminine qualities of pity and sympathy for suffering.

In *Six Guns and Society* Will Wright points out that in "classical westerns" like *The Plainsman,* the strong and the weak have a special relationship:

> In the classical Western we have an aristocratic tendency with a democratic bias. . . . The weak must be protected from duties and responsibilities beyond their capacities and from attacks on their persons or properties; but otherwise, they are the equal of those who are strong and must therefore be respected and deferred to. Now if in this description we substitute "women" and "men" for "weak" and "strong," we will have a fairly accurate account of the relations between men and women in American society, at least until the mid-fifties, when the classical Western began to disappear.[15]

Calamity Jane forfeits privileges by not being a complete woman, by not wearing dresses, being passive, ladylike, and utterly incapable of taking care of herself. She does not receive the deference offered to Bill Cody's wife. Nevertheless, when it comes to actual threats against her person, she can always rely on her gender as a way out. We see relatively little of the Calamity Jane who is capable of driving the stagecoach and fighting off attackers.

When she tends bar in Deadwood City we do see her stop a villain with her whip for trying to leave without paying for his drink. For the most part, though, she is pleading for the stereotypically feminine concerns of saving her man's life before his honor, putting her private needs above the interests of the larger society. At the same time Jane is a distinctly atypical female heroine in that she actively pursues the hero, begging Wild Bill to tell her he loves her and constantly planting unwelcome kisses on his mouth, all but one of which he wipes off with disgust. Within the world of the film, Jane just can't win as a masculine or feminine figure, but for the audience she is a rather appealing anti-hero. Her existence is explained and justified from the viewer's point of view, even if not from the point of view of the other characters in the film. Although Bill reveals covert homosexual tendencies in his fear of women and his powerful attachment to Bill Cody, his character needs no explanation for those around him. In the typical thirties' western, the hero's manliness is established as much by his disdain for women as it is by his ability to fight. Often he would rather die, in a very literal sense, than settle down and marry.

The Jean Arthur version of Calamity Jane is a transitional figure, something between the more appealing female heroine of the twenties and early thirties and the driving, conniving woman of the late forties and fifties. She has the determination to capture her man, but she is totally open, blunt, and honest about it. Molly Haskell observes that between 1930 and 1934 "women were entitled to initiate sexual encounters, pursue men, even to embody certain 'male' characteristics without being stigmatized as 'unfeminine' or 'predatory.'"[14] The 1937 Calamity Jane pursues her man, but she is a friendly character, hardly seen as "predatory." Unlike the heroines of the early thirties, Calamity Jane has no sexual appeal for the hero, and her openly aggressive behavior is comical, at times almost pitiful.

Even though women were pursuing unwilling males, relations were still light, friendly, and playful, a situation embodied by the popular partnership of Roy Rogers and Dale Evans during the forties. Their plots were hardly original, but the repetitive triumph of this team over the standard interchangeable villains seemed to fulfill the same need for adventure that the earlier serials had done. Dale Evans began her screen career as a saloon girl who was "rescued" by Roy Rogers. The switch from black lace evening gown to gaucho pants and boots is actually one of clothing rather than character. In most westerns, beneath the frivolous exterior, the saloon girls are as tough and independent as any man. They must be masculine in spirit in order to survive the violence of the saloon life. Dale Evans becomes the wholesome (nonprostitute) version of this type of woman by maintaining her strength, underplaying her sexual attributes, and aligning herself with one man. What she gives up in independence she gains in respectability.

This connection between the saloon girl and the masculine woman is evidenced by George Marshall's casting of Marlene Dietrich as Frenchy in *Destry Rides Again* (1939), the film that introduces sex and the element of self-parody to the western. She is perfect for the part, of course, not because of a long-time association with westerns, but because of her cabaret connections, playing roles in which she had the toughness often associated in people's minds with masculine characters. Robert Warshow comments on the cowboy and the saloon girl:

> Those women in the Western movies who share the hero's understanding of life are prostitutes (or, as they are usually presented, barroom entertainers)—women, that is, who have come to understand in the most practical way how love can be irrelevance, and therefore "fallen women." In Western movies, the important thing about a prostitute is her quasi-masculine independence.[17]

Destry Rides Again presents the makeup and clothes of the saloon floozy as devices to fool men, a kind of psychic drag designed to advertise the merchandise as pretty and vulnerable, when in fact it is decoration on an essentially masculine spirit. With Dietrich's formerly established image of androgynous femme fatale, the film comically exploits the subtle connection between the masculine and feminine elements of the saloon entertainer, giving us insight into the male reaction against the superficial elements of her femininity. When Dietrich leaves James Stewart holding a lady's parasol and looking foolish, the twist resonates with allusions to *The Blue Angel* (1930), in which she manages to get the professor to put on her stockings for her. In an attempt to put himself on a more equal footing by removing the deception, Stewart asks Dietrich to take off her makeup because she would "look prettier without it." What he is really saying is that he would feel more comfortable if she were more direct, more like the masculine spirit hidden by her feminine trappings. The treatment of Dietrich's character in *Destry Rides Again* could have been entirely comical, except that the fallen woman of the censorship era must die, as usual, in order to be truly reformed.

The forties brought in the predominant image of woman in elegant eastern dress for the parlor or the saloon, although there were a few notable exceptions to this rule. *The Great Man's Lady* (1942) finds Barbara Stanwyck drenched by a storm, in the middle of a cattle drive, wearing an unflattering macintosh, an image that conforms to and reinforces her iron-willed screen personality. Teams like Johnny Mack Brown with Nell O'Day and Evelyn Finley with Tom Keene continued to showcase the considerable stunt-riding ability of the women as well as the men. In general, though, westerns of this period tended to support the image of the "feminine" woman. The condescending tone of the title *Frontier Gal,* a 1945 film featuring Rod Cameron and Yvonne De Carlo, typifies the predominant attitude. In the 1949 film *Yellow Sky,* Anne Baxter undergoes the transformation from the man-hating, independent figure clad in jeans and boots to the softened, dependent creature who is tickled by a fancy hat she receives from Gregory Peck. Films of the later forties often show couples beginning a relationship with real antagonism and ending it in uneasy peace. The women in the forties' westerns are often belligerent, treated with the "you're cute when you're mad" attitude, to which they usually respond by finally yielding to the man.

Although these images offered little in the way of role models, they did have an influence on fashion that indirectly moved women toward greater liberation. They introduced western dress, particularly blue jeans, to a whole generation of teenage girls. Blue jeans and sloppy shirt were considered appropriate only for casual wear, but they contained the seeds of a revolutionary concept: women no longer needed to be constantly beautiful. They could wear practical, rugged clothing without being considered peculiar, and this change in fashion eventually led to a more profound change in the scope of women's activities.

During the late forties and early fifties films took a schizo-phrenic turn in the depiction of the masculine woman. On the one hand, we see the appearance of strong female figures like Joan Crawford's Vienna in *Johnny Guitar* (1954), Barbara Stanwyck in *Cattle Queen of Montana* (1954), and Jane Russell as Calamity Jane in *The Paleface* (1948) and as Belle Starr in *Montana Belle* (1952), and Yvonne De Carlo in *Calamity Jane and Sam Bass* (1949). On the other hand, the glamorous Rhonda Fleming becomes the queen of the technicolor westerns and Doris Day turns Calamity Jane into the girl next door who just wants to sing her way into domesticity. The contrast between Gene Tierney's 1941 soft-spoken, ladylike portrayal of Belle Starr and Jane Russell's 1952 hard-edged, masculine version of the same character indicates the shift in attitudes toward women. They were no longer belles to be protected and cherished.

During World War II and after, when women proved them-selves capable of maintaining their place in the working world, many men began to wonder just how much of the economic pie the women were going to take. For a time, the western under-went a series of chameleon-like changes, for although directors weren't sure what the new western should or could be, they knew that westerns of any variety made money. Thus, in much the same way that many nonsingers were drafted into musicals during their heyday, studios and actors all began to jump on the western bandwagon at a time when surefire successes were at a premium. During this transition period, the feminine, ladylike cowgirl becomes the sexy cowgirl, a trend that didn't seem to appeal to male audiences already concerned about the apparent omnipre-sence of females.

Many of the westerns of the fifties try to glamorize their sub-ject by throwing in voluptuous women in tight blue jeans, creat-ing some truly bizarre combinations. In a review of the current and forthcoming westerns, a 1953 *Time* article commented that the western had changed "since the good old days (Buck Jones, Tom Mix) when a cowboy preferred his horse to a girl, especi-ally when we see actresses like Marilyn Monroe, who 1) wears 'Tailored Levis,' 2) fights off Indians on a raft with an oar, 3) sings two songs, 4) battles a wildcat barehanded and wins."[18] As outlandish as this description seems, *River of No Return* (1954) is by no means atypical in the period. The film offers a crazy-quilt of Indian attacks, father-son pathos, near rape, and rationalizations for shooting a man in the back. The work departs from the earlier western themes particularly in its brutal approach to male-female relationships. In one scene, Robert Mitchum almost rapes Marilyn Monroe, but their tussle is interrupted by the appearance of a wildcat. In the final scene, Mitchum enters the saloon where Monroe is singing, grabs her in a fireman's rescue hold, and carries her off with him, caveman style. The incongruity between this behavior and statements like "You'll make me forget you're a woman" indicate a basic ambivalence about how women should be treated—revered and protected as feeble females or bullied as untamed wildcats. Monroe's pants represent a purer life than the glitter of the saloon entertainer's costume. Her redemption from saloon life is embodied in the final gesture of the film, as she tosses off her sparkling shoes, the last remnants of her old way of living. Here and in her saloon performances there is a parallel with Dietrich's situation in *Morocco;* Monroe, like Dietrich, leaves her shoes in the dust, abandoning glamor in order to follow the man she loves.

Although glamor and sex appeal were striking features of many western heroines of the fifties, this was not the only popular type available. If a woman couldn't be sexy in blue jeans like Rhonda Fleming, she would be cast as a hard-driving toughie like Barbara Stanwyck or as the goofy, harmless tomboy, probably the most popular masculine heroine image of the fifties. Tomboy figures combined a number of contrasting features, none of which represented any real threat to the status quo. Portraying the masculine cowgirl as a kind of buffoon helped alleviate anxiety over competition from women while it also offered a female figure who would not be overly dependent on an unwilling male.

The almost pathologically energetic and cheerful Betty Hutton is a typical example of the typecast tomboy of the postwar era. She once commented that people working with her had to get insurance policies, so often were her co-performers actually injured by her boisterous antics.[19] Hutton stars in the 1947 *Perils of Pauline,* a screen biography of Pearl White, reinforcing the image created for her in *Incendiary Blonde* (1945), in which she played Texas Guinan, who first acted in action films. In 1950, the film version of the musical *Annie Get Your Gun* gave expression to the popular cliché that women must hide their abilities in order to get a man. In the film, Hutton as Annie gets Frank Butler (played by Howard Keel) by learning how to shoot crooked; and the actress makes a statement about her own marriage that indicates a similar situation in her off-screen life: "But when a real man comes up against a situation where he gets second billing, he walks."[20] Three years later, with *Calamity Jane,* Hollywood filmmakers sent "yet another dog after the scraps from *Annie Get Your Gun's* box-office banquet."[21] Doris Day offers the same brand of kid-sister appeal in yet another film in which a woman clothed as a man must put on a dress and act helpless to have any sex appeal. Tomboys and masculine women in these films are fools, unable to be the women they secretly long to be, so that their skills in the male domain seem insignificant.

In Jane Russell's *The Paleface* (1948) and *Son of Paleface* (1952), the comedy treats some fears more directly. In *The Paleface,* Russell's Calamity Jane feigns helplessness, letting Potter (Bob Hope) believe that he is killing Indians and managing the situation. Here is a striking parallel with what many men may have seen as the deceit of women before the war in pretending to be incapable of both running a household and holding an outside job. The war had necessarily undermined the myth of feminine helplessness. Both the *Paleface* films ridicule the notion of man's inherent prowess in self-defense, and they also include subtle allusions to the covert homosexual and bestial elements of the western themes. As in countless Bob Hope movies, he inadvertently kisses or fondles other men, thinking they are women. *Son of Paleface* spoofs the idea of the cowboy liking horses better than women by having Roy Rogers sing a love song, "Four-legged Friend," to his horse, instead of romancing the very willing "Mike" (Jane Russell). Unlike De Mille's 1937 Calamity Jane, Jane Russell is in complete control, maneuvering the helpless Bob Hope and hitting him over the head with her gun butt whenever he gets a bit frisky. The woman is perfectly capable, and yet she chooses to hide her abilities and make an idiot of the man.

The antidote to this anxiety-ridden comic situation is Doris Day's *Calamity Jane.* This film carries more gender-related gags than any Andy Warhol/Paul Morrissey work, but all of them are designed for a wholesome, innocent audience. They begin with the confusion caused when the Deadwood City theater owner promises a show featuring a woman, Frances, who turns out to be Francis, a man (played by Dick Wesson). To avoid a riot Francis has to go on stage dressed as a woman, singing a song about having honey for a special honey bee—special, indeed. When his wig is lifted off by a roving slide trombone, Jane steps in to save the day by promising to get Adelaide Adams, a famous entertainer, to come to Deadwood. Wild Bill Hickok (played by Howard Keel) swears that if she succeeds, he'll come to the performance dressed as a squaw with a papoose, and of course, that's exactly what happens. The woman isn't really Adelaide Adams, but her maid, Katie (played by Allyn McLerie), who goes to live with Jane for protection from the men in Deadwood City.

In this film we see the same kind of female-female relationship as in *The Plainsman,* but here it is further developed because both women are single. Calamity Jane takes the newly arrived feminine heroine out to her place, helping her down from the buggy with masculine gallantry, holding her two-handed by the waist as she descends. Katie is horrified at how dirty and unattractive Jane's house is, but to the tune of "A Woman's Touch" she transforms it into a cozy, kitschy home. When Jane tries to become a woman by wearing a dress, she lands in a mud puddle; right after this, Wild Bill sees her and bursts into gales of laughter. She tries again, and when she arrives at the local dance wearing a white dress, people are so amazed at her beauty that they hardly recognize her. Even Wild Bill suddenly begins to appreciate her. When the two characters realize that they can't have the people they think they want, they decide to settle for each other, and the film ends with a double wedding of the two couples.

Calamity Jane attempts to explain away the masculine woman by showing that all she really wants is to get married and settle down. The film promotes the idea of settling for less and being convinced that it is more than enough. One song praises the life of the small, unsophisticated Deadwood in comparison to Chicago, and another song, "Once I Had a Secret Love," helps Jane believe that she will be much happier with Wild Bill Hickok than she would have been with the handsome lieutenant she thought she loved. The final bit of settling for less occurs at the end of the film, when Jane relinquishes her role as stagecoach driver. The final shot shows Jane in a wedding dress, atop the coach but no longer holding the reins, for Bill has taken over that function. In keeping with the tradition of the musical comedy, the film takes a discordant note in society and makes it harmonize; society accepts Calamity Jane because she reconciles herself to the role demanded of her.

At the same time that this male wish-fulfillment film was playing in local theaters, Nicholas Ray was preparing a very different kind of western to come out in 1954, *Johnny Guitar*. Despite its idiosyncratic qualities, the film is representative of new developments in the western, particularly in its treatment of the female leads. The fifties are a transitional period; according to Will Wright, beginning in the mid- and late fifties, "Women are no longer representatives of society requiring protection and exuding morality; they are now individuals in their own right, capable of joining the elite group and making it, by their presence, even more independent of society."[22] In earlier westerns, strong men protected the weak, and there was a clear distinction between good and evil, a distinction that was to become hazy in the westerns of the sixties. During the transitional period, there is little confusion over good and bad, but "instead of the strong man protecting the weak woman, the strong couple now asserts its independence from the weak and cowardly persons who make up the social group."[23]

Most of the earlier film treatments of couples demonstrate the standard pattern described by Wright. All of the prefifties versions of Calamity Jane and Wild Bill Hickok show them as an exceptional couple, with Jane as the dependent member of the team. Their relationship to society is that of protector without special privileges. Society may turn on them or reject them temporarily, but eventually they are integrated into the society, and this usually means that Jane becomes more traditionally feminine. A "gun-toting girl" like Anne Baxter in *Yellow Sky* (1948), "though she was brought up among the Apaches, has a feminine heart, and she goes riding off with her man."[24] The happy ending demanded that the woman take her place behind the man, and that the couple take its place in supporting society's values.

In *Johnny Guitar* the protagonists (male and female) break from a society that is led by a vicious, vindictive woman, played by Mercedes McCambridge. Joan Crawford, as Vienna, is most assured when she is dressed in black pants and a shirt, as in the opening and closing sequences. She is at her lowest ebb when she dresses like a woman in virginal white and yields to her "feminine heart." According to the film's internal dress code, woman is most dangerous when she takes on the role of prostitute, wearing the red dress of a woman who has been with many men. In Vienna's character we see the melding of the two female figures capable of participating in the distinctly masculine ethos of the western. The combination of cowgirl and prostitute contains strength and physical readiness as well as an almost offhand, aloof attitude toward love. Nicholas Ray underscores the connections between the three stock female types found in westerns by using clothing in a strictly codified way. Even reviewers who were unsympathetic to Ray's efforts commented on how well Joan Crawford wears pants or on how "her beautiful slacks and costumes are much more appropriate to a Noel Coward rough and tumble satire."[25] *Johnny Guitar* is indeed a satire, even if some people don't get it, and it plays on all of the conventions of the western in a highly stylized way.

The focal point is Ray's experimentation with sexual role reversal. The subtle link between woman-as-man and woman-as-prostitute is articulated by Vienna's fulfillment of both roles. The key element linking the two is the woman's control over the relationship, maintained by her emotional invulnerability. At the same time that Crawford portrays the masculine female, Sterling Hayden plays the pacified, feminized male who has given up his gun for a guitar. It isn't long before we see the gunfighter beneath Johnny Guitar's veneer as well as the womanly female beneath Vienna's stern exterior. In neither case is this hidden fidelity to gender the most admirable feature of the character's personality, for there is a neurotic, grasping quality to Vienna's dependence and a psychotic element in Johnny's hotheaded aggressiveness. In their relationship with each other, Johnny takes on the whining, wounded pout of the stereotypical female, whereas Vienna tortures him with her emotionless explanation of how she managed to build her saloon while he was in jail: "For each brick, each plank, each beam of this place, I—" whereupon Johnny cuts in with an almost tearful, "Don't."

As the film progresses Vienna softens, wears dresses, and comes close to filling the role of the standard western heroine, always calling for peace and law-abiding behavior. More daring than the standard heroine, Vienna is ready to sacrifice herself to save the life of the young boy, Turkey, and in a later scene she exhibits a John Wayne stoicism as the townspeople come to lynch her. After her last-minute rescue by Johnny, she sheds the white gown, once again putting on black pants and a shirt, the functional clothing of a fugitive. At the same time, she sheds the passivity of her role as martyr, perhaps because she realizes the extent of the danger as Emma's leadership of the townspeople galvanizes Vienna into an active defense. This process reverses the standard film treatment of the masculine heroine, for instead of showing how the female dressed as a male cannot survive, the film shows us the female wearing a dress on the verge of being hanged, surviving only when she switches back to the pants she wore in the beginning.

In a number of westerns of the sixties, as well as in certain earlier ones, the villain's obsession with the hero is so overwhelming as to constitute a covertly homosexual love-hate relationship. This is certainly the case with Vienna and Emma, whose obsessive hatred of Vienna goes beyond animosity to the savage fury of a betrayed lover. Vienna's relationships with Johnny and the Dancin' Kid are almost insignificant as compared to her involvement with Emma. Vienna's feelings for Johnny and the Kid are merely sexual and emotional, whereas the conflict with Emma is a struggle out of which only one of them can emerge alive.

The sexual ideology of the film is strangely paradoxical. On the one hand, Vienna contradicts social norms and offers an alternative to the stereotype of the heroine. It is shown that she need not be passive in order to get her man, and indeed the man (or men) is a peripheral interest at most. Survival is the issue in this film, and in order to survive, Vienna must undergo the same kind of masculinization that the heroines of the early serial films did, for circumstances will not allow her the luxury of wearing a white gown or carrying on a romance with her lover. On the other hand, Vienna's freedom from femininity results in the same kind of enslavement to violence that she begs Johnny to avoid. In the end she is forced to shoot it out with Emma, even though she has argued for peace throughout the film. What is most significant is the fact that it is another woman who forces her to betray her ideals. McCambridge plays the frustrated, puritanically asexual creature that Vienna would have become in order to be accepted by society.

The issue which emerges during the late forties and early fifties in films like *Johnny Guitar* is the growing sense that the individual can no longer become part of the community, and that the society is inimical to the well-being of the individual. The communal values of cooperation, protection of the weak, peaceful solutions to conflict, and mutual acceptance of a moral code become vaguely linked with the notion of a Communist conspiracy. At the same time, the idea of controlling violent or antisocial impulses is identified with Momism. The fifties fears concerning the disappearance of the individual had the paradoxical effect of driving people toward greater rigidity and conformism, particuarly with regard to sexual roles. The fifties are marked by the emergence of sexual extremes—the ultrafeminine Monroes and Mansfields with large breasts and tiny waists, and the supermasculine Lancasters and Mitchums with their large shoulders and narrow hips.

In the sixties women almost disappear from the western, but those who remain hold their own in a hostile, violent environment. No longer is woman the representative of society, the civilizing, pacifying force. In *The Misfits* (1961), a modern western, Marilyn Monroe is identified with the wild mustangs, free things that cannot be captured or tied down. In *El Dorado* (1967), "Joy dresses like a man, always carries a gun, and kills the arch-villain in the final shoot-out, saving Thornton's life."[26] *Time*'s review of *Cat Ballou* describes Jane Fonda's participation in the train robbery as "a throwback to Pearl White's perilous heyday."[27] At the same time that Fonda grows into her gun-toting persona, we see the "feminine" side of Kid Shelleen (Lee Marvin), as Jackson Two-Bear trusses him into the corset he wears for gunfights. As in *Cat Ballou,* the heroine (Kim Darby) in *True Grit* (1969) hires a professional to help avenge her father's death. John Wayne as Rooster Cogburn says admiringly of the young girl, "She reminds me of me." In Sam Peckinpah's *Ride the High Country* (1962), Mariette Hartley, as the cross-dressing female lead, "is at the very centre . . . the soul of its action, her growth (the girl finally accepting a suitable costume) faithfully paralleling Judd's own progress."[28]

By the beginning of the seventies, westerns with women dressed in men's clothing and fulfilling masculine functions had become so commonplace that modern audiences may assume women always wore pants in the old west. Reversals of traditional dress no longer operate as a meaningful code in the western; indeed, the genre may have played itself out for a time. In *The Electric Horseman* (1979), a film depicting the cowboy as an anachronism, we finally see the ultimate reversal—a woman riding off into the sunset, carrying the sweet memory of her affair with an innocent, idealistic cowboy.

Tomboy, Pal, Companion

The western has always provided an ideal setting for the return to youth, whether it be the nation's, our own, or both. Outside the western, the same need is fulfilled by the female cross-dresser who acts as buddy, making no sexual demands and offering no competition for the male. We see this androgynous character in the 1926 and 1931 versions of *Kiki;* the sound version was played by Mary Pickford, already experienced as a boy in her version of Little Lord Fauntleroy. The depression prompted *Wild Boys of the Road* (1933), a sentimental treatment of the problem of the nation's young people who were riding the trains and living in hobo camps. In this film we see young girls wearing boys' clothing in order to travel, unimpeded by feminine dress or the accompanying sexual harassment. *Sullivan's Travels* (1942) provides a sexier version of the companion, with Veronica Lake as the girl who wears boys' clothes in order to accompany the protagonist on his journey to discover the real life of poverty.

All these films are able to create situations of male-female intimacy without fear of offending public decency, simply because the woman who is dressed as a male in such situations often loses her sexuality—at least according to film custom. Even in a film as late as *A Walk on the Wild Side* (1962) Jane Fonda makes no move to flirt with Laurence Harvey until she gets out of men's clothes and into a dress that she considers sexy. With the exception of the fifties' use of jeans as a seductive novelty, film precedent has it that women traveling as men are not molestable or even attractive, perhaps because dealing with two sets of pants is too difficult for audiences to imagine. Nevertheless, these road pictures offer the viewer a great deal of latitude in imagining what happens between the scenes.

The popularity of the tomboy reached its peak in the years after the Second World War. A number of these films showed women participating in the masculine realm, often dressed in appropriate male attire, but reduced the threat of such women by placing them under the tutelage or control of a man. In Preston Sturges' *Sullivan's Travels,* Sullivan, the idealistic movie director, takes charge of the girl who follows him through the hobo camps of America. In *The Seventh Veil* (1945), James Mason plays the part of a psychotic pianist who trains his inhibited and imprisoned ward (Ann Todd), a young woman forced to be his faithful companion. When he discovers that she is in love with the artist who is doing her portrait, he tries to break her hands. In *Pat and Mike* (1952), a cheerier vision of this relationship, there is a twist on the trainer-trainee situation because Hepburn plays such a capable figure. Nevertheless, it fits in with the Pygmalion pattern that has the man creating, controlling, or training the frisky thoroughbred. By reducing the woman almost to the level of an animal, these films make the woman's feistiness less threatening.

One of the most appealing examples of this type of film is Clarence Brown's *National Velvet* (1945). Velvet Brown (Elizabeth Taylor) is just a slip of a girl, and even though Mickey Rooney may not be a macho type, he controls Velvet, just as her father controlled her mother when he trained her for the English Channel swim. The film appeared at a time when people were longing for a comforting story. In the war years, animal pictures such as *My Friend Flicka* (1943) and *Lassie Come Home* (1943) were popular, perhaps because people wanted to believe that at least animals would not betray us, even if human beings had revealed a treachery and barbarousness hitherto unimagined. As the perfect counter, a film like *National Velvet* shows the audience that not only animals but people as well can be trusted.

The gold of the picture rests in the hearts of the two women, Velvet Brown and her mother. Although *National Velvet* offers the inspiring model of a young girl overcoming all odds to win the Grand National Steeplechase, the film subtly undercuts her success. Velvet's mother was an exceptional woman who swam the English Channel, but in the film we see her only as Velvet's mother. When she gives Velvet the prize money to enter the Pie in the Grand National, she tells Velvet to try for it because it is all she will have for the rest of her life. Velvet decides to ride rather than get a cynical paid jockey, and she willingly cuts her hair short, winning the race in a male disguise. She then must forfeit the prize because she is a girl and thus excluded from the competition. This situation sadly supports the notion that a brief moment of glory is all she will have. Velvet is offered a Hollywood contract, but she is happy to be "sensible" and stay with her family in an environment that will prepare her for a female role in society. The film supports the status quo (or what many people at the time wanted it to be) by showing women, young and old, happily choosing the nest over an exotic career.

With *Pat and Mike* (1952) we see George Cukor's more feminist version of the woman-as-trainee in a movie that fits in with a wave of sports movies like *The Fighter* (1952), *Jim Thorpe, All-American* (1951), and *Follow the Sun* (1951). Cukor includes the conventions that support the image of woman as property; for instance, Mike (Spencer Tracy) simultaneously puts his dim-witted prize fighter, his horse, and Pat (Katharine Hepburn) on a strict diet and training schedule. Cukor then undermines these stereotypes by having the woman do such unconventional things as save the man from thugs by using her jiu-jitsu skills. Most critics considered the film fine comedy, and yet it is obvious from the comments of reviewers that the feminist message was controversial and not necessarily to everyone's liking. For example, Manny Farber writes, *"Pat and Mike* is an almost charming fairy story about two subjects that give most sports writers the creeps—a female athlete and the more mercenary type of language-mangling underworld-haunting manager."[29] Farber's comment is a fairly typical reaction to an atypical film.

Much more in keeping with the general direction of film depictions of tomboys was *Tammy and the Bachelor* (1957), a somewhat belated selling campaign for the wholesome country virtues of simplicity, loyalty, and idealism. Debbie Reynolds, as Tammy, is favorably contrasted with the rich city girl, a representative of the decadent, materialist, modern ethos that includes everything from jitterbugging to disdain for the land. The film opens with Tammy offering to go with her grandfather (Walter Brennan) to look for survivors of a plane crash. When he says that the "whirlpool ain't no place for a girl," she insists that she has strong arms and a strong stomach as well. Tammy and her grandfather nurse Pete, who is amazed at the naïveté of Tammy, whose manners and beliefs are as simple as the jeans she wears. She doesn't have the typical feminine weaknesses; rather, she is vulnerable because of her sweetness, her faith in human goodness. She is unspoiled by the social customs and sexual role playing, a fact revealed by her behavior once she arrives at Pete's house. At breakfast the father of the family holds her chair for her as she sits down, and when Pete arrives, she jumps up to repeat the same procedure for him.

Tammy swears that she cannot wear "fancy silks," and when she finally does put on a gown, the aunt tells her that we "have to sacrifice for beauty." Throughout the film Tammy's unpretentiousness contrasts sharply with the materialism, superficiality, and frivolity of Pete's rich fiancée. After Tammy gives up on capturing Pete's heart, we see her once again back in the swamp, wearing her jeans. Pete makes his inevitable return and proposes to her. Tammy's jeans, her straightforward manner, and her disdain for "citified" ways, all represent traditional populist values of independence and antimaterialism. At a time when corporate values and loss of individuality were becoming rampant, this film is a throwback, a failed attempt at a retro portrait of a time that never was.

A Member of the Wedding (1953), based on Carson McCullers' novel, takes a more profound look at the phenomenon of the tomboy who is unable to accept the sex role designated for her by society. Julie Harris plays Frankie, a social outcast with short-cropped hair and a boyish figure who finds herself unable to adjust to the idea of her brother's marriage. Abandoning hope for turning herself into a proper girl, she decides, after much raving and agonizing, to stow away with the honeymooning couple in order to be close to this mysterious love between man and woman. At the same time, John Henry (Brandon De Wilde) displays his own sexual confusion. In an attempt to capture the attention of Frankie and the cook Bernice (Ethel Waters), the little boy parades around the kitchen wearing a woman's hat and high heels and carrying a purse. The dialogue of the film centers on the meaning of maleness and femaleness within society. Although it is overly melodramatic, the film is one of the first serious efforts at dealing with the adolescent's difficulty in adjusting to the sexual identity imposed from without.

The Career Woman

The wave of male impersonation films of the early thirties was followed by a new manifestation—the mannish woman in business and the professions. Molly Haskell points out that "while the Hays office, having assumed the mantle of our national superego, suppressed the salutary impulse of female sexuality, it was also largely responsible for the emergence of the driving, hyperactive woman. . . ."[30] The sexual innuendo and comic situations of cross-dressing become too risqué for the production code, and we see the asexual, masculine woman emerge in the films of the late thirties and the forties. A stock comic situation is the grumpy heroine's conversion to the joys of marriage after a standard battle with a male.

Many of the films that remain popular today offer an alternative to the domestication of the woman. In *His Girl Friday* (1940) and in a number of the Hepburn-Tracy films the story ends with the couple still struggling to maintain the precarious balance of power that marks a vibrant, open relationship. These films are admired by feminist critics, but the relationships often lack the fillip of overt sexual play present in pre-code pictures. Much more common is the film that offers a conversion fantasy: women who don't like men or who like their work (including tomboys, career women, feminists, implied lesbians, etc.) can be converted to the joys of sex by the right man. The women in these films are not necessarily cross-dressers, but they wear clothing that is brittle in its no-nonsense, professional aura. Such films were popular throughout the late forties and fifties, and even as late as the early sixties we see works that zero in on the "problem" of the career woman.

A number of films of the early fifties can be viewed as attempts to reconcile the apparent conflict between a career and the traditional feminine role. In *No Sad Songs for Me* (1950), Margaret Sullavan plays the part of the wife who, upon learning that she is terminally ill, sets herself the noble task of finding a wife and mother for her husband and child. She is the controlling agent in this tale, and the replacement she chooses for herself—the new "draftsman" (Viveca Lindfors) who comes to work with her husband—is even an improvement on the old model wife. She looks great in pants, can do everything the first wife could do, and can also be a real companion and help to the man in his work. As John Garfield points out in *Gentleman's Agreement* (1948), a man no longer wants just a wife; he wants a buddy who has the strength to stand by him and help him in his career. *No Sad Songs* shows us very literally the death of the traditional wife and the takeover of the "new woman" who has career interests and capabilities as well as the usual womanly attributes. Along with such films that show contemporary women moving into traditionally male careers came loosely historical films such as *The Girl in White* (1952), in which perky, wholesome June Allyson plays the first woman ambulance intern. Although the trend in the fifties was toward films that would reconcile the society to the existence of career women, even during the sixties we see films that attempt to show career women as unsatisfied misfits.

A New Kind of Love (1963) tells a rather old kind of story about a woman who wants to lose herself in her work and ends up losing herself to a man instead. Joanne Woodward, whose image as a tomboy is reinforced by numerous films, plays Sam, a man-hating fashion designer. Because she was once burned in love, she has resolved to have nothing to do with men, even though she is flying to Paris, that notoriously amorous city. Paul Newman, a journalist, calls her "sir" the first time he meets her, because of her mannish attire, hairstyle, and gestures. Once in Paris, on the day of Saint Catherine, Woodward has a change of heart and prays to the saint for a husband. Only after she has altered herself to the point of looking like a prostitute does Newman notice her and want to interview her for a story. During this masquerade, she amazes Newman with tale after tale of her supposed sexual adventures, all of which she steals from the experienced Parisienne played by Eva Gabor. When the truth is revealed, she is finally integrated into the society as she reforms the playboy ways of Paul Newman and eliminates the boyish ways of her former self. The assumption of the film is that the mannish woman is miserable as such; she must find a man in order to be fulfilled. The playboy male is shown to be superficial and incomplete without marriage, but countless males fantasize about coping with just such superficiality as the drunken orgy and the one-night stand.

Several films of the fifties make an interesting set of connections between feminine clothing and capitalism versus masculine clothing and Communism. In *No Time for Flowers* (1952), Viveca Lindfors plays a frumpy Prague secretary whose mannish clothing, manner, and outlook are defeated when she falls for a capitalist who brings her nylons, lipstick, and champagne. A common magazine advertisement of the day shows a beautiful woman wearing a chic but inexpensive rayon suit, American made, alongside a plain woman wearing a blocky, mannish, and expensive Russian-made suit. This ad unites Americanism, feminine fashion, and rayon in a single blow. At the same time that hardness in women is identified with Communism, softness in men becomes the correlative symptom. According to Raymond Durgnat, during the fifties "there is a haunting fear that a 'liberal' policy towards Communism is the policy of men who are, not exactly feminized, but neutered, castrated, by their scruples."[31]

The best-known film playing on the connection between capitalism and feminine pulchritude is Rouben Mamoulian's *Silk Stockings* (1957), which spoofs politics, materialism, and sexuality all at the same time. We see Cyd Charisse change (behind a translucent screen) from the dowdy, uniformed Party member to the steaming sex siren we all secretly know she is and, as in previous films, it is the luxury of traditional feminine clothing as much as it is male charm that converts her to the capitalist cause. This remake of the *Ninotchka* story done by Garbo in the thirties was not considered very successful, but it was a smash hit compared to the earlier, little-known film *The Iron Petticoat* (1956). Katharine Hepburn plays the part of a Russian pilot who flies to an American base in Germany because of her disappointment over not receiving a medal she felt she deserved. Bob Hope is hopelessly miscast as the charmer who seduces her to the luxuries of female clothing and western attitudes. The figure of the severely dressed, sexless Communist appears in countless films of the period, usually in contrast to the voluptuous warmth of American women.

There is a certain cold comfort for males in the thought that women are like children or the stereotyped Indians of the westerns; they can all be bought off with a few baubles. At the same time, all men are not millionaires, and even those who are rich would like to be loved for themselves rather than for their money. Hence, we see the popularity of films that show us the simple country girl, unconcerned with material possessions, like Tammy. Yet films like *Tammy* or *Silk Stockings* were seen even at the time of their release as anachronistic, futile attempts to recapture some spirit of past innocence. Commenting on *Silk Stockings,* the *Time* reviewer sums up: "Hollywood should keep abreast of the times enough to know when not to spoof a superannuated spoof."[32] The reviewers of the Tammy films responded in a similar vein by pointing out that very young girls and old ladies might appreciate the cuteness and innocence of the old-fashioned character.

Just as the Hays Code's squelching of sexuality had given birth to the hard-driving, aggressive career woman of the forties film, the forties strong woman had created a demand for a simpler, homier heroine. According to Molly Haskell, the Rosalind Russell figure "was not a favorite with men," because of her combination of wit and sexual appeal.[33] It is also likely that she was no great favorite with certain women who, by choice or by necessity, never hoped to be like the forceful career women Russell portrayed. Indeed, a certain number of the women who had entered the job market during and after the war wanted nothing so much as to find a man who would support them. Films like *How to Marry a Millionaire* (1953) reveal the masculine anxiety over female materialism, but they almost invariably allay that anxiety by showing the woman following her sentimental heart rather than her mercenary reasoning. If the films of the thirties fulfilled people's wishes by showing streams of glamorous people with no financial worries, the films of the fifties showed people placing their interest less in material values and more in the virtues of family, home, and country. This is not surprising, since the

United States was undergoing a financial boom, and the area that was the most in need of fantasy solutions was the crumbling family structure.

The Cabaret Tradition

The German cabaret tradition is responsible for a large number of the night club versions of women as men, a motif originally popularized in film almost solely by the Sternberg/Dietrich combination. In his autobiographical *Fun in a Chinese Laundry,* Sternberg describes the sexual ambiguity common in cabarets when he was in Germany:

> At night, when I went out to dine, it was not unusual for something that sat next to me, dressed as a woman, to powder its nose with a large puff that a moment ago had seemed to be a breast. To differentiate between the sexes was, to make an understatement, confusing. Not only did men masquerade as females, wearing false eyelashes, beauty spots, rouge and veil, but the woods were full of females who looked and functioned like men.[34]

When Sternberg came with Dietrich to the United States, he was well aware of her androgynous appeal, despite the misleading advance publicity describing her in rather mundane terms. Sternberg comments:

> I had seen the "modest little German *Hausfrau,*" whom all these preparations were to frame, wearing the full-dress regalia of a man, high hat and all, at a Berlin shindy, and so outfitted her, planning to have her dress like a man in one of the café sequences when she would sing in French and circulating among the audience, favor another woman with a kiss. The formal male finery fitted her with much charm, and I not only wished to touch lightly on a Lesbian accent . . . , but also to demonstrate that her sensual appeal was not entirely due to the classic formation of her legs.[35]

Sternberg presented a short scene to the studio officials in which Dietrich was dressed in white tie and tails, and they objected vehemently, swearing "that their wives wore nothing but skirts."[36] Sternberg adds that "having her wear trousers was not meant to stimulate a fashion which not long after the film was shown encouraged women to ignore skirts in favor of the less picturesque lower half of male attire."[37] Women in earlier films had worn pants for practical purposes, but never before had they been considered sexy, an attitude to be irrevocably altered by Dietrich's example.

Marlene Dietrich has aroused as much critical interest as any star in Hollywood, and much of it centers on her androgynous quality. Peter Bogdanovich explains his fascination with Dietrich in terms of the masculine quality she projects. Ordinarily, men identify with and prefer male stars (and vice versa), for, as Bogdanovich puts it, "part of my affection for film stars lies in wishing I were like them and it therefore follows that my interest would be more in the men."[38] Dietrich's allure lies in her ability to appeal simultaneously to male and female audiences, an important factor in the viewer's appreciation of film. As Handel and Mayer point out in *Hollywood Looks at Its Audience,* "It is quite common for the dreamer, male or female, to imagine himself or herself in the place of the hero or heroine of the particular film."[39] It is pleasurably disconcerting for either sex to identify with Dietrich, for the experience calls on both sexes to experience a liberating sexual duality. According to Haskell, Dietrich "is Sternberg's creation, his anima, and yet she absorbs so much of him into her that she is not an 'other' as object, on the far side of the sexual gulf, but an androgynous subject."[40] Such was the identification between the two that Sternberg was reported to have said, "I am Miss Dietrich—Miss Dietrich is me."[41]

In almost all of his films, Sternberg tests sexual boundaries, exploring fearful as well as pleasurable fantasies in ways that leave the viewer wondering whether Sternberg worships or loathes women. Sexual power is a central theme of his films, and in Sternberg's world characters' manipulation of each other usually involves the female taking on male characteristics. As is true of many films that employ cross-dressing, Sternberg's masculinization of the female is often accompanied by the feminization of the male, with the role exchanges reinforced by visual cues.

In *The Blue Angel* (1930), Emil Jannings as the professor serves and pampers Dietrich, even helping her put on her silk stockings. *Morocco* (1930) presents several unlikely reversals involving the ordinarily masculine Gary Cooper; he wears a rose behind his ear, plays with one of Dietrich's dolls, and holds her fan to shield a kiss with Dietrich from the audience's view. In *Shanghai Express* (1932), Dietrich puts on Clive Brooks' hat at the same time that she encircles him with her plumed neckpiece. Dietrich's masculine Catherine of *The Scarlet Empress* (1934), dressed in Hussar's uniform, is the fulfillment of a character that begins the film as a timid, doll-like puppet. As the film progresses, she soon proves herself more of a man than Peter (Sam Jaffe), who, dressed in the flowing robes and long, loose hair of the period, often looks as much like a little old lady as a crazy little man.

The seemingly endless succession of costumes, including everything from bird plumage to military officer's hat, is the embodiment of the boundless sexual and intellectual possibilities contained within the single character played by Dietrich. In this sense, she is always the same figure, regardless of the film, for she is never a one-dimensional personality—never completely cruel, never completely serious, and above all never completely comprehensible. At a more concrete level, Sternberg's constant obsession with clothing and the voyeuristic appeal of objects hanging between the viewer and the viewed may all stem from his youthful labors in a New York millinery shop and later in a lace house. One can easily imagine the impressionable fifteen-year-old immigrant losing himself in reveries as he would clean the shop, filled with lace, feathers, artificial flowers and fruit, hat forms, manikins, and the lingering perfume of the day's customers. These erotically charged visual experiences would become the building blocks of Sternberg's film world.

Voyeurism is central to Sternberg's concept of man's relationship to woman, for in his schema, to gaze is to worship. Man's desire to look at woman does not, as many feminists claim, make her a mere object; rather, in Sternberg's world, it gives her almost unlimited power. Indeed, the title *The Devil Is a Woman,* although supposedly created by Ernst Lubitsch, gives the devil, traditionally an almost all-powerful male figure, the female identity that Sternberg considered ultimately triumphant. According to Andrew Sarris, in Sternberg's films, "The Girl will possess a mystical authority over the life of the Boy, and it is this authority which marks Sternberg's attitude toward women long before the debut of Marlene Dietrich."[42] After his farewell film with Dietrich (*The Devil Is a Woman*), Sternberg continued to create films of sexual reversal, if not celebrating androgyny, exploring it with all the thoroughness and morbid curiosity of a child examining a squashed bug. *Shanghai Gesture* (1941), with Gene Tierney (as Poppy), Ona Munson (as Mother Gin-Sling), and Victor Mature, is yet another film replete with the exoticism and sexual ambiguity characteristic of Sternberg's work. Henri Agel notes that "the 'femme fatale' who clothed her bewitching carnality in all climates, the aridity of Africa (*Morocco*), the Vienna of *Dishonored*, the China of *Shanghai Express,* the Hispano-Hollywood of *Devil Is a Woman,* has become in *The Shanghai Gesture* a fatal man, and androgyne as well, with the oily and animal face of Victor Mature. . . ."[43] Emlyn Williams as the pretty, demonic Caligula in the never-completed *I Claudius* represents the same kind of destructive androgynous figure as the one played by Mature. In *Jet Pilot* (1951), Janet Leigh is the aggressor, a Russian jet pilot who is supposed to seduce John Wayne to the Communist cause (of course, a ridiculously hopeless premise). Despite the casting of a totally masculine John Wayne and a very unmasculine Janet Leigh, the film gives us the typical Sternberg sexual interchanges and female aggression in the sequences that show the refueling of the jet planes. Here, the character of Leigh, which doesn't succeed in being truly masculine or androgynous even in a flight suit, takes on its masculine features when it is encased in a bullet-like jet plane. As in *Ninotchka, Silk Stockings, No Time For Flowers,* and *The Iron Petticoat,* the theme of Communism repressing sexuality appears; it is only as Janet Leigh peels off the flight suit and succumbs to the attractions of capitalism that she becomes sexually expressive.

Sternberg's final film makes explicit the relationship between viewing and worshiping. In *The Saga of Anatahan* (1953), based on a true story, Sternberg expresses his notion of the organic unity of the male and female relationship. The twelve Japanese sailors chant to "the Queen Bee," the only woman in their midst, "You and I, like an egg—you, egg yellow, I egg white—I embrace you!" This chant indicates the symbiotic aspect of the combination as well as the centrality of the female figure, the yolk, that consumes the white as it grows. Andrew Sarris observes that once again in this final work, Sternberg goes against the grain of popular thought by offering another tale of female supremacy:

> When the girl on the island is first introduced to the survivors, Sternberg's camera remains focused deliriously on the girl's beauty. This emphasis might be compared with a similar situation in Renoir's *La Grande Illusion* where the Allied prisoners pause to stare at the impersonation of a chorus girl by a British soldier. Renoir's approach is humanist in the sense that he asks his audience to respond to the fraternal feeling of sexual longing shared by the prisoners. Sternberg, by contrast, asks the audience to respond to the spectacle of the woman herself, to the dark, mysterious beauty which obliterates reason, honor, dignity. . . . For Sternberg, Woman, in Truffaut's phrase, will always be supreme.[44]

If Sternberg's obsession with the strong woman and the weak man existed before and after his collaboration with Dietrich, she also carried the masculine image to the films she did without Sternberg. In *Desire* (1936), she wears the double-breasted sports coat that was soon to become the fashion, and in *The Garden of Allah* (1936) she is handsomely outfitted in the boots and riding pants necessary for a desert safari. In her "comeback" film, *Destry Rides Again* (1939), Dietrich wears dresses, but her tough prostitute character (Frenchy) dominates the sheriff, played by mild-mannered Jimmy Stewart. She gets into a barroom brawl, chases Stewart with a gun, and even saves his life by placing herself between him and a fatal bullet. *Seven Sinners* (1940) finds Dietrich once again as the saloon girl, and in the number that wins John Wayne's heart she is wearing the sailor's full dress uniform. In *The Spoilers* (1942), Dietrich remains in women's clothes, but John Wayne gets decked out in her plumes, looking foolish while he tries to confront Randolph Scott. As in *Destry,* Dietrich saves a man from death by shielding him from a bullet in Fritz Lang's *Rancho Notorious* (1952). Lang has Dietrich looking chic in men's clothes through the major part of the film, a costume innovation that prefigured Nicholas Ray's outfitting of Joan Crawford in *Johnny Guitar* (1954). Billy Wilder's *Witness for the Prosecution* (1958) casts Dietrich as the strong-willed, mysterious Christine

Vole, who, in the flashback scenes, wears a Nazi uniform and sings to her own accompaniment on an accordion.

Almost all these films portray Dietrich as the vamp, but none worships her as the goddess she played in Sternberg's films. Especially in the films clustering around the prewar and World War II years, the vamp is diminished by being either humorous or utterly villainous, slapped around or killed—humiliations to which Dietrich was never subjected in Sternberg's films. Her identity as a foreigner, and a German no less, undermined her appeal for popular audiences during the war, but she never lost the basic androgynous identity established in her early films.

Alexander Walker points out that Dietrich's personal background and film persona owe a great deal to the gentlemanly military tradition. He argues that "the male dress she often puts on in her films is not necessarily sexual in its undertones: generally it has a military association, too."⁴⁵ Instead of viewing the male dress as military rather than sexual, it might be wiser to see that there is something distinctly sexual in the military motif, particularly in the German context. The gender-related elements of submission and aggression are inextricably bound with the strict military tradition. One can hardly deny the sadomasochistic appeal underlying the mystique of the uniformed man, raping, pillaging, suffering tortures, perhaps, but always glorified for actions that would be considered bestial and savage in any other setting.

What the Dietrich persona has in common with the military tradition is her unemotional adherence to a code, her refusal to yield to pain or emotion, and what seems at times to be an almost sadistic sense of amusement in the face of danger or death. In *Dishonored* (1934), Dietrich refers to her prostitute's clothing as the "uniform" she wishes to die in. While one of the soldiers in the firing squad cannot bear to shoot at her, she applies her lipstick with all the sangfroid of the hero, showing no emotion whatsoever in the face of her own death. By the end of *The Scarlet Empress,* Dietrich, as Catherine the Great, is in uniform as she gallops up the stairs to claim her power; the ecstasy of her expression is in complete contrast to the doll-like blankness of the "feminine" Catherine of the opening scenes. The line between stoicism and masochism is a fine one, but whatever term one chooses, it is this seeming immunity to pain that marks the Dietrich character. The idea of Dietrich bursting into hysterical tears is as incongruous as John Wayne in petticoats, and this seemingly masculine unwillingness to reveal emotion places Dietrich, along with heroes like Wayne, in the military camp.

The tradition of the military woman or the tuxedoed femme fatale established by Dietrich's cabaret performances remained a significant motif in Hollywood films, but the image was laundered and sweetened when the cynical foreigner faded from vogue. As film censorship took over and the United States witnessed the events that led to World War II, military and tuxedoed females were still around, but now the foreign vamp was diminished, replaced by a variety of less threatening models, one of the most popular being the diminutive Shirley Temple. In *Captain January* (1935), she wears a tiny sailor's uniform, and in *The Little Colonel* (1935), *Poor Little Rich Girl* (1936), and *Wee Willie Winkie* (1937) she wears a soldier's costume.

Hepburn in *Little Women* (1933), as Jo, masquerades as a moustachioed cavalier in one scene, and in Dorothy Arzner's *Christopher Strong* (1933), she plays an aviatrix who commits a noble suicide as the ethical solution to a forbidden love affair. *Spitfire* (1934) shows Hepburn as a tomboy faith healer, and in 1936, she plays the title role in *Mary of Scotland* and the lead in *A Woman Rebels*. The latter two films were not instances of cross-dressing, but they further establish her as a dominant woman, an image that helped her gain the "box-office poison" label she received when *A Woman Rebels* flopped.

With *Woman of the Year* (1942), Hepburn appears in the mannish business suit of the forties, but, as if she and the studios had learned their antifeminist lesson, this plot was more congenial to popular tastes; her character realizes that marriage is more important than a career is for a woman. With *Pat and Mike* (1952), Hepburn reestablishes her feminist grounding, only to have it snatched out from under her in the execrable film, *The Iron Petticoat* (1956), another tired echo of the Ninotchka theme. That same year, she plays a frumpy spinster who wears pants to do her farm chores, in the more successful but equally nonfeminist film,

The Rainmaker (1956). Hepburn's career is checkered with films that argue for female independence and those that demonstrate just the opposite sentiment.

At the peak of her career, in the mid-thirties, she is the true androgyne, without the mysterious glamor of Garbo or the subtly suggested sadomasochistic allure of Dietrich, but with a freshness and ethical surety rarely granted to actresses of the American screen. This image is captured most effectively in *Sylvia Scarlett* (1935), a film that was unacceptable to audiences in 1935 for precisely the same reasons that it is fascinating to present-day audiences.

The True Androgyne

Sylvia Scarlett was not a big money maker at the time of its release, and George Cukor, ever eager to gauge his films in terms of dollars and cents, all but disowns the film because it was not a popular success. The *Newsweek* review of the film discusses the fact that Katharine Hepburn had to undergo as many trials during the filming of the picture as the heroine Sylvia does in the story. "First the shy star had her hair—one of her most attractive attributes—lopped off like a man's."[46] Doing all of her own stunts, Hepburn nearly broke her hip in a fall from a window and nearly drowned during the filming of the drowning rescue scene. Despite *Newsweek*'s emphasis on the difficulties involved, Hepburn had been enchanted by the part when she read it, and Cukor recalls the time the crew spent filming as playful and idyllically happy.

Time begins its review with the controversial statement that "*Sylvia Scarlett* reveals the interesting fact that Katharine Hepburn is better looking as a boy than as a woman."[47] As much as modern audiences can look at old Hepburn films and see her as enchantingly beautiful, the audiences of her day found her a bit unconventional, probably in exactly those features that make her ideal for male impersonation—a wide, strong jaw, rather large teeth, prominent cheekbones, and relatively small eyes. Moreover, her brusqueness, outspoken manner, and forceful, abrupt gestures—all qualities that add to her appeal for modern audiences—combined to make her unpopular for the period in which audiences rankled at her aggressiveness and apparent disdain for convention.

Hepburn was certainly ideal for the part of the gamine in *Sylvia Scarlett,* eager to join in the larceny and yet constantly flubbing the con games, at times because of her unwillingness to actually hurt anyone, at other times simply because of her inability to stay out of the way and keep her mouth shut. The film opens with Sylvia disguising herself as a boy in order to go to England with her father, a lace smuggler. It is never exactly clear why she has to become a boy, but she faithfully maintains the pose throughout the major part of the film. Sylvia and her father meet up with Cary Grant, and after sizing each other up, they agree to work con games together in England. The first one fails because Sylvia loses control and shouts at a fellow criminal, "Thief!" in English, thus revealing that she is not the French boy she pretends to be. At another point in the film she ruins her pose by bursting out laughing. Finally, they manage to steal some jewels while visiting the maid of a rich woman, but because Sylvia cannot bear to see the poor girl blamed for the loss, she exposes the plot once again. As they sit in their room afterwards, desperately considering what to do to get some money, Sylvia naïvely proposes, "Why don't we all get jobs and go to work?" to which the men react with utter disgust.

All these situations point to the kind of "moral ascendancy" that Margaret Mead sees as belonging to the woman in American society. Cukor's treatment of the theme differs from the majority of films that present woman as self-righteous civilizer. Unlike the goody-two-shoes flavor we find in the standard, moral movie heroine, the honesty of Sylvia's character is the one element that saves the group of scoundrels from being common criminals. The glamor is taken out of crime or violence by a film like *Sylvia Scarlett,* which offers instead a pastoral tranquillity that is almost Shakespearian in its appeal. Like Rosalind/Ganymede in *As You Like It,* Sylvia dreams up the scheme of returning to nature, and the group decides to become troubadors, frolicking and entertaining beside the sea.

During the tour the sexual complications begin to mount. First, the maid (Dennie Moore) who has joined them has designs on the nubile young boy she assumes Sylvia to be, teasing her and asking, "When are you going to grow some whiskers?" She paints a moustache on Sylvia, wondering whether to turn her into Chaplin or Ronald Colman, and after she finishes the job, she kisses Sylvia on the mouth in a very unmotherly way. Aside from Sylvia's apparent revulsion at the lesbian elements of the situation, she feels sorry for her father, who is blindly in love with this shallow woman. The next difficulty arises when Cary Grant tells her she'll "make a proper hot water bottle" for him to sleep with, and she must constantly cope with the problem of disguising her gender from him.

When the group meets the artist, played by Brian Aherne, it is obvious that Sylvia likes him and that he takes a shine to her/him as well. He comments that there is something in the boy (Sylvia) that gives him a queer feeling, but he interprets it as simply something that "needs painting." Sylvia steals some women's clothes and visits him, and he comments that he now understands why he talked to her as he did even when she appeared to be a boy. The artist first laughs at her and then tries to kiss her; finally he grows into the more sympathetic response of teaching her "the tricks of the trade" of being female so that she can defend herself against the tricks men will play on her. Both characters learn something in this scene, for the pose that a woman takes in order to get a man is shown to be as laughable as Sylvia's posing as a boy.

In the process of the film, Sylvia matures and becomes the ideal woman, an impression that is strengthened when Cukor contrasts her with the other characters in the film. As soon as Sylvia meets the artist's mistress (Princess Natalie Paley), she tries to emulate her by dressing up as a lady. Both Paley and Moore (the maid) serve as perfect foils to Sylvia by showing the higher- and lower-class versions of womanhood. Moore, as the maid with a stage career in mind, is frivolous, superficial, and cruel in her faithlessness. Paley's character is tempestuous, high-spirited, and impulsive—the high-class model of what Moore would be if she were richer, more beautiful, and more intelligent. She, too, is cruel and thoughtless, and her behavior even provokes the disguised Sylvia to strike her. Aherne's revulsion at this action high-lights the thirties double standard that allows women to strike men, but not even a young boy is allowed to strike a woman.

The resolution of the film finds the upper-class mistress leaving with Cary Grant, while Sylvia and the artist search for them. Sylvia accidentially slams the car door on the artist's hand, and therefore ends up driving, still wearing the boys' clothes she has worn throughout most of the film. In the end, Sylvia has her artist, without having to compromise or give up the bluntness that constitutes her charm. Grant, the natural deceiver, and the princess find themselves together, both of them clinging to and paying for their ridiculous notions of what it means to be male and female. The two characters are caught up in deception, while Sylvia and the artist are liberated from it.

What is most significant about this treatment of male impersonation is the fact that the female doesn't have to reform her own masculine ways in order to have a man. Although she plays with her female identity and the notion of pretense, her behavior is acknowledged as play; it doesn't last, and it isn't taken very seriously while it is taking place. *Sylvia Scarlett* avoids two popular and contradictory film assumptions about woman's ethical function. Women are often presented as the inhibiting, stifling moral force, the opponents of all that is free, natural, or adventurous. As Molly Haskell points out, "The flight from women and the fight against them in their role as entrappers and civilisers is one of the major underlying themes of American cinema."[48] At the same time, films often show a woman as having no ethical code but a devotion to the survival of herself, her man, and her family. Sylvia Scarlett definitely has commitment to a moral code, one that makes her willing to risk her own life to save the mistress of the man she loves. She is not the entrapper or the civilizer, though, for she displays the butterfly qualities of a Peter Pan, not a Pollyanna or a puritan. Sylvia's character offers a delicate balance of ethical principles and a spirit of fun, a combination all too rare in film heroines of later decades.

We see this kind of playful, high-spirited androgyny in a number of films of the period, including *As You Like It* (1936), *Queen Christina* (1933), and *First a Girl* (1935). *As You Like It* follows the Shakespeare play, thus ending with the normal comic resolution of a return to proper roles for all involved. *Queen Christina* is more ambiguous, leaving us with the final image of a lone figure, noble, grieving, yet self-sufficient. *First a Girl* is similar to *Sylvia Scarlett* in that it shows a lower-class couple falling in love with a princess and her fiancé. Jessie Matthews plays the part of the woman whose husband happens to be a dance hall female impersonator. When he falls ill, she takes over his part and pretends to be a man pretending to be a woman. She wears men's clothing offstage, smokes and plays cards, and then wears scanty, glittering bikinis and feathered headpieces for "her" show. The film provides the usual comic situation of cross-dressers: "The two men and Miss Matthews in male garb, drawing cards to determine who sleeps alone and who shares the double bed in the last available room in a French inn."[49] During that same year, Gladys Swarthout plays the dual roles of Rosita Castro and the masked Don Carlos in *Rose of the Rancho* (1935), an echo of her earlier stage male impersonation as the page in the opera *Romeo and Juliet.*

It is difficult to explain why *Sylvia Scarlett* endured, becoming a minor cult classic, while a number of other similar films faded into complete obscurity. Probably the primary factor is the presence of Katharine Hepburn, but then what constitutes her timeless appeal? As with the Sternberg/Dietrich combination, the magical chemistry between actress and director was essential to Hepburn's rise to stardom. George Cukor had the ability to exploit Hepburn's qualities; the combination was complete when her saucy, flippant, independent character was counterbalanced with the truculent, unflappable screen image of Spencer Tracy. Hepburn was a heroine that women could emulate and men could find, if not appealing, at least not too threatening to enjoy. Hepburn's willingness to adapt to various roles contributed to her screen longevity, for she could provide a fairly consistent, positive role model that was often modified according to popular tastes. She offered a contrast to the figures played by stars like Bette Davis and Joan Crawford, who, although they rarely wore men's clothes, managed to take on a number of negative masculine attributes to become figurative castrators and literal murderers, or else dependent, love-starved neurotics.

If Dietrich was too foreign to remain a popular favorite throughout her career, Hepburn seemed to capture the features of American womanhood admired by women and men. She has the almost rawboned look of determination of the pioneer woman, combined with the spontaneity and high spirits of the aristocratic thoroughbred, an irresistible blend of the homey and the elegant. Audiences also developed the sense that there was little distance between the various roles that created Hepburn's screen image and the carefully guarded private woman behind the screen. As more women began to look for a sense of independence and individuality, Hepburn came to be an accepted role model of the woman who liked men but had her own life to lead.

Just as actresses often reflected their private attitudes and tastes in their screen roles, so the public's imitation of these roles came to be reflected in private attitudes and needs. The public's desire for a masculine heroine may be viewed as thinly veiled disdain for women, or it may be seen as a drive for liberation from confining stereotypes. The wide range of masculine and feminine heroines can be seen as a reflection of women's uncertainty over their proper role, or it can be taken as society's willingness to accept a number of roles for women. No doubt the truth lies somewhere in between, for although women do enjoy a greater amount of freedom in their dress and behavior, children also experience this kind of freedom because their status is low enough to allow for experimentation and play. The question remains whether women or men will ever be able to achieve a comfortable balance.

CHAPTER FOUR

1960–1985:
NEW DIRECTIONS

The Decline of Censorship: Homosexuality and Transvestism Come Out

IN THE EARLY SIXTIES, with changing attitudes toward sexuality in general, the taboo subjects of homosexuality and transvestism began to appear in popular movies. What is striking in the last twenty years is the unprecedented variety of approaches to cross-dressing in both serious and comic contexts. Wilder's *Some Like It Hot* and Hitchcock's *Psycho* offered significant new models in the treatment of female impersonation, shocking audiences and critics and breaking the bounds of "good taste" until those boundaries ceased to be standardized. The sixties witnessed the first relatively open treatment of homosexual themes in such films as the two 1960 British works, *Oscar Wilde* and *The Trials of Oscar Wilde.* For American audiences, the topic was considered acceptable for mass audiences in 1961, as long as the word "homosexuality" was not used. The British film *Victim* (1961) was banned in American theaters because it named its central character's sexual preferences, whereas the American films *Advise and Consent* (1961) and *The Children's Hour* delicately skirted the clinical labels that were so offensive to censors.

By the end of the decade lesbian love affairs were the subject of films designed for popular, adult audiences. In keeping with the greater freedom allowed to female characters as opposed to male characters in film, fairly explicit female sexual play is commonplace at a time when the first kiss between males is still a shock for the audience. In *Reflections in a Golden Eye* (1967), Brando's hurried, climactic kiss is greeted with horror and revulsion by his "victim." Not until 1970, in Hal Prince's *Something for Everyone,* do we see in a major studio release a homosexual kiss between two consenting adults. Meanwhile, films like *Thérèse and Isabelle* (1968), *The Fox* (1968), *Les Biches* (1968), and *The Killing of Sister George* (1968) show women kissing nipples, licking navels, and simulating masturbation and climax. These works represent a new trend that brought what had been the porno-arthouse film into popular neighborhood theaters. The change in treatment of homosexual and lesbian characters altered the significance of cross-dressing, because transvestism took on the connotation of sexual perversity, whereas in earlier popular films it had represented more purely asexual, social deviation.

The Rise of the Underground Film

At the same time that the mass-oriented cinema was beginning to touch on homosexual themes, the underground cinema was showing homosexual activities quite explicitly. The rise of the underground film was to have an enormous effect on what topics were available and how directly they could be treated in major studio releases. Jack Smith's famous *Flaming Creatures* (1963) was among the first successful avant-garde films to wed the confusion of abrupt camera movement, jump cuts, and unfocused shots with the disorienting blur of gender distinctions often associated with homosexuality and transvestism. A few earlier films had depicted transvestite behavior—*The Savage Eye* (1959), in which a female divorcee drops acid and goes to a "drag ball," or *Star Spangled to Death* (1959), which shows Jack Smith slumming in drag—but *Flaming Creatures* was the first to catch on as an underground standard. The supposedly intentional technical crudity does not undermine the interest of the film, and at times, the nonstandard techniques highlight the content. During the orgy scene, the jiggling of the camera humorously suggests the excitement of participation of the camera operator as he undergoes the earthquake of orgasm.

If Smith's work has any message it is the playful glorification of the transvestite, homoerotic, transsexual world created in his film. Smith makes a subtle link between vampirism and sexuality by having a woman (who turns out to be a man) emerge from a coffin and become a vampire who chases her victims with the same zeal shown by the orgy participants. In a sense, the concept of masculinity feeds on femininity, and vice versa. The repeated shots of jiggled penises and breasts underscore the notion of the interchangeability of masculine and feminine appendages; they are all playthings for our amusement, when they are stripped of the mysterious significance created by the larger society and even of the serious sadomasochistic connotations suggested by Kenneth Anger's *Fireworks* (1947) or Jean Genet's *Chant d'amour* (1952).

The confusion over the gender of actors in the film provides an interesting parallel with the filmmaking process itself. Even bad impersonations of women can sometimes leave us with the feeling that the actor/actress is really a woman until we see the telltale penis or some other definitive gender cue. In much the same way, even a badly produced film can create an illusion of reality until we see something like a jet stream in a tale of the old west, at which point the illusion is interrupted. Our demand for verisimilitude, formed and nurtured by the Hollywood tradition, is not fulfilled in the same way in avant-garde cinema. In *Flaming Creatures*, the satirical theatricality is deliberately underscored by filmic ineptitudes. The abrupt jolting of the camera, for example, reminds us that this is a movie, not merely an act of voyeurism. The home-movie quality of avant-garde films goes beyond limitations of budget and technique to make a statement about the nature of the art. The homosexual subculture celebrates dramatic artifice, a theatrical sense of the absurd that promotes an aesthetic of artful self-consciousness in film. For many avant-garde filmmakers, the purpose of films is not to make us lose ourselves in illusion, but to call our attention to the fantastic elements in the everyday world and to jar our comfortable assumptions about the nature of that world.

Self-reflexive techniques pervade the underground cinema, but they are employed for a variety of reasons. Indeed, lumping together a wide variety of films under the relatively recent and somewhat misleading label "underground film" suggests nothing more than the fact that such films do not ordinarily receive wide distribution or acceptance by popular audiences. *Flaming Creatures* was one of the first sexually explicit films to receive widespread publicity because of the New York City police's seizure of the film, along with Genet's *Chant d'amour,* and the arrest of Jonas Mekas, editor of *Film Culture,* in March of 1964.[1] This brought to the public eye the issue of censorship of underground films, and the notoriety created public interest in many films that might otherwise have remained truly underground. It is ironic that attempts at censoring such films had, during the sixties, the unintended effect of publicizing and thereby popularizing the previously taboo subjects of homosexuality and transvestism.

During the sixties, the Warhol/Morrissey productions gave birth to a whole new series of transvestite actor/actresses, with gender reversals constituting a central theme in the majority of their works. Mario Montez's impersonation of Harlow in *Screen Test I* (1965) and *Harlot* (1965), the transvestite sheriff in *Lonesome Cowboys* (1969), and the elaborate cross-dressing in *Chelsea Girls* (1967) are still being screened in art houses and film classes today. In praising *Lonesome Cowboys,* George Cukor comments on the unabashed boldness of such films:

> And I relish the moments of unexpected deliciousness—Viva playing a rather emotional scene to the sheriff, who's calmly making up and getting into drag. There's such a candor about these pictures, and nobody has any reserve at all. I'm just full of admiration for them. . . .
>
> Nobody has any kind of guilt in these pictures. None of the attitudes are conventional, you never see a tear—that's extremely refreshing![2]

Films like *Blonde Cobra* (1962), *Chumlum* (1963), and *Himself as Herself* (1966) all explore the connections between transvestism, transsexualism, and homosexuality in ways designed to alienate and disgust the popular audience, while the films confirm the communality and the sense of alienation from the larger culture experienced by the subculture of the gay community. The improvisational style, supposedly deliberate crudeness, and disjointed plotlessness of these films are all signals of the subculture's rejection of mass values of tidiness, order, traditional hierarchy, and conventional form.

Underground films and the older "camp" favorites that influenced them fulfilled a variety of functions. In analyzing social functions of films, Jarvie outlines several major categories.[3] Certain films offer a model of behavior for an audience that is not part of the social group being portrayed. The audiences watching the glamorous stars of the thirties often wished to imitate the dress and habits of these characters to fulfill status aspirations. In a somewhat different way, this same reasoning applies to the recent popularity of films that feature stars like Greta Garbo, Marlene Dietrich, Bette Davis, and Mae West, women whose campy glamor, aggressiveness, and theatrical manner serve as behavior models for certain male homosexuals. Another category of films presents characters and situations that are familiar to the audience, and these movies reinforce values and customs already held by the viewers. Like the patriotic films of the forties, the avant-garde films of the sixties legitimate the behavior of a particular segment of society. The final category involves the film that establishes a rapport among audience members and acts as a social lubricant. This aspect of film-viewing was particularly important to the vocal patrons of silent movies. In recent years, the communal quality of film attendance has reemerged among teenagers and members of intellectual and sexual subcultures. Avant-garde and cult favorites offer alternative world views and establish a sense of group solidarity among their fans.

The daring techniques and subject matter of avant-garde cinema also had an enormous influence on popular films. Andrew Sarris points out the important link between so-called underground films and conservative Hollywood productions:

Films such as Jack Smith's *Flaming Creatures,* crudely put together for a pittance, probably have done more to liberate Hollywood from its idiotic self-censorship than have all the pious editorials on the subject. By making the unthinkable thinkable, Jack Smith's outrages against decorum extend the boundaries of artistic freedom.[4]

During the sixties what had been truly underground cinema found its way into the more respectable art houses designed for a somewhat larger audience, and with this step up, these films became the subject of *Newsweek* and *Time* reviews. By the end of 1966, Warhol's *Chelsea Girls*—described in *Time* as a "very dirty and dull peep show,"[5] and in *Newsweek* as the "natural expression of a class," touching "more nerves than a multifariously perverse world will ever admit"[6]—had grossed over a million dollars. Films like Shirley Clarke's *Portrait of Jason* (1968) and Frank Simon's *The Queen* (1968) explored homosexuality and transvestism in documentary style, introducing many viewers to a world they had not previously acknowledged or even known existed.

Other directors brought deliberate tastelessness to the underground screen in humorous put-ons of serious subjects. John Waters assaulted conventional taste and attitudes, first in short pieces like *The Diane Linkletter Story* (1968) and later in *Mondo Trasho* (1969) and *Multiple Maniacs* (1970), which feature Divine, a three-hundred-pound female impersonator, in the lead role. In *Multiple Maniacs* Divine is raped by a man wearing a dress, and she is later seduced in a church by a woman who gives her an anal "rosary job" while reciting the stations of the cross. Divine then goes on a killing spree, is raped by a huge mechanical lobster, and finally enters the streets, chasing hordes of screaming people while she cries out that she loves being a maniac. Waters' most notorious film, *Pink Flamingos* (1971), achieved infamy for the scene in which Divine eats dog feces, a sight that most audiences just weren't ready for. Waters' *Polyester* (1981) also features Divine and, in a bid for greater acceptance with the mass audience, Tab Hunter, an actor who has graced locker doors as both a heterosexual and a homosexual pinup.

As with the Warhol/Morrissey stars, Divine is grotesquely glamorous in her predatory sexuality, and the fact that she is really a man is never acknowledged within the narrative of the films. This incongruity adds an interesting dimension to our response, for just as we remind ourselves that she isn't really eating feces or killing people, we must often remind ourselves that "she" isn't even really a woman. Her portrayal of a sadistic, domineering female is so convincing that we find ourselves thinking of her as feminine, even though she/he is not. Waters' films create a sense of liberation as we laugh at the grotesque absurdities and enjoy being temporary maniacs. What rescues his work from utter depravity is the fact that the violence and sexual abuse are portrayed in a deliberately formulaic, ritualized manner, with no attempt to create realistic special effects. Films like *Pink Flamingos* and *Female Trouble* (1975) are intentionally revolting, creating humor out of sacred, taboo subjects such as death and defecation, thus expanding our notions of the possible topics of humor and art. At the time of their release these films were hardly popular successes, and yet they created a cult following that remains healthy (or unhealthy, as some might choose to view it) to this day.

Toward the end of the sixties, critics began to recognize the connections between the underground mentality and the attitudes of the larger society. Richard Schickel calls Warhol's *Lonesome Cowboys* "a cartoon version of Leslie Fiedler's famous theorizing about the homosexual components in our basic, sustaining masculine mythology."[7] Our society's overemphasis on masculine virtues and male power structures seems to spring a leak in films of the sixties and seventies, with men taking on female characteristics almost as if to compensate for the imbalance. Homosexuals in our society, called on to put on a cover "performance" of heterosexuality, developed a gay sensibility that is apparent in the aesthetic of many underground, quasiunderground, and eventually popular films. The principle operating in the films and lifestyle of this group is the notion that art (and artifice) is life and vice versa. The gay community's blurring of the boundaries between male and female roles, gay and straight behavior, may contribute to the paradoxical, contradictory quality of such films. A sense that it is a home movie and therefore natural and realistic is countered by the sense that the actors are completely theatrical and artificial, constantly putting on their audiences with wild stories and exaggerated gestures and costumes. In his review of Warhol's *Chelsea Girls,* Andrew Sarris observes: "Warhol's people are more than real, because the camera encourages their exhibitionism. They are all 'performing' because their lives are one long performance, and their party is never over."[8]

If we look at a popular model for gay female impersonators we see this same pattern in the performances of Mae West. On the one hand she exhibits an unabashed frankness about her sexual impulses and past escapades. On the other hand, we never see her character actually open up or speak in a "straight" mode; we only see the ironic, theatrically wisecracking persona who lusts but never loves, who uses but is never used, and who sees through society's pretenses but is never seen through in her own pretense of invulnerability. Robert Sklar notes:

> West's comedy is the comedy of turnabout, making people laugh by saying exactly the opposite of what they are accustomed to hearing. Small wonder her flamboyance and brazen sensuality have led some commentators to connect her with the stage tradition of female impersonators: women in American society had not been permitted to behave that way, though male performers in women's dress had acted out men's anxieties and fantasies about women. . . . She did it in the same way as men, as an aggressive, free, independent sexual being.[9]

The price she paid for this toughness was a loss of dimension and variety in her roles. Like the stoic male hero of countless films, West's character has a kind of flatness. Her lines are delivered in a nasal monotone (not unlike John Wayne's) that emphasizes certain words ("Come up and *see* me sometime"), but her voice never captures the fluidity and range of pitch characteristic of most heroines' voices.

The rebellious aspects of West's characters were a shock to many of her contemporaries, but to the alienated counterculture of the sixties her aggressiveness was a refreshing alternative to the limitations of established sexual stereotypes. Underground audiences admired her, and filmmakers created female impersonations that had many of the same strengths and self-imposed emotional boundaries. These artists recognized a particular mentality in American culture—that of aggression, individualism, and a disdain for domesticated tameness—but in placing these features on women and female impersonators, they delivered a challenge to the establishment's double standard for men and women. Conventional critics and audiences sensed the threat in this overturning of values, but despite their protests they were waging a hopeless battle against attitudes that were to subtly permeate even the wholesome family film.

The Family Film:
Comedy's Attempt to Reconcile Dichotomies

The standard comic treatment of cross-dressing which had occurred in "family" films of the forties and fifties underwent a subtle alteration during the sixties. While the decrease in censorship was a powerful force in blatantly sexual films, even in films designed for the whole family there were hints at the desirability of experimentation, albeit within the bounds of good taste, whatever that had come to mean. Comedies had traditionally operated to bridge the boundaries between young and old, rich and poor, male and female. The somewhat androgynous male had always occupied a comfortable niche in this scheme. Even covertly homosexual types had existed in early films in the form of butlers, unmarried uncles, and widowers. Because homosexuality was a taboo subject, the character was indicated by the most banal stereotypes in order to get the point over strongly, if subliminally, to the audience. Bachelors and widowers were stock comic characters whose dislike or fear of women was an accepted part of their humorous appeal. Unlike the widowers and Belvederes of earlier years, the bachelor or widower of the late fifties' and early sixties' family films is not allowed to remain in sexless bachelorhood, but he is encouraged to break loose and experiment. That does not mean that he becomes aggressive, but his passivity is one of acceptance rather than rejection of women's advances. Fear of women had become suspect in an age in which the existence of homosexuality was beginning to be acknowledged by the general public.

A number of the movie actors who dress in women's clothes in family films already have an androgynous appeal, offering the kind of companionship that does not threaten any woman. Their bisexual or sexless appeal is made apparent when we see just how effective they are in imitating women's behavior. An excellent example of this type is Bing Crosby in Blake Edwards' *High Time* (1960), a comedy that is basically in keeping with earlier "innocent" treatment of cross-dressing. Within the bounds of the family approach, though, the film makes an argument for the idea that people should be tolerant of variation from the norm. *High Time* tells the story of a middle-aged, wealthy owner of a restaurant chain (played by Bing Crosby), who decides to get the college education he has always wanted. He is not only a huge success with all the youths of the college, but he also lackadaisically, but successfully, woos the pretty French teacher of the school. He even joins a fraternity, and as part of his initiation he must dress as a woman and get his dance card signed by the crusty judge who hosts the annual fancy dress ball. Before he accomplishes this feat, he ends up dancing with his own son, who is horrified to realize that this peculiar woman is his father. Then, in the lady's room, he is introduced to his own daughter, who swoons when she recognizes him.

Crosby's mannerisms are no more feminine when he is in drag than they are when he is dressed as a man, but he is surprisingly pretty and effectively feminine as a women. The careful makeup job accentuates his eyes, and we realize that Crosby does make a more attractive woman than he does a man. His features are rather delicate, and his soft, highly modulated voice resembles a woman's without much attempt at disguise. All this points up the fact that Crosby's looks, gestures, and voice are vaguely feminine even when he is not wearing women's clothing. Crosby may kick up his heel behind him (usually taken as a distinctly feminine gesture in our culture) while he dances in drag with a man, but this same movement is repeated in a later part of the film when he is in his male persona.

The unabashed attitude toward female impersonation is in keeping with Crosby's image as a star, and the easygoing quality of his screen image also fits in with the message of the film. Stereotypes are overturned in a spirit of harmless fun, and the intent is not so much to undermine traditional values as to show that society's established structure can accommodate variations, as long as they are polite, friendly, and relatively passive. Crosby dances with the male chemistry teacher, but when he goes out on the balcony with him, Crosby casually lifts off his wig and makes no apologies. Then, after he has finally pulled the judge onto the floor for a quick gallop, he tosses the wig into the judge's lap and exits without embarrassment.

Crosby succeeds in this film, and in so many of his other films, by being passive, a trait often associated with feminine behavior. His appeal for innocent young girls and middle-aged ladies is that of the nonthreatening, kind-hearted, almost androgynous male. If he has any sex drive, his polite, unassuming attitude prevents him from directly acting on such impulses, and it is this lamblike innocence that draws women to him. If his method reassures the ladies, the success of this method insures him against accusations of effeminacy, and thus makes him acceptable to men as well.

Although there is not really all that much to tolerate in the world of *High Time,* the theme of the film is tolerance. When Tuesday Weld, the symbol of modern young womanhood, enters a different phase each year, with an appropriate costume to match, Crosby accepts it much more readily than her contemporaries do. When she goes through the stage of liking "mature" men, Bing passively endures her attentions, and comments that she is "finding herself." Of course, what keeps the film from being an open vision of human possibilities is the fact that none of the variations from the norm are any more profound than Tuesday Weld's changes in costume. The movie never challenges the audience with anything more shocking than the proposition that an older man has the right to join a fraternity and dress like a woman as a prank. Thus, although the film purports to present a liberal message, it supports the status quo by refusing to acknowledge the existence of truly antisocial behavior.

In 1964, with *Goodbye Charlie,* Vincente Minnelli deals somewhat more directly with the private fantasies surrounding female impersonation. The basic premise of the film is that a man named Charlie dies and is reincarnated in the body of a woman. Debbie Reynolds plays the part of the transformed Charlie, formerly a despicable womanizer who has been shot to death while trying to escape the bedroom of another man's wife. As the story progresses, we learn that in his old life Charlie had been so selfish and deceptive in his dealings with all of his acquaintances that only three people bother to show up at his funeral: his best friend (Tony Curtis) and two of his former mistresses. When Charlie appears in the body of Debbie Reynolds, Curtis is at first unable to believe that his friend is actually housed in this new female form. After Charlie recounts detail after slimy detail of his former life, Curtis is finally convinced, and he agrees to help Charlie reestablish herself in her new life. At first Charlie is horrified at being a woman because of the utter disdain he had for the creatures he victimized throughout his life. As the story progresses, Charlie grows to appreciate her new equipment, beginning with her introduction to her body in an attractive pants outfit that Curtis provides for her.

Charlie presents herself as the wife of the former Charlie, and she immediately sets to the task of making money, since Charlie left nothing but debts. She arranges a luncheon with the two women who had attended the funeral, blackmailing them with her knowledge of their illicit affairs with "her husband." When Curtis reveals to her that the two women she blackmailed were the only people who came to the funeral, Charlie becomes almost hysterical with remorse, confessing that she has never felt this way before. She is suddenly capable of feeling guilt, and she longs for love and affection. Curtis is overwhelmed by the sight of her tears, and he lies down beside her on the bed, stroking her and comforting her in her vulnerability. It then dawns on him that it is really Charlie, his old friend, inside that female body, and he leaps up, shouting, "We were almost making out!" Charlie, aroused by her feminine urges, sees no reason why they can't get married and live together, but for Curtis the overtones of homosexuality inherent in the relationship are too much to handle. This apparently irreconcilable conflict is resolved in the end by having Charlie leap into the sea and die once again. When Debbie Reynolds returns, this time playing the part of a real woman, the stage is set for an inevitable romance and happy ending.

Goodbye Charlie is by no means a good film, but it is an excellent indicator of what filmmakers considered appropriate fare for popular audiences in 1964. There are a number of references to the sex drives of Charlie in her new body, and the elements of voyeurism and narcissism are comically exploited. The film alludes to the possibility of homosexuality while it also acknowledges the existence of sexual aggressiveness in the female, albeit as experienced by a male personality. Charlie luxuriates in her female attributes, and it seems that the switch from male to female also instills a sense of obligation to others, a lessening of the drive to exploit people.

Raymond Durgnat discusses trends in film and television depictions of sex roles, noting that *Goodbye Charlie* is a typical covert expression of the American male's anxieties of the sixties:

> It takes one stage further the vein of sophisticated (as opposed to farcical) transvestite comedy which is currently obsessional in screen and television comedy. The tendency of our routinizing, intellectualizing, push-button civilization, to soften, and, in a sense, feminize men, while maintaining them in a state of anxious passivity and frustration, is fairly obviously responsible, and it's not so much a sign of homosexuality as an expression of despair; it becomes easier to mentally change one's sex into the naturally passive one than to live out one's own fully.[10]

Durgnat's analysis seems accurate, except in his assumption that females are naturally passive and that feminization must necessarily be a frustrating and painful experience. He ignores the more positive, reconciliatory elements of works that celebrate gentleness, sympathy, and sensuality (not, of course, that these are exclusively female traits). The attempts of early sixties comedies to reconcile these dichotomies apparently succeeded as little with the general public as they did with Raymond Durgnat; audiences flocked to a different kind of film that expressed directly their hostility and fear over changes in sex roles.

The Shockers: Audiences Lose Their Innocence

While films like *High Time* were gazing into the past, yearning for the days when all conflicts could be resolved by tolerance, a much more disturbing and influential vision turned toward the future in films—a future in which even the sanctity of motherhood would be tainted by suspicion, hostility, and violence. Alfred Hitchcock's *Psycho* (1960) was the first major work in American film history to explore the psychotic manifestation of female impersonation. The character of Norman Bates was to become synonymous with a newly discovered phenomenon, the pathological "Momma's boy." Norman Bates so despises and yet so identifies with his domineering mother that after her death he preserves her body by stuffing her, and he "becomes" his mother by dressing in her clothes, killing anyone who threatens that totally closed, restricted relationship. The film was based on the novel inspired by a real incident in which "a man kept his mother's body in his house, somewhere in Wisconsin," but under Hitchcock's direction the macabre tale becomes a profound and complex work of art.[11]

The film teaches us not only to mistrust exterior reality, but to mistrust the filmmaker as well. Although Hitchcock was not particularly concerned with the subject of cross-dressing per se, some of the touches that make the film so cinematically innovative were necessitated by the inherent deceptiveness of impersonation. Hitchcock comments on his reasons for using a long high-angle shot when "Mother" (Anthony Perkins) kills the detective, Arbogast:

> . . . I could shoot down on top of the mother, because if I'd shown her back, it might have looked as if I was deliberately concealing her face and the audience would have been leery. I used that high angle in order not to give the impression that I was trying to avoid showing her.[12]

The second high-angle shot occurs when Perkins carries his mother's body to the cellar, and in discussing this shot, Hitchcock reveals more of his own feelings about his technique:

> I didn't want to cut, when he carries her down, to a high shot because the audience would have been suspicious as to why the camera was suddenly jumped away. So I had a hanging camera follow Perkins up the stairs, and when he went into the room I continued going up without a cut. As the camera got up on top of the door, the camera turned and looked back down the stairs again. Meanwhile, I had an argument take place between the son and his mother to distract the audience and take their minds off what the camera was doing. In this way the camera was above Perkins again as he carried his mother down and the public hadn't noticed a thing. It was rather exciting to use the camera to deceive the audience.[13]

Hitchcock creates a brilliant synthesis of form and content here. By calling attention to the filmmaking process itself, he distracts the audience from an inconsistency in the actual content of the film (the fact that Norman's mother is actually a stuffed, dead woman). At the same time, he uses content, the argument between Norman and his mother, to keep the audience from noticing the camera's peculiar movements. This kind of interplay between form and content is typical of much of Hitchcock's work, but it seems that this subject called on the director to exceed himself in manipulation and deception because of the very nature of the cross-dressing situation. What makes his solution to the problem of concealing true identity so elegant is the fact that this angle also creates tremendous suspense, a sense that some evil presence is looking on from above. The length of the shot from above builds so much tension that a cut to any other camera angle comes as a shock. No director after Hitchcock was to master the theme with such purely filmic devices. Rather, other directors turned to the expertise of the female impersonator to fool audiences when the plot demanded such deception.

According to Hitchcock, *Psycho* was one of his most successful films in cinematic as well as financial terms. For no more than $800,000 in production costs, the film had grossed $15 million by 1967.[14] He was delighted by the fact that those profits reflected an astute reading of his audience—as Hitchcock puts it, "They were aroused by pure film."[15] *Psycho* is a culmination of Hitchcock's work, combining his recurrent themes of voyeurism, the doppelgänger, and extreme sexual repression. Hitchcock had dealt with the transvestite character early in his British career in *Murder* (1930), in which a woman is suspected of being a murderer until it is discovered that her fiancé (who leads a double life as a transvestite trapeze artist) is the real culprit. Much later in Hitchcock's career, in *To Catch a Thief* (1955), he directs Cary Grant as a reformed cat burglar who finally catches the woman who has been impersonating him, robbing houses in imitation of his own style.

Almost all of Hitchcock's work abounds in images of the sexual repression he had observed at a personal level and saw mirrored in the American scene. James Naremore, in his *Filmguide to Psycho,* points to the connection between such individual concerns and the social panorama of American life:

> Of course Hitchcock is a popular filmmaker, and with *Psycho* he desired mainly to stir the emotions of his audience. He achieved that end perfectly, but at the same time he was able to bring to the surface and joke about the underside of American life. Incest, latent homosexuality, voyeurism, necrophilia—all these themes

are touched on repeatedly in his American films; in *Psycho* he declares them openly, playing them off against a background of capitalist and puritan repressions.[16]

Hitchcock remarks on the need "to design your film just as Shakespeare his plays—for an audience."[17] Hitchcock was keenly aware that, although contemporary critics might pan his film as grisly and shocking in its combination of blood and wit, the public was ready for just such a shock.

Hitchcock's careful manipulation of form and content is informed by his astute understanding of the expectations, demands, and responses of his audience. This sensitivity points to two of the essential differences between pre-*Psycho* and post-*Psycho* treatments of serious female impersonation. In earlier films the audience had been aware of the deception, but in the sixties and seventies, filmmakers increasingly chose to leave viewers in the dark, often until the end of the film. In part, this is a difference in the prevalent genre featuring female impersonation before 1960—comedy—and the more serious films, often with shock value, after 1960. In older comedies (and in the vaudeville throwbacks still occasionally produced in the sixties and seventies), usually the audience must be aware of the deception in order to appreciate the jokes. This shift in audience awareness is comparable to the change that took place from the Shakespearean to the Jacobean period in drama; the former, more optimistic vision allowed the audience knowledge and some sense of insight and order, whereas in the darker world of the Jacobean drama, the audience is almost as much victimized by the shocking spectacles before them as are the characters within the play.

In *The World in a Frame,* Leo Braudy discusses Hitchcock's works as closed vehicles, in which all the parts fit together and "the audience is a victim, imposed on by the perfect coherence of the world on the screen."[18] *Psycho* victimizes the audience by leading our vision, with the camera directing attention to forbidden images that often create involuntary responses of shock and fear. Perhaps more pervasive and disturbing than the intrusion of sudden violence is the sense of inevitability in the film's conclusion. Like Hawks' *Male War Bride* and other closed films, *Psycho* ends with a scene of very literal entrapment. The camera peers through a tiny window for the final shot of Norman Bates, locked forever in one small room; his own personality (whatever he had) is trapped now in the persona of his domineering, controlling mother, who cannot even allow the flies in the room their freedom of flight. In *Psycho* the only alternative to complete repression of sexuality is violence, and the film's conclusion neatly locks this threat into a padded cell.

Hitchcock's film established a successful precedent that filmmakers of the sixties and seventies would imitate, almost always with less depth. William Castle's *Homicidal* (1961) was one of the first films after *Psycho* to employ gender disguise to create suspense and a surprise ending. Although the film is in no way so well made as *Psycho,* the plot has even more intricacies and the disguise is much more sophisticated and elaborate. Throughout most of the film, the audience assumes that Emily, a very beautiful blonde, is a psychopathic killer. After an opening sequence, in which Emily marries a stranger and then, for no apparent reason, stabs the county clerk who has married them, we are introduced to Warren Webster. Mariam Webster, Warren's stepsister by another mother, is suspicious of Emily, whom Warren brought back from Sweden. We soon learn that Mariam is in line for an inheritance if anything should happen to Warren, who is to receive the family property on his twenty-first birthday. It appears that Emily is out to kill Mariam so that Emily will be the heiress if Warren dies. Mariam discovers that Emily and Warren are married, and meanwhile the police believe that Emily was the one who committed the murder.

While all of this is going on, Emily keeps threatening to kill Helga, the mute paralytic who was once Warren and Mariam's nursemaid. Mariam is frantic to make Warren realize that his wife is a murderer, and she goes to his house to warn him. Emily succeeds in killing Helga, and when Mariam arrives, Emily is about to kill her as well. When Mariam calls to Warren for help, Emily pulls off her wig and says in Warren's voice, "Warren can't help you now." The police arrive just in time, and Warren falls down the stairs, stabbing himself with the knife intended for his victim. In the final scene at the police station, we learn why Warren/Emily wished to kill his two victims, the clerk and Helga, who had been present at his birth. Warren was actually born a girl, and his mother raised him as a boy in order to insure that he/she would receive the inheritance, which stipulated that it would go to her child only if it was a son. The county judge and

Helga were the only people aware that Warren Webster was really a female and therefore not the rightful heir.

The final twist of the film occurs after the story is completed, when Warren and Emily appear side by side in split-screen projection, and we learn that the two characters were played by Jean Arless, a name that could indicate actor or actress. It is virtually impossible to determine whether Jean Arless is a man or woman, so effective is the portrayal of each gender. The only hint is the possible dubbing of Emily's voice, but even that is difficult to determine because the entire soundtrack seems slightly out of synch. As Emily, Jean Arless is a totally convincing woman with a flawlessly smooth complexion and lovely mouth and eyes. As a man, Jean Arless has the broad shoulders and shadow of a beard that cue the male gender. The acting, direction, and production of *Homicidal* are mediocre at best, but moviegoers had never before seen such an authentic dual role performance in terms of gender presentation.

Homicidal patently imitates *Psycho* in a number of respects. It is filmed in black and white (no doubt for budgetary reasons) and Castle attempts to employ a number of the horrific elements included in *Psycho:* the early unexplained murder, the shrieking music accompanying scenes of violence, the darkly lit gothic mansion, and the mysterious old invalid. The film also offers a contrast between the safe hometown atmosphere in which Mariam lives and the nightmarish house in which Emily, Warren, and Helga live. Although dozens of factors point to imitation of Hitchcock, there is little artistry in Castle's attempt to create another *Psycho.* Castle had been producing gimmicky horror films throughout the fifties, including *The Tingler,* for which the seats were equipped to deliver a slight shock at appropriate moments during the film. Unlike *Psycho, Homicidal* has almost no connection to a social reality outside the world of the flat characters in the film. The film makes no attempt at a psychological explanation, but in offering the financial motivation for murder, it indirectly touches on the notion that women are economically victimized by laws and customs that favor male heirs. This association seems purely tangential to the plot of the film, and the intent seems to be simply to shock and entertain. Like the circus sideshows that once featured two-headed calves, films like *Homicidal* are curios that have faded into obscurity precisely because they have nothing more than shock value.

Jean Arless (right) makes his/her movie debut in William Castle's *Homicidal* (1961), in which the end of the film shows the actor/actress appearing as male and female in a split screen. (Courtesy of Columbia Pictures)

Lee J. Cobb appears in drag to talk with Andrew Duggan as the President of the United States in Gordon Douglas' *In Like Flint* (1967). (Courtesy of Twentieth Century Fox)

Susannah York (left) and Beryl Reid play a lesbian couple who dress as Laurel and Hardy to attend a costume party in Robert Aldrich's British production, *The Killing of Sister George* (1968). (Courtesy of Cinemabilia)

A similar female couple appear in Mark Rydell's film version of D. H. Lawrence's *The Fox* (1968), with Sandy Dennis (as Jill Banford, left) and Anne Heywood (as Ellen March). (Courtesy of Claridge Pictures)

An anonymous transvestite applies makeup to complete a Doris Day imitation in Frank Simon's 1968 documentary *The Queen.* Participants from all over the country vie for the title of "the queen" in a transvestite Miss America contest. (Grove Press, Vineyard Films, Si Litvinoff, and MDH Enterprises production. Courtesy of Cinemabilia)

Luchino Visconti's *The Damned* (1969, Praesidens/Pegaso) shows Helmut Berger doing his impersonation of Marlene Dietrich in *The Blue Angel*. (Courtesy of Cinemabilia)

John Hansen plays the title character in Irving Rapper's *Christine Jorgensen* (1970), the story of one of the first publicized transsexuals. (Courtesy of Cinemabilia)

Raquel Welch plays the female version of Myron, after a sex change operation turns him into Myra in Michael Sarne's *Myra Breckenridge* (1970), based on Gore Vidal's novel. (Courtesy of Twentieth Century Fox, Robert Fryer production)

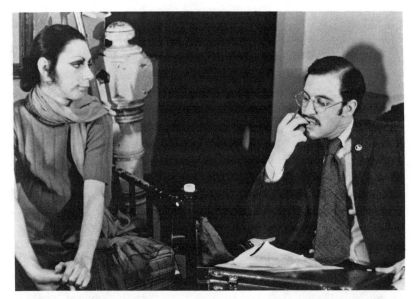

Paul Morrissey's *Trash* (1970) stars one of Andy Warhol's favorite female impersonators, Holly Woodlawn (left), who appeared in a number of other Warhol/Morrissey productions. (Courtesy of Cinemabilia)

Tricia's Wedding (1970) presents "The Cockettes," a collection of female impersonators. (Courtesy of Cinemabilia)

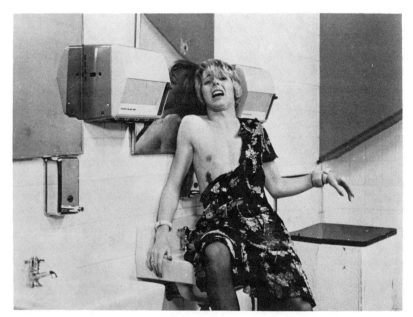

In Richard Rush's *Freebie and the Bean* (1974, Warner Brothers), a central scene features the exposure of the character played by Christopher Morley, who is revealed as a thoroughly effective female impersonator. (Courtesy of Cinemabilia)

Tim Curry's "sweet transvestite transsexual from Transylvania" encounters the extremely straight Brad (Barry Bostwick) and Janet (Susan Sarandon) in Lou Adler's *Rocky Horror Picture Show* (1975), directed by Jim Sharman, a cult film of unprecedented popularity. (Courtesy of Twentieth Century Fox)

In Jack Smight's *Fast Break* (1978), Mavis Washington (right) plays Bobby, the team's star forward who has just unbound her breasts to reveal her gender. (Courtesy of Columbia Pictures Industries, Inc.)

Renato Baldi (Ugo Tognazzi), right, gives instructions to his maid, Jacob (Benny Luke), left, in *La Cage aux folles* (1979), directed by Edouard Molinaro. (Courtesy of United Artists)

John Lithgow plays transsexual ex–football player Roberta Muldoon, greeted here by Jenny Fields and Garp (Glenn Close and Robin Williams) in George Roy Hill's film version of John Irving's *The World According to Garp* (1982). (Courtesy of Warner Bros., Inc.)

Dustin Hoffman plays Dorothy (alias Michael Dorsey), who takes a firm approach with John Van Horn (played by George Gaynes), in Sydney Pollack's *Tootsie* (1982). (Courtesy of Columbia Pictures Industries, Inc.)

Peter Weir's *The Year of Living Dangerously* (1982) features Linda Hunt as the male character Billy Kwan, a role for which she won an Academy Award for best supporting actress. (Courtesy of MGM/UA Entertainment Co.)

One fascinating aspect of this film is the self-consciousness of the opening and closing commentaries. These sequences deliberately call the audience's attention to the fact that it is a movie and that we are unable to determine the true gender of the central player. Like *Homicidal* and the Hitchcock television series of the sixties, *The Rocky Horror Picture Show* later uses the "analysis" of an outside commentator as a kind of comic relief, and Charles Gray, who plays this character, even bears a striking resemblance to William Castle. It is significant that Hitchcock performed this function in his television pieces, whereas in his films he indulged in brief appearances that only true followers of his films would notice. This suggests that Hitchcock took his films seriously and saw the television introductions as an inherently unserious gesture that would automatically distance viewers from the subject by making them aware of the storylike quality of the violence they would witness. This same kind of self-consciousness was to become a prominent feature in cross-dressing films of the seventies in which a campy sense of black humor often calls our attention to the exaggerated absurdity of the type-cast characters and twisted plots.

The Spy and the Impersonator

Parodic elements in violent cross-dressing situations appeared in the spy movies, with their aesthetic of extreme emphasis on clothing, mechanical gadgets, and artifice. What better place for the transvestite, whose spy status resides in the most effective disguise of all, that of false gender? The image of masculine females and feminized males is obsessive in spy films and, as with movies like *Ninotchka* (1939), *The Iron Petticoat* (1956), and *Jet Pilot* (1957), the sexual repression and role reversals of the Communists are contrasted with the pinup sexuality and traditional male dominance of the West. Exaggerated gender signals constitute one of the primary attractions of spy films. On women we see prominent breasts and tiny waists, accentuated by low-cut dresses and bathing suits; the hero usually has a well-muscled, broad-shouldered body with a hairy chest. We rarely see hairy-chested heroes in earlier films, no doubt because of the association with hidden gender cues like pubic hair and sexual parts. The breasts and buttocks of women have been emphasized in some form throughout film history, but only in the sixties do films begin to exploit in a parallel way the visual sexual appeal of male chests and buttocks. In earlier films, a hairy chest, with its hint of animality, was often a noticeable feature of the villain, while the smooth-chested male was the hero. The threat of unisex in the sixties drove some filmmakers and their patrons to look for an antidote to this muddling of sex distinctions, and one result was the supermasculine James Bond and his ultrafeminine playthings.

The accretion of gender dues on characters like James Bond and his women is countered by opposites—the dykey spy or the perversely effeminate villain, whose clothing and physical characteristics are subversive in their ambiguity. In these very popular spy films, which glorified the masculine attributes of bravery and cocksmanship, anxiety over sex roles emerges in the image of the transvestite (both male and female). *From Russia with Love* (1963) presents Rosa Klebb, the sadistic lesbian, wearing tough masculine boots that are especially equipped with retractable knife blades. In *Goldfinger* (1964) James Bond battles with a widow who turns out to be a male assassin in disguise.

In Like Flint (1967), directed by Gordon Douglas, is typical of the anxiety-ridden spy films that attempt to banish forever the specter of the liberated woman. James Coburn plays Flint, the all-powerful hero who uses and disdains women in order to establish his superiority over them. Lee J. Cobb, the bumbling sidekick, is the perfect foil, and it is naturally this character who dresses as a woman so as to impress Coburn with his ability to be a "master of disguise." Cobb enters the Fabulous Face Spa, the headquarters for a group of women conspiring to take over the world. In contrast to Cobb's humiliating entry as a woman, Flint takes the man's way, going underwater through a grate to find himself miraculously in the women's steam room—an adolescent fantasy come true. The negative fantasy of the film is the fear that women will take over (or perhaps already have taken over) the world. The women involved in this enterprise are all beautiful, rich, and famous, and they all view men as weak, stupid, and unnecessary creatures. Because this film panders to the male wish for supremacy, however, the women's scheme ends up failing through pitifully poor planning. They foolishly overlook the fact that their success hinges on the willing cooperation and submissiveness of the man who plays the part of the President of the United States and on those who are in key government positions around him. When these men revolt, the powerless women must turn to Flint for rescue from worldwide disaster.

Both the wishful and fearful fantasies are transparent in this film. As Flint points out, his never-failing success with women arises from his refusal to compete with them. He is so virile that he can service his own harem and still find energy to seduce those evil women who are devoted to female supremacy. In the plight of Lee J. Cobb we can see exactly what the character of Flint is defending against. Forever the bumbling victim, Cobb is easily captured by a deadly combination of beauty and drugs, and he finds himself in the humiliating situation of being set up by an attractive young woman. As soon as she gets him in bed in a compromising position, lights go on, flash bulbs go off, and the man discovers that of course he will be blackmailed. This symbolic emasculation is followed by the more thorough feminization of dressing as a woman. He doesn't succeed in breaking up the conspiracy, and his attempt only leaves him victim to catty remarks about the impossibility of beautifying such an ugly creature as himself/herself.

The one other instance of cross-dressing in the film gives tantalizing intimations of what might have been a truly interesting conspiracy. The scene in which the real President is replaced by a double uses two boys who are eventually revealed to be women. If this idea had been carried through the film, having all the men in the government replaced by surgically altered females, the film might have had much greater complexity. Of course, the writers would have been obliged to think of a more convincing reason for the women's failure to take over the world.

Like *Male War Bride, In Like Flint* reflects contemporaneous issues, concerning itself with the anxieties created by the women's movement of the late sixties. The film pits the superhero first against the authoritarian, bee-like hive of women and, once their organization has crumbled, against the unscrupulous power-hungry men who plan to take over the world. The plot is not satisfying because the enemy is not powerful and we never doubt Flint's eventual victory. Although *In Like Flint* assures the masculine triumph, the film follows the pattern of the anxiety-ridden *Male War Bride* in several key respects. It is tied to topical issues, and it offers extreme, flat characterizations rather than complex, varied individuals. Moreover, the film plays to the male sense of usurped power and injured pride. The same impulse governs films that support the status quo (like *Flint*) and those that bemoan the fate of men in a woman's world (like *Male War Bride*). The particular manifestation varies, but the desire to place man in the superior position is invariably expressed by depicting masculine women as aberrations, and womanly men as degraded, absurd victims. Lee J. Cobb is merely the flipside of James Coburn, and like the film's predecessors of the thirties, forties, and fifties, *In Like Flint* must ridicule the unmanly victim in order to glorify the manly hero.

The European Art Film Meets American Entertainment

At the same time that spy films and shockers intrigued popular audiences with images of sexual extremes and gender ambiguity, other films were dealing with these issues in ways designed to appeal to a more sophisticated audience. As underground topics became more acceptable to viewers, foreign directors like Bergman, Fellini, and Visconti explored the resonances of the transvestite theme. All through the fifties, the popularity of foreign films had been growing in the United States. *Life* magazine noted: "Between 1948 and 1958 movie box-office grosses fell by nearly 50%—but only for theaters showing the Hollywood product. Art theaters, showing European films ranging from Brigitte Bardot sex farces to Ingmar Bergman's medieval morality plays, were thriving."[19] The treatment of cross-dressing in foreign films of the sixties was not necessarily sympathetic, but the theme was presented seriously as a legitimate symbolic device, in distinct contrast to its ludicrous presentation in the majority of earlier American films.

The use of cross-dressing in foreign films is marked by wide variety. Bergman's *The Magician* (1959) offers Ingrid Thulin disguised as a young male assistant in one of the many illusions in the film which call on the audience to look beneath surface realities. In *Hour of the Wolf* (1968), Johan first watches an old woman remove her face (quite literally), and then he is made up by Lindhorst, the archivist, and presented with the nude corpse of Veronica. He is expected to make love to her in front of a crowd while he remains in his emasculated, madeup condition. In Fellini's *Satyricon* (1969), the wedding of a hideous old man to a beautifully painted and coiffed young boy serves as a symbol of the decadence which abounds in this film rendition of ancient Rome. Visconti's *The Damned* (1969) opens with Martin (Helmut Berger) doing a drag imitation of Marlene Dietrich. The film's ad campaign featured a still of Martin/Marlene with the statement, "He was soon to become the most powerful man in Nazi Germany." Female impersonation in all these films becomes the representation of social malaise, inversion in the natural order of things, and eventual doom for the society that spawns such behavior.

By 1968, the screen was exploding with images of sexually ambiguous characters, particularly lesbians, in such films as *The Fox, Les Biches, Therese and Isabelle,* and *The Killing of Sister George.* Foreign filmmakers were thriving, while American companies still had not caught up with the public's desire for "mature" treatments of sexuality. In films directed at a less popular audience, American filmmakers were presenting homosexuals and drag queens, but the public was not yet ready for such presentations, or so movie-makers thought. The portrayal of the lesbian offers an interesting set of features, a combination of titillating fantasies and anxieties about women who turn to other women for sexual and emotional gratification. Such characters seem to exist because men of the period fear their existence, but these women are pictured as incomplete and neurotic in their relationships, as if to show women how they will be punished if they participate in lesbian activities. In the meanwhile, male and perhaps female viewers can appreciate the voyeuristic charm of seeing women fondling each other.

British imports were booming in American theaters, and one of the most popular films for the intelligentsia was Robert Aldrich's *The Killing of Sister George* (1968), featuring the well-known character actress Beryl Reid as the bull-dyke member of the team (Sister George), and Susannah York as the femme member, Alice "Childie" McNaught. The picture's release in the United States coincided with the formation of the rating system still in operation today (with certain modifications), and the film received considerable attention, no doubt due to its X rating. Despite its appeal to prurient interests, the film has little that is actually titillating, aside from the final seduction of Childie by Mrs. Crofts (Coral Browne). In this scene, we are given an enormous closeup shot that fills half the screen with Susannah York's breast, which seems impervious to the assiduous workings of the other woman's tongue.

None of the characters in the film is likable, but the director attempts to make the central character sympathetic and multi-faceted. As unappealing as the character of Sister George is (she makes Childie eat cigar butts), we can't help feeling a little sorry for her by the end of the film simply because she is so beset by misfortune. At the opening of the film, George appears to be at the peak of her television career, but we soon learn that her popularity is waning, and the studio would like to phase her out of the production. Childie, George's kept woman, is a frail little thing who "spoils" George's cigar-eating punishments by appearing to enjoy them. Childie is jealously attached to her doll collection, and her emotions keep pace with her choice in hobbies. When she learns of George's loss in popularity, she shows little sympathy and quickly sets about looking for a new sugar momma. George tries to reinstate herself with the studio by writing dozens of fan letters in her own behalf, but to no avail.

One of the most interesting and lighthearted scenes of the film offers us a glimpse of gay night life in a drag bar, to which Childie and George go dressed as Laurel and Hardy. This comparatively happy scene is interrupted by Mrs. Crofts, who informs George that she is to be cut from the series—run over by a ten-ton truck. Things go no better in George's love life, for Childie finally confesses that she has been out with Mrs. Crofts and plans to live with her. In the final scene of degradation for George, Mrs. Crofts introduces George to a woman who will offer her employment as the voice of Clarabelle Cow, an offer that drives George to make a fool of herself at the annual company party. George returns to her apartment only to find Mrs. Crofts making love to Childie, and at this point the venom pours forth in a series of bitter accusations. Finally, George goes back to the studio set where she used to work, destroying whatever she can. In the final shot, she stands alone, mooing in desperation, an echo of the rooster crowing in the closing scenes of *The Blue Angel*.

Many of the details of the film are somewhat humorous in isolation, but together they form a pathetic picture of one old woman with no future, no job, and no one to love, and a younger woman with a future of moving from one domineering mother figure to the next until she can no longer pass for a child. The stereotypes of lesbians in the films represent the two types offered in other films of the period. Childie's character is much like that played by Sandy Dennis in *The Fox* or Jacqueline Sassard in Chabrol's *Les Biches*. The femme character is often a woman whose almost catatonic acceptance cloaks the passive/aggressive impulses of one too filled with self-hatred to feel any love for others. The butch figure is treated with somewhat more variety, as exemplified by Anne Heywood's sensitive rendition of March in *The Fox,* or Stéphane Audran's coolly sophisticated bisexual in *Les Biches*. In both films, it is the aggressive, sadistic woman who finds it easy to switch from women to men. In *Sister George,* the aging butch is left on her own when she loses the power and status that her career had given her. Rather than offering female relationships as an alternative to the power-oriented aspects of heterosexual love, these films present women operating on the basest principles of attachment, choosing partners on the grounds of their strength, success, and ability to dominate. Any sign of weakness is greeted not by sympathy but by abandonment. Conflicts are resolved through violence, be it self-inflicted or outer-directed.

Aldrich's depiction of the neurotic lesbian as male imitator is unflattering, yet essentially sympathetic. If we contrast *Sister George* with an American female impersonation film of the same year, we see a portrait of the psychotic male that is even more shallow and repressive, but this American product includes touches of black humor. In *No Way to Treat a Lady* (1968) Jack Smight's treatment of role reversals demonstrates the newly increased freedom of the screen while it exploits old stereotypes. The only change we see characters undergo is that some of them die or change costumes; none of them grows or learns anything, and neither is the audience invited to change in its already established attitudes. What at first appears to be simply a series of disguises on closer inspection proves to be a subtle attack on a carefully selected set of subcultures, for whom the larger population may feel suspicion, fear, or downright loathing.

Christopher Gill's (Rod Steiger's) first disguise of the film is that of the Irish priest, whose celibacy may conjure up in the minds of a noncelibate, non-Catholic audience questions concerning the sincerity, heterosexuality, or normality of priests in general. We get the mild suggestion that the priest is not so asexual as he should be when we see him turn to stare at a miniskirted passerby. When he proceeds to kill a woman, we are assured that he is abnormal, no matter that he turns out not to be a priest after all. In the next disguise character and victim are German, a nationality ever popular among villains and victims of the American cinema. For the killer to disguise himself this way fits in well with the Hollywood stereotype of Germans as heartless murderers who take pleasure in torturing and killing others. The way Steiger kisses and cheerfully tickles his victim in this scene underscores the sadomasochistic element of the character's image. When Steiger carefully paints a kiss on his victim's forehead in lipstick, the audience is encouraged to suspect that this murder is essentially feminine in inspiration.

In the next disguise, the homosexual hairdresser is an easy stereotype. The unfounded yet surprisingly common female fear of attack (for who knows what purpose) by a homosexual is concretized by the scene in which Steiger strangles the woman he is fitting for a wig. In his call to Morris (played by George Segal), his favorite police officer, Christopher is highly emotional, almost in hysterical tears, confessing that he has been a "bad boy." His ability to express emotion in this persona could be seen as an indication that homosexuality is closest to his true inclinations. At the same time, this portrayal is a further fulfillment of the demands of the standard homosexual portrayal—hysterical, guilt-ridden, trapped by his own sick compulsions. The film's use of the homosexual disguise plays on ignorant people's fears and misconceptions instead of performing the more difficult task of creating full characterization.

The policeman disguise which follows reinforces the notion of Gill as Morris' double, the expression of the officer's subconscious desire to kill his own mother, a nagging, domineering woman who constantly undermines his ego. The flattery of imitation points to Christopher's homosexual attachment to Morris, and it indicates his desire to win Morris' approval by cleverly executing his murders and conferring with Morris about them. Christopher's anger at the murderer who has impersonated him by also killing women thus reveals jealousy over the rivalry for Morris' attentions.

Steiger's impersonation of a prostitute completes the set of Hollywood connections among homosexuals, domineering mothers, drag queens, prostitutes, and psychotics. Prostitutes, by trading in sex, become threatening figures who, like the domineering mother, exercise control over the male. The drag queen's identification with this figure is an expression of hostility as much as it is an imitation born of admiration or affection. By imitating her, the weak male emphasizes those qualities of bitchy independence which he does not express through his own masculine personality. Killing the tough prostitute, whose deep voice and worldly manner resemble the female impersonator, satisfies Christopher's desire to destroy the woman who has dominated him as well as the woman in himself. In her review of the film, Renata Adler notes that "there is the peculiar casting of someone who is obviously a female impersonator as one of Steiger's victims, although nothing is made of this in the plot."[20] Although the plot does not exploit this element, the almost identical appearance of Steiger and the supposedly female prostitute effectively connects prostitute and drag artist because the similarity is authentic. At the same time, the prostitute's epithet, "fairy," delivered in anger, takes on an ironic twist for the sophisticated viewer who recognizes that the "woman" looks like a man in drag.

The final disguise is not really in keeping with the previous easy targets for bigotry, unless we see the southern accent of Steiger's final character as a mark of the outsider. Christopher has a different type of victim in mind as well—Morris' young girl

friend (played by Lee Remick)—and he is driven by jealousy, a
sense of betrayal. Not only has Morris called him a pervert, but
he has refused to believe that an imposter and not Christopher
committed the latest crime. The tie between Morris and his
double is the key relationship in the film. The stereotyped Jewish
mother played by Eileen Heckart is the comic, low-class embodiment of Christopher's dead mother. Christopher Gill is the psychotically active, homoerotic alternative for Morris' passively
neurotic, heterosexual character. Morris passes from one nagging
mother to the next when he decides to marry. Lee Remick plays
the part of a woman who knows that the way to win his mother's
heart is to comment on how dumb, klutzy Morris is only good for
one thing—"to boss around." Christopher, taking matters quite
literally into his own hands, commits the kind of crimes that
Morris (and very probably a portion of the audience) would like to
perform on Morris' relentlessly obnoxious mother.

But what is the upshot of all this? If the audience is so inclined, it gets its kicks by watching the murder of a series of
mother figures, finding that Smight "manages to stay funny" and
"squeezes legitimate comedy from the corrosive camaraderie of
Steiger and Segal."[21] On the other hand, one may see the film as
presenting murder as a solution to conflict, a thrilling prospect
because none of us has to assume any responsibility for the violence or the misogyny. When it comes time to understand the
Steiger character, the audience can neatly slip into the Segal character who, when asked for forgiveness, simply remains mute. For
all the supposed insights into Christopher's psychosis, the film
closes with the standard horror film treatment of the doppelgänger motif. Kill the bad half and the good half will live happily
ever after in a society purged of destructive impulses. The Segal
character seems in no way perturbed by the events he has witnessed, and the audience is left with a clear-cut, unsatisfactory
moral. Christopher's actions are "no way to treat a lady," and to
quote Christopher's final speech, Morris "knows how to treat a
lady"—suppress that hostility and submit. What makes the
finish of the film rather melancholy is not the death of the villain
(for whom we never really feel any sympathy), but the imagined
future of the hero, who has discovered no alternatives to existence
as the eternally henpecked victim of female domination.

If one has any doubt about the misogynist overtones of the film, one need only look at the ad campaign: two hands in a strangling position with the words, "No way to treat a lady—or *is* it?" Hints of the *Psycho* theme are apparent in Smight's focus on domineering mothers who allow no outlet for the aggressive impulses of their sons. At the same time, *No Way* contains much of the black humor and self-conscious exaggeration that was to become a hallmark of American films featuring sexual reversal. Unlike the films clustering around the turn of the decade, however, *No Way* seems to be fairly serious in containing its playful violence and misogyny with middle-class respectability, marriage, and a happy ending.

Whereas American films tended to undermine the seriousness of the transvestite theme through parody, the European treatment, though just as confused, was often still haunted by World War II. Part of the seriousness of European approaches sprang from a different concept of the film's function in society—to awaken audiences to the social ramifications of private moral deterioration.

In Luchino Visconti's *The Damned* (1969), Martin (Helmut Berger) symbolizes the victimized, corrupt youth of World War II Germany, and female impersonation is the form of decadence that epitomizes his corruption. Ingrid Thulin, as Sophie von Essenbach, Martin's mother, wears stark white makeup and blood red lipstick, which makes her vampiresque and corpse-like even before she dies. Martin accuses her of creating his hatred through her "will to subjugate with idiotic wigs and makeup." We see Martin become progressively more depraved, first in his cabaret impersonation of Marlene Dietrich, then in molesting a little Jewish girl, in raping his own mother, and finally in forcing her and her lover to commit suicide. Although Martin is the central focus, Visconti paints him as the victim of essentially feminine impulses by portraying his mother as the glittering, coldly aggressive tigress always lurking in the background. She goads her lover to kill her husband and take on the Essenbach name and fortune, and Martin is thus cast in the role of a not-so-innocent Hamlet, avenging the usurpation of his industrial throne.

Throughout the film, Visconti confuses the issues by creating a number of popular yet false associations. The image of Dietrich in the opening scenes may symbolize Nazi Germany for some, but in fact Dietrich detested the Nazis and was very active in her support of Allied efforts. As John Simon points out, "Visconti plainly knows the homosexual milieu, yet falsifies it for the sake of sensationalistic effects."[22] Although Visconti might have wished to sensationalize his work for economic benefits, Pauline Kael may have come closer to an understanding of the real impulses behind the film's confusion of political and sexual realities:

> *The Damned* is . . . not so much a political movie as a homosexual fantasy. It's really a story about a good boy who loves his wicked mother, and how she emasculates him and makes him decadent— the basic mother-son romance of homoerotic literature, dressed up in Nazi drag.[23]

Whatever Visconti's motives, the misogynist overtones in the arrangement of "facts" are typical of cross-dressing movies of the day. It seems that, having acknowledged the psychopathy of certain homosexual or transvestite characters, filmmakers were searching for a readily identifiable source of blame; the loved and hated mother was an ideal culprit in numerous films of the late sixties and early seventies.

Violence and Camp Sensibility: "Polymorphous Perversity"

Throughout the sixties, British and European directors addressed the issues of male, female, and bisexual identities, topics that attracted American audiences; but the seriousness of foreign approaches did not satisfy popular tastes in America. The suffering, violence, and shame of these sexual reversals soon became the object of ridicule in American films, with the humor calling for an uneasy truce between the general public and disturbingly "aberrent" elements of society. In many of the films of the late sixties and early seventies, the titillation offered by sex and violence is condemned by certain characters, but rarely do we take the moralizing seriously. We see a great deal of irony, self-parody, and veiled allusions to other films, reminding the audience that this is, after all, only a movie. Critics noted that such films seemed to be working at cross-purposes, as is evidenced by John Simon's comments on Russ Meyer's *Beyond the Valley of the Dolls* (1970): "The film emerges curiously schizoid: Meyer's exaggeratedly male, aggressive brainless lustfulness (or bustfulness); and Ebert's smartass, campy, in-joking put-ons."[24] With films like *Beyond the Valley of the Dolls, Myra Breckenridge* (1970), *Performance* (1970), and *Something for Everyone* (1970), filmmakers seemed to be trying to produce something for everyone and coming up with nothing for anyone, according to many critics.

Despite the critics' rejection of these films, they were important transitions. European films that examined psychotic role reversals in a somber way were often greeted by boredom, anger, and rejection by popular audiences. Within the context of film history these negative portrayals represented a crucial stage of development. It is as if the screen reflected the nightmares of a collective consciousness, confronting for the first time the taboo possibilities of sexual inversion. After the serious images of tortured, depraved homosexuals, lesbians, and transvestites, American parodies began subtly undermining these stereotypes. The move toward parody was a way of coping with anxiety, a distancing mechanism that allowed audiences to work through feelings of hostility by seeing their fears as exaggerated and thus ludicrous. The important distinction between this kind of absurdity and farce in the earlier cross-dressing films is that impersonators of the late sixties and early seventies are generally powerful figures. In recognizing that power, filmmakers acknowledged the fearful aspects of androgyny at the same time that they undercut the validity of our fears. Ridicule shifts from the cross-dressing characters themselves to the anxieties of the audience.

By the late sixties the cult of sex and violence had reached such a peak that it could no longer be taken very seriously by filmmakers or their audiences. Critics responded almost en masse by being insulted at the mix of violence, ambiguous sexuality, humor, and psychedelic sequences. Although one may not agree with their specific reasons for feeling insulted, it seems that they were accurate in their reading of the intent behind "sexploitation" films. Producers and directors were quite willing to exploit sex and violence as long as such films made money. In 1968 *Variety* reported that 48 percent of current box-office admissions were in the 16 to 24-year-old age group, and that "the more 'adult' films have become, the more they appeal to teenagers and the less they appeal to their elders."[25] While a certain number of films were trying to appeal to family audiences and older viewers with inanities like *Yours, Mine, and Ours,* or *With Six You Get Egg Roll* (1968), another segment of the film industry was producing the sex-violence combination guaranteed to draw a younger audience that was eager to taste the newly available forbidden fruit. Such films did not need to be "mature" in their treatment of character, but they did have to present a sophisticated, cynical sense of humor, glossy color and costumes, and a sensitivity to the youth market's attitudes toward sexual identity.

The youth-market filmmakers were discovering what underground directors knew to be an important aspect of the explicit portrayal of human sexuality, namely its humorous potential. In an *Atlantic Monthly* article on *Lonesome Cowboys,* Dan Wakefield comments: "The opportunity to deal relatively freely with sex on screen is perhaps a more complicated and frightening opportunity than anyone bargained for. One solution is to play it primarily for laughs."[26] A serious portrayal would also go against the counterculture's perception of sexuality as anything but the gravely mysterious business that their elders insisted it was. To many youths and homosexuals, it seemed that most of their difficulties concerning sexuality arose from the larger society's insistence on the sacredness of established sex roles and customs.

The humorous portrayal of transvestites in counterculture films was laced with violence; the male-female characters were shocking in their sexual aggressiveness, their unabashed rejection of standard heterosexual values and manners. What seemed to worry critics most was the thought that there was a substantial segment of heterosexual society to which these supposedly homosexual films appealed. In commenting on *Performance* (1970), Richard Schickel calls it "the most disgusting, the most completely worthless film I have seen since I began reviewing," and he goes on to note the connections between "disgusting" movies and the tastes of the drug culture: "No critic I know of has come right out and publicly labeled any of these films as whoring after a rather special minority, drug-users."[27] John Simon makes a more astute, but equally negative, observation on the connection between form and content in these films:

There is something promiscuous and amoral about the very con-
struction and editing of the film. The first half is gangster melo-
drama jazzed up with bizarre visual effects and spiked with
homosexuality and sadism; the second half is mostly dropping
out and turning on, polymorphous perversity, exchanges of gender and identity, psychedelia and rock music. . . . The film . . .
is predominantly homosexual in spirit.[28]

Simon's final observation reveals the primary basis for many
critics' rejection. Members of the establishment were shocked to
discover the depth of bitterness in a portion of society hitherto
repressed and unacknowledged. Critics were even more dismayed
to realize that not only homosexuals but heterosexual members of
this counterculture could identify with the content and apparently chaotic form (or formlessness) of these products. Youths
who had been raised on television's mishmash of commercials,
melodramas, comedies, and crime programs found it easy to
switch mental channels as they watched films that threw together
comedy, violence, old movie footage, musical interludes, and
purely visual light shows. Unlike their elders, youthful audiences
viewed the sexual diversity and apparent amorality of these films
as a liberating license to pursue their own impulses. The very
casualness of sexual encounters depicted in such films eased some
of the sense of desperation that had surrounded young people's
decisions about sexual activity in the fifties.

With the screen's new freedom to reveal body parts, particularly breasts, the depiction of cross-dressing became a more complicated task. Many filmmakers of the sixties and seventies
became extremely careful in depicting female impersonation, either relying on clever cinematic craftmanship (as did Hitchcock
in *Psycho*), turning to the skills of the true female impersonator
(as in Castle's *Homicidal*), or simply substituting real females or
males in crucial scenes. In *Seeing Through Clothes,* Anne Hollander
notes the degree of sophistication required to pass as the opposite
sex in an age when anyone can wear pants, which were at one time
a completely sufficient gender cue:

A number of women in fact and fiction are supposed to have
served in various armies with the sex undetected. The uniform
evidently anounced their sex to everyone's satisfaction, as did the
boy's clothes in which women were also supposed to have traveled
without discovery. . . .

> And when neither sexual nor class distinctions is well defined
> by dress, the less well-defined things about clothes and bodies
> that do distinguish the sexes and classes are automatically more
> carefully scrutinized.[29]

If a film plot relies on the audience believing the character to be
male or female, the disguise must be effective in its minutest
detail, the direction must avoid revealing the slightest incongruity, or the acting must be done by a stand-in.

Films of the early seventies show increased use of a male and a
female to play the role of a single cross-dressing character. In *Dr.
Jekyll and Sister Hyde* (1971), Ralph Bates plays Dr. Jekyll and a
very sexy Martine Beswick plays his alter ego, Sister Hyde. Roy
Ward Baker's version of the tale carries a particularly misogynist
message by adding a gender twist to the story. The gentle, idealistic doctor, in a search for the elixir of life, uses female hormones because he has observed that women live longer, healthier
lives, and they don't lose their hair as often as men do. The low,
base creature that emerges when Jekyll takes the elixir is none
other than a woman, complete with a narcissistic love of mirrors
and an uncontrollable urge to shop for clothes. The female within
Dr. Jekyll wars for control, and she murders ruthlessly in order to
survive. She criticizes her "brother" for being weak-willed and
overly concerned with the dictates of his conscience, something
Sister Hyde is totally lacking. What is fascinating about this film
is its choice of characteristics for the female: longevity, immunity
to disease, beauty, heartlessness, narcissism, and manipulative
sexual passion. Many of these attributes are negative, and yet
they imply power and aggressiveness, features that had been relatively rare in standard presentations of the feminine.

Other films use a real male actor to play the part of a girl raised
as a boy, or an actress to play the part of a boy raised as a girl. In
William Fraker's 1973 film *A Reflection of Fear,* Sondra Locke plays
a psychotic young girl who is eventually revealed to be a male
raised as a girl by his mother. Throughout the film she carries on
a dialogue with her male self, who commits a series of brutal
murders. We discover that the mother and child were abandoned
by the father, thus engendering such hatred for men that the
mother decides to raise her male child as a girl. When the father
returns to take the child away, the male persona of the "daughter"

turns on the father and kills him, punishing him for his rejection of the family. In an exaggerated way, this film recreates a situation in the American family often commented on by sociologists. The noninvolvement or absence of the father in the home became a real concern in the sixties, and many people blamed the rebelliousness and juvenile delinquency of suburban teenagers on the father's failure to participate in the child-rearing process.

Another film of the same year deals with the reverse situation of a girl who is brought up as a boy. In Paul Bartel's *Private Parts* (1973), George, who is supposed to be a cross-dressing female, is played by John Ventantonio, a rather effeminate and yet definitely male actor. George's mother, Martha, runs a hotel inhabited by a variety of weirdos, including a homosexual priest and an aging lesbian who keeps calling for her favorite young woman, Alice. (It is interesting that Lucille Benson, who plays the hotel owner, later appears in the television cross-dressing show, *Bosom Buddies,* as the manager of a women's apartment building—an in-joke for viewers who have seen her in both roles.) Martha is convinced that women are corrupt creatures of the flesh, and in order to save her daughter from temptations, she has given her male hormone injections and raised her as a boy. As in *Reflection of Fear,* the attempt to suppress sexuality results in psychopathic behavior. When George cannot convince young women to submit to his bizarre form of sexual gratification (injecting them with his own blood in his/her best substitute for intercourse and ejaculation), he gets upset and murders them. The use of a real man to play the part is necessary to keep the audience from guessing the end of the story, in which we learn that "George" is a woman. This fact is revealed (using a stand-in) by giving a close-up shot of the strongest cue for female gender in our culture; George's mother uncovers the breast, which has been bound, in order to feel the heart and see if George is really dead. The importance of the breast is indicated by an attending policeman's comment: "Boy, with knockers like that, I could go for this guy myself."

The breast is an important image in many American films, although it is presented in earlier films so subtly that only the glands and not the conscious mind would register its impact. In cross-dressing films, breasts take on added resonances, combining the appeal of returning to mother, appreciating breasts as a focal point of adult sexuality in our culture, and experiencing that sexuality through the imitative possession of false breasts. Esther Newton notes the importance of breasts in stage impersonations of females:

> The "breasts" especially seem to symbolize the entire feminine sartorial system and role. This is shown not only by the very common device of removing them in order to break the illusion, but in the command, "tits up!" meaning, "get into the role," or "get into feminine character."[30]

In early female impersonations, breasts were a focal point of the comedy, as in Chaplin's *A Woman,* in which he keeps losing his "breasts" as they fall out of position. Even as late as 1935, Joe E. Brown's version of Thisbe in *A Midsummer Night's Dream* makes a few stabs at mammary humor. When Thisbe kills herself, Brown first puts the sword down his/her dress, but when this proves too chilly a death, he sticks the sword into the baggy, lopsided breast, which wanders from armpit to stomach in the process. Had the film been made a few years later, certainly the sequence would have been altered to remove the direct thrusts and touching of the artificial breasts. Not until *Psycho* in 1960 do we see the reemergence of the breasts linked with the psychological underpinnings of transvestism. As James Naremore points out, "in *Psycho,* the half-slip and the massive brassiere become obsessive images," for the breasts "are especially desirable to a psychopath with an unnatural love for his mother."[31]

The fascination with breasts becomes much more blatant as the decade passes, and it reaches a high point (or what some felt was a low point) in Michael Sarne's *Myra Breckenridge* (1970), based on Gore Vidal's novel. At the opening, Myron, who is to undergo a sex change operation, wants to know what his "tits" will be made of, and in the closing scene, his first question, as he grabs at his flat chest is, "Where are my tits?" In 1968, when casting for the part of Myron/Myra, Vidal reported that " 'not one' actor so far had come forward for the part of the young man."[32] Even if a female impersonator had appeared for the part, he would have needed breasts to play the role convincingly. It is essential that the film have real breasts for display in those closeups that highlight them as the central visual attraction, no doubt one of the main considerations in casting Raquel Welch as Myra.

Myra Breckenridge is intended to offend and shock its audiences primarily by directly treating the sadistic aspects of homosexuality and attacking the middle-class values that Mary Ann (Farrah Fawcett) calls "normal—what everybody does." As Myra puts it, her "goal is the destruction of the traditional man," and in her attempts to seduce Mary Ann, she apparently wants to destroy the traditional woman as well. In the end, Myra is unable to seduce Mary Ann, and the Myron within her is eventually conquered by Mary Ann's saccharine charms, which come to represent all of America—the plastic food, the intellectual bankruptcy, and the shallow wholesomeness that remains sweetly impervious to Myra's assault.

The film intentionally undercuts its own cinematic tradition by intercutting excerpts from a wide variety of old movies. As a self-reflexive fantasy satire, *Myra* does not hold together or bear detailed analysis of structure. It appears to contradict its own revolutionary intent by closing with a kind of retraction of the ideals Myra/Myron touts throughout the major part of the film. Yet on its way to a bittersweet, tongue-in-cheek reconciliation, the film makes a number of minor comments on popular American values and prejudices. Repeated references to "fags" reveal a major preoccupation of the film, and when Myra punches Uncle Buck (John Huston) for calling Myron a "fag," it is clear that such remarks are not taken kindly by Myra, even if they are true. Terms like "fairy," "queen," or "fag" are derogatory when delivered by an outsider, but, as with the term "nigger," an insider's use of them may range in connotation from an acceptable insult to an endearment signifying in-group cohesion. When Myra asks a black student at Buck's acting school if he is a fag, the young man lifts one jeweled finger to his mouth in coy evasion, a gesture that indicates effeminacy as clearly as does his wearing of numerous necklaces, bracelets, and glitter.

The dual standard that allows Myra/Myron to call someone a fag and punch someone else for using the same term is but one of many contradictions. Myra's stated purpose is to destroy the traditional male; yet she is clearly fascinated by Leticia Van Allen (Mae West), whose hobby of using "manly men" as studs Myra apparently admires. The same contradictory ambivalence operates in Myra's attraction to Mary Ann, and in her worship of the old films that helped to form the American mentality she detests.

In its apparent ambiguity regarding sex roles, *Myra* is typical of the period.

Feminist critics have observed the misogynist and antifeminist aspects of homosexual female impersonation, which often sarcastically highlights negative elements of the "feminine" stereotype—frivolity and fashion-consciousness, bitchiness and superficiality. With female impersonation at its focus, *Myra* offers an orgy of costumes, primarily in red, white, and black, and varying from military style to ultrafeminine frills. After a film clip of Marlene Dietrich singing in navy uniform, Myra appears in an identical uniform, lecturing about the male desire to rape. Myra later appears in a riding habit and crop, a costume that reinforces her "Lady Domineer" image. When she performs her mock examination of Rusty, the all-American boy, she wears a white uniform, underlining the association between sadistic authority and nurses, who are featured as anything but angels of mercy in films of the seventies (*One Flew Over the Cuckoo's Nest* [1975], *Coma* [1978], etc.). In the following rape scene, Myra emerges dressed as Wonder Woman, but wearing a large white cowboy hat just like Uncle Buck's. Then, as she performs the dildo rape of Rusty, we see Myra in knight's armor, calling out, "Charge," and thrusting her spear aloft. Myra's costumes vary from the white full-skirted sundress of the opening scenes to the somewhat mannish white business suit she wears for discussing business matters. Myra is a kind of superwoman partly because of her facility for shifting costumes, personae, and sexes, a changeability that is to be admired and envied rather than looked down on as fickleness.

The film offers an essentially negative portrait of American womanhood and manhood as well, with not much choice between the cynical sharks like Uncle Buck and Myra, who ruthlessly abuse their inferiors, and the mindless robots like Rusty and Mary Ann, who slavishly follow what they can dimly make out as "normal" behavior. Whereas most cross-dressing films clustering around 1970 were simply following box-office instincts, with little eye to social criticism, *Myra* seems to be an exception to this trend in fluffy violence, intended only to titillate rather than enrage. *Myra* was received with fear and loathing by all the major critics—fear that this was to be the new trend in film treatments of sexual themes, and loathing that such a film had made its way into existence. *Time*'s reviewer comments:

> Michael Sarne, *Myra*'s director and co-author, deserves special discredit for the repulsive dildo rape scene and the obscene device of interspersing the film with clips from movies of favorite old stars. Thus, in the context of *Myra*, Laurel and Hardy are made to look like fags. Even more outrageous is the use of Marilyn Monroe sequences during the rape. Only one clip educed any illuminating commentary about *Myra*. A tough old cop sergent from some obscure war movie growls, "That's what I call disgusting." Precisely.[33]

Newsweek's Joseph Morgenstern calls it a "nightmare version of Hollywood's most recent dreams, . . . a horrifying movie."[34] *Myra*'s dildo rape of Rusty is the focus of most reviewers' shock; not only is anal intercourse considered unnatural, but it is compounded by the fact that a woman is the aggressor and a heterosexual male the victim.

A number of features in *Myra* are common to other crossdressing films produced around the turn of the decade, offering a catalogue of sadomasochistic fantasies. In *Beyond the Valley of the Dolls* (1970), the archvillain, Z-man, emerges at the climax of the film in a Wonder Woman costume, revealing two minuscule breasts he has been cultivating with hormone injections. We also see the recurrent connections between sexual perversity and Nazism in Z-man's butler, who serves drinks while wearing his old SS uniform. A similarly aggressive assault on the audience occurs in Frank Zappa and Tony Palmer's *200 Motels* (1971). Originally shot in videotape, the film takes the audience from surreal cacophony with the London Philharmonic in psychedelic colors to the mundaneness of "Centerville—a real nice place to raise your kids up." This juxtaposition of the bizarre and the ordinary is used in the film's presentation of doubles or two versions of essentially the same reality. Ringo Starr plays Larry the Dwarf, who bears a striking resemblance to the mustachioed, turtlenecked Frank Zappa that we see lurking in the wings (and supposedly in the television set) for brief moments. Flo (Marl Volman of the group Flo and Eddy) plays himself, and he also does a drag imitation of a blonde groupie infatuated with the rock musicians. At one point in the film, the real groupie sits down on the lap of Flo's drag version of the groupie. The film's psychedelic visuals, plotlessness, and John Cage–style music are disorienting and potentially off-putting; Jay Cocks describes the work as "an act of undisguised aggression against the audience—rather like a mugging in a movie theater."[35] For a certain segment of society, this film represents an attack not on themselves but on middle America and its values. Like *Pink Flamingos, Chelsea Girls,* and other underground films, *200 Motels* was to gain a substantial cult following, thus creating a continued demand in small movie houses for this "failure" long after successes of the same year had faded into the twilight zone of late night television.

Alongside these cult successes, other films were coming out with more serious and less successful treatment of impersonation and sexual reversal. In Hal Prince's *Something for Everyone* (1970), Michael York plays a bisexual object of lust, just as he does in *Cabaret* (1973). *Triple Echo* (1973) features Brian Deacon as an AWOL soldier who first wears dresses as a disguise and eventually wears them for pleasure. In Robert Fuest's *The Final Programme* (1973), the new messiah is a bisexual creature who destroys her masochistic followers. These films were attempts to jump on the bisexual bandwagon, but they flopped with popular and underground audiences, as well as critics, in part because they took themselves too seriously. Audiences of the seventies delighted in unexpected sensational effects, and filmmakers turned increasingly to the newly discovered skills of the female impersonator to create these surprises.

Real Impersonators Make Their Cameo Debuts

Substantial numbers of the movie-going public enjoyed seeing themselves as sophisticated and experienced, and recognizing female impersonators came to be a mark of the urbane viewer. In *Midnight Cowboy* (1969) the audience can pick up on the surface innocence and the covertly homosexual elements in Voigt and Hoffman's relationship because of the repeated homosexual cues that serve as a backdrop to their friendship: Voigt's two attempts at homosexual prostitution, his unwittingly homosexual cowboy image, and his encounter with two female impersonators who manage to fool him completely. *Cabaret* creates a similar contrast between the surface innocence of British Michael York and the worldliness of the German cabaret folk. Sally Bowles (Liza Minnelli) is the American go-between who sends a German female impersonator to take her place in entertaining a rich business man in the cabaret. She also inadvertently introduces York to his first homosexual encounter, an incident that the audience becomes aware of before she does. Here, as in *Midnight Cowboy,* the sophisticated viewer catches on and participates in the conspiracy as an insider—so that the viewer's emotional ties are with the impersonator and the homosexual rather than with the naïve character who is fooled. Even when the audience may not recognize an impersonator as such, the unattractiveness of the people being deceived automatically puts us on the side of the impersonator in a film like *The Magic Christian* (1970). Yul Brynner's rendition of "Mad About the Boy" is so flawless that the audience will probably not recognize him as a man, let alone as Yul Brynner. When he pulls off his wig, the horror expressed by a fat bourgeois gentleman is ridiculous, making the scene all the more hilarious and flattering to the impersonator.

The professional quality of such impersonations influences amateur attempts, and we see more authentic performances in conventional films. Michael Cimino's *Thunderbolt and Lightfoot* (1974) takes the ever-popular bank robbery plot and makes it funny by undermining the manly images of the robbers. Clint Eastwood as the hard-bitten Thunderbolt is the perfect opposite to the smiling, carefree Lightfoot played by Jeff Bridges. Lightfoot joins the crew of bank robbers and serves as a distraction during the robbery by dressing as a miniskirted blonde and flirting with the bank guard. As the feminine member of the team, Lightfoot laughs more and expresses himself more playfully, but he is not a stereotypically passive or ludicrous character. Far from making Lightfoot the object of ridicule, his creative and enthusiastic performance as a woman makes him a hero. It is fascinating to see how easily the clean-cut image of the all-American boy—slim, dimpled, and grinning—transfers itself to the coy charm of the all-American girl, giggling and tossing her long blonde hair.

Not all the films that feature convincing drag imitations present the character so favorably. One of the most authentic impersonations of the seventies occurs in Richard Rush's *Freebie and the*

Bean (1974), an anarchist parody of the *Dirty Harry* film style. This was one of the last films of the seventies to have a female impersonator as an actual villain. As with *Midnight Cowboy,* the presence of a real female impersonator amplifies the underlying homosexual elements of the buddy motif. We see the same kind of teasing male camaraderie in *Freebie and the Bean* as in *Thunderbolt and Lightfoot,* but the conclusions drawn are very different. Throughout the movie, James Caan, as Freebie, the macho member of a detective team, makes remarks to the Bean (Alan Arkin) that establish in a jovial way that the Bean is the "wife." When the Bean tries to get Freebie to put on a helmet during one of their many disastrous chase scenes, Freebie pushes him off, saying, "What are you, a hairdresser?" Freebie accuses him of "turning into a shrew," and later he comes right out and says, "You'll make somebody a lovely wife." All these digs are demeaning to the Bean and to women, yet they are delivered in an affectionate way; at one point Freebie even tells the Bean that he loves him. Against the background of this heterosexual male love relationship, the eventual killing of a patently homosexual female impersonator takes on a deeper resonance.

At the climax of the film, the audience and Freebie are convinced that the Bean is dead or dying, and Freebie's ensuing battle with the deadly impersonator begins to convince us that Freebie may not survive either. In a series of balletic turns and kicks, what had appeared to be a beautiful young woman loses his/her wig and is revealed as the effeminate young man of an earlier bubble-bath scene. His method of fighting is peculiarly graceful, yet devastating, and his strength and finesse almost succeed in destroying Freebie. When Freebie finally shoots him, his victory seems hollow without his friend alive to enjoy it. On the way to the hospital with the supposedly dead Bean, Freebie hears a voice from under the blanket saying, "I need a taco," reassuring Freebie and the audience that the Bean is very much alive. With all the criminals dead, Freebie and the Bean continue in their carefree destruction of property and order, forever chasing through the streets in celebration of the boyish battles of friendship between two men who will never grow up. As in films of the earlier seventies, the transvestite in *Freebie and the Bean* fulfills a kind of ritual function at a symbolic level, the locus for evil and discord. Once this threatening figure is destroyed, the exclusive society of two men is purged of sexual perversity, and harmony (no matter how chaotic) is restored.

Critics viewed the film as an unhealthy throwback and commented on the repressive racist and sexist elements. *Time's* reviewer noted the streak of sadism, and *Newsweek's* reviewer called the film a "new low for male chauvinist piggery," a film that "represents the cretinization of the Butch Cassidy–Sundance vogue for male romances."[36] As anachronistic as the film seems in its blatant sexism and its images of random destruction, the police corruption and victimization of the innocent were representative of the state of affairs in an era that had witnessed the Chicago Democratic convention, the Vietnam War, and the Watergate conspiracy. What was objectionable about the movie was its attempt to romanticize this corruption and violence.

The Transvestite Becomes Human

Although certain films of the seventies featured the transvestite as a villain, movies were clearly changing in the depiction of sexual ambiguity. While many female impersonators of the sexploitation years were pathologically strong characters, real threats to society, other transvestites (particularly of the later seventies) were blossoming into a variety of human, often sympathetic characters. An excellent example is Roman Polanski's *The Tenant* (1976), a work in which the outsider, the misfit, offers us insight into the problems of confused identity and alienation. Although the outsider suffers, he also sees and understands more of society's ills than the comfortable insider does. A variety of offbeat heroes in the seventies appear as the representatives of unconventional wisdom. The female impersonator in such films may be a source of such knowledge; or the hero's (or heroine's) intimacy with the female impersonator may indicate the hero's sensitivity, tolerance, sophistication, or simple disregard for social custom.

One of the first and most popular films of the seventies to offer the outsider as hero was Arthur Penn's *Little Big Man* (1970), with Dustin Hoffman as the unconventional protagonist, Jack Crabb.

A central theme of the film is the notion that the qualities that make us human are internal rather than external. The Cheyenne (or "human beings," as they call themselves) accept the outsider, Little Big Man, just as they accept their own transvestite Little Horse, who is distinctively feminine in dress, voice, and gesture. The image of the feminine male is balanced by Jack's sister, who is so masculine that when the Cheyenne first capture her, they feel for her breasts to make sure she is really a woman. In a later encounter with her long-lost brother, she tries to teach him how to be a proper gunslinger, but the endeavor proves to be too macho for Jack's tastes, and he leaves the defense of the family honor to his capable sister. Each time Jack returns to the Cheyenne in one of his bounces back from the white culture, he is greeted with affection by Little Horse, who offers him womanly support and sympathetic friendship. Jack's appreciation of Little Horse is a sign of the tolerance Jack has learned from the Cheyenne, whose values seem eminently humane in comparison with the barbaric hypocrisy of the whites. *Little Big Man* encourages us to laugh at the frivolities and peculiarities of both cultures, but the laughter dies and our ultimate sympathies lie with the gentle, pastoral people, as we see them being ruthlessly driven from their lands, slaughtered by gun-carrying soldiers on horseback who kill women and children without pity or remorse. If we see the values of the Cheyenne as essentially feminine, in contrast with the aggressive, patriarchal white culture, the film makes a strong statement for the Indian values.

Other westerns of the seventies offered alienation as the key feature in the individual's relation to society. The classical western's model of society as basically sane and ordered had disappeared almost entirely, and in its place we see the confrontation of isolated outlaws and lawmen who are practically indistinguishable from each other. Arthur Penn's *Missouri Breaks* (1976) is the tale of a cattle rustler (Jack Nicholson) and the "regulator" who pursues him (Marlon Brando), with the choice between these two unconventional characters amounting to the option of Nicholson's anarchy or Brando's fascism; there is no stable, reasonable alternative in between. Brando's wearing of a granny dress and bonnet as one of his disguises sounds an eerie echo of *Psycho,* as we witness this deadly voyeur taking aim with binoculars and a long-barreled rifle. Penn's depiction of the almost loving hatred between pursuer and pursued is reminiscent of Nicholas Ray's focus in *Johnny Guitar* on the obsessive relationship between Mercedes McCambridge and Joan Crawford. *Missouri Breaks* self-consciously alludes to and overturns old movie conventions surrounding outlaw and lawman. The sexual component of this relationship is hinted at in the scene in which Nicholson points his gun at Brando, who is luxuriating in a bubble bath. The classical western love between a man and his horse is also parodied when Brando shares a carrot with his horse, ending in a mouth-to-mouth embrace. As with many of the situations of *Missouri Breaks,* when Brando does something eccentric, like putting on a dress, the humor has a poisonous edge. The chilling image of the little old lady as regulator is close to the core of American fears of momism, but rarely do films make such an explicit connection between the soulless law enforcer and the matronly disciplinarian who has more love for order than for humanity.

A very different portrait of female impersonation appears in Polanski's *The Tenant,* a film that uses cross-dressing as a metaphor for the complete loss of identity. Polanski plays the central character, Trelkovsky, who moves into an apartment whose former tenant tried to commit suicide by flinging herself out the window. Trelkovsky becomes more and more obsessed with the former tenant's identity, and he is convinced that there was a conspiracy to drive her to madness and suicide. He even goes to visit her in the hospital, and there he finds a totally bandaged, faceless androgyne who cannot speak to him. Frightening signals of conspiracy (such as a load of refuse dumped at his doorstep) gradually turn into signs of Trelkovsky's own insanity, as we see his trancelike ritual of putting on the woman's clothes and makeup every night. Touches of the surreal, typical of Polanski's work, add to the confusion; Trelkovsky finds a tooth hidden in a brick in the wall, and we are left to wonder whether it is a mysterious sign planted by conspirators or merely a figment of his tortured imagination, put there by himself. His final act of abandonment to the mysterious female identity takes the form of suicide, in imitation of the former tenant. Dressed as a woman, he throws himself out the window onto the street as onlookers applaud—an echo of a scene from Cocteau's *Sang d'un poet* (1932).

Many critics were confused by the film, and some saw it as a failed black comedy. *Newsweek's* Janet Maslin comments that "*The Tenant* doesn't seem to have been designed as a self-parody, but it certainly comes across that way."[37] In *Time,* Jay Cocks gives Polanski a little more credit for control over his subject:

> Like much of Roman Polanski's work, *The Tenant* is a comedy tipped with poison. . . . Polanski has a carbolic wit and discovers unplumbed depths of amusement in emotional deformity, physical abuse and psychic shock waves.[38]

Commonweal's Colin Westerbeck is similarly puzzled by the tone of the film and asks, "What is the movie itself supposed to be, anyway, a horror film or a comedy?"[39] Penelope Gilliat offers a more sensitive interpretation of Polanski's intent in her review in *The New Yorker: "The Tenant* is no piece of whimsy about drag. It is a serious, exact film about the ache of exile. Exile from a country. Exile from a gender."[40]

Polanski details for us the gradual breakdown of Trelkovsky's identity, conveying his sense of displacement by creating in the audience a similar sense of normlessness. Trelkovsky doesn't have a job or friends—no niche in society and no apparent chance of finding one. Even his private world and his attempts at female impersonation are pitiful; with his lips painted a garish red beyond their natural boundaries and his cheeks heavily rouged, he is all dressed up with no place to go. The viewer may well feel the urge to laugh nervously, but it is the same kind of humorless giggle that escapes when one encounters insanity in a busy city street. Just as in *Repulsion* (1965), Polanski leads us to identify with the central character by having all the action of the film take place with that character. In fact, we get such an insider's view of the action that we are sometimes unsure which events are inside the character's mind and which ones really happen. As in *Cul-de-sac* (1966), female impersonation signals a character's search for identity, a struggle designed to enlist our sympathy and challenge our iron-clad sense of ordinary reality.

An equally sympathetic but far more optimistic treatment of female impersonation, Richard Benner's Canadian film *Outrageous* (1977), examines professional impersonation as a form of personal liberation. The film showcases the talents of Craig Russell (a professional impersonator in real life) as a homosexual hairdresser named Robin, and Hollis McLaren as his schizophrenic friend, Liza. The film is sympathetic to both characters, who will "never be normal" because of their defiant longing to live lives of "dazzle." The script abounds with in-joking double entendres, as when Robin decides to quit hairdressing: "I'm sick of doing everyone else's head!" Whereas earlier films about nonconformists often ended with their odd characters conforming or crumbling under the weight of an oppressive society, *Outrageous* allows its central characters final victory, small enough to be believable, yet large enough to give a sense of triumph. When Liza finds Robin working as a successful impersonator in a club in Manhattan, she receives acceptance from the patrons of the club, and she also announces her own decision to write literature for the misfits of the world. Like many small counterculture films that received limited initial distribution, *Outrageous* continues to play in theaters designed for intellectual and for homosexual audiences.

And Justice for All (1979) demonstrates the trend of the late seventies toward sympathetic portrayals of female impersonators and transvestites in more popular movies. The film opens with a black transvestite being put in jail for attempted robbery of a taxi driver. The inmates shout and whistle as he passes by their cells, and this scene of taunting immediately wins audience sympathy for the transvestite. Al Pacino eventually agrees to be his defense lawyer, and during their conversations, the young man wears his blond wig and tells Pacino that sometimes when he is dressed up he can "look really fine." As we learn his story, we see that he was a passive participant throughout the robbery, and as he explains his situation to Pacino, he becomes almost hysterical at the thought of what will happen to him in prison. Pacino sends a lawyer friend to present the parole request; the case is badly handled, and the young man is sentenced to a prison term. Pacino then learns that the man killed himself shortly after his sentencing. The film is confused in its nebulous message about random corruption and injustice in the judicial system. Nevertheless, the essential idea of "justice for all" signals an increasing popular acceptance of the principle of tolerance for individual diversity combined with suspicion of the lawmakers who deliver judgment and punishment.

What all these films have in common is the seriousness with which the transvestite character is treated. For the first time, the impersonator or feminized male is viewed as an unusual but legitimate part of humankind. Moreover, the very fact that there is such a variety of types in these films indicates filmmakers' and audiences' growing awareness of the diversity of such characters. It may be argued that these films not only reflected a change in popular attitudes but also influenced mass market audiences to see homosexuals, transvestites, and feminine men as human beings.

Comedy and Farce Carry On

To say that serious treatments of cross-dressing were having a profound influence on popular attitudes is not to argue that the farcical tradition had died out. Indeed, it was alive in a series of "B" comedies, including Lindsay Shonteff's *The Second Best Secret Agent in the Whole World* (1965), Jerry Lewis' *Three on a Couch* (1966), Blake Edwards' *What Did You Do in the War, Daddy?* (1966), Richard Lester's *A Funny Thing Happened on the Way to the Forum* (1966), and Bruce Bilson's Walt Disney production, *The North Avenue Irregulars* (1979). The impersonations in such films are generally caricatures of women, and in the shallow, demeaning quality of the disguise is reflected the limited, negative view of women implicit in the choices made. Other kinds of films were still having fun with manly matrons, but if they did so at the expense of women, they were no more gentle with manly virtues. The British contributed enormously to this fund of absurd humor based on gender and role reversals, bringing with them a light-heartedness. In Stanley Donen's *Bedazzled* (1967), Dudley Moore plays the beleaguered Stanley, a short-order cook who sells his soul to the devil for seven wishes that will bring him love and happiness with Margaret, the woman of his dreams. He is tricked by semantics in each of his wishes, one of which results in perfect spiritual love; the catch is that Stanley and Margaret are both nuns. The joke is on Stanley, but the filmmakers are also spoofing religion, celibacy, heterosexuality, and the whole notion of platonic love. This same kind of irreverence toward religion and sex is demonstrated in Monty Python's *Life of Brian* (1978), a film that features Peter Cook in drag as Brian's mother, as well as a male transvestite who is convinced that he should have been born a woman. One of the most cunning reversals of the film takes place in the public stoning sequence, in which a group of women (acted by men) put on fake beards so that they can attend the stoning, a rousing event that women are not allowed to watch. These films derive their humor from the absurdity of the situations as well as the artlessness of the disguises. A less successful American attempt at farcical drag and drug humor is Cheech and Chong's *Up in Smoke* (1978), in which Tommy Chong wears false breasts to facilitate hitchhiking, and Cheech Marin wears a tutu and sings about being a queen who wears panty hose. These films present female impersonation as good clean fun, striking a blow for the cheerful anarchy of comedy.

One of the most successful and sophisticated cross-dressing comedies of the decade is the French-Italian film *La Cage aux folles* (1978), directed by Edouard Molinaro. The French had often dealt with female impersonation in a rather playful way. In Louis Malle's *Le Souffle au coeur* (1972), a young boy's identification with his mother takes the form of putting on her makeup and wearing her robe. In one scene he lays out her underwear and dress on the bed and falls on the bed in an ecstasy of incestuous love. The eventual mother-son sexual encounter is presented as an initiation rite, a benign introduction to the joys of sex. In Malle's *Zazie dans le metro* (1960), Zazie visits an uncle in Paris who is a female impersonator, but this potentially shocking experience turns out to be just another phase in her education. The carefree, relaxed quality of these films appealed to the intelligentsia in the United States, but *La Cage aux folles* captured popular audiences as well, and set a record for earnings of a foreign-language film.[41]

In the classical tradition of comedy, *Cage* amuses audiences by betraying expectations and overturning conventions. The film opens with what appears to be a middle-aged homosexual getting a doctor to convince his star female impersonator to get on stage for the scheduled performance. We soon learn that Renato (Ugo Tognazzi) has a deeper relationship with his star, Zaza/Albin (played by Michel Serrault), than simply that of manager and performer. Theirs is a friendship that has lasted twenty years—a true marriage, complete with boy child (conceived by a woman, of course). When Renato learns that his son, Laurent, wishes to marry a girl, he reluctantly accepts the situation. Laurent's request that Albin leave the house so that the future in-laws can meet with each other is more than either Albin or Renato is willing to accept. Albin attempts to impersonate Laurent's mother, but when his biological mother appears, the parents of the future bride demand to know who the boy's mother really is. Renato points to Albin (Zaza) as the boy's real mother, an affirmation of love as the essential element of motherhood. As a final twist, the father of the bride-to-be must dress as a woman and go out through the gay nightclub, La Cage aux Folles, in order to escape the reporters who are ready to heap scandal on his head. When his own chauffeur asks him "How much, Madame?" he almost blows his own cover, screaming in horror that he is not a woman. The comedy is resolved with the traditional wedding, attended by a very untraditional set of parents of the groom, Renato and his lovely wife, Albin.

Cage highlights the close connections between the effeminate homosexual's mannerisms and the sex-linked gestures of women. The use of the feminine name, Zaza, the consistent use of feminine pronouns and adjectives in referring to her, and the clothing and tastes all point to the deep identification Zaza/Albin feels with the female role. The beginning of the film seems to carry misogynist connotations as well as antihomosexual stereotypes in the depiction of Zaza and his/her relationship with Renato. Zaza's high-pitched whine, his hysterical accusations of infidelity, and his listing of Renato's romantic failings are all associated with the worse aspects of "feminine" behavior. Zaza complains that he lost weight and Renato didn't even notice; Zaza bought a new outfit just to please Renato, but Renato didn't mention it, etc. What makes these things comical is the very fact that it is a man who is behaving in what is considered to be a feminine way, demonstrating supposedly womanly concerns. Finally, Zaza is satisfied when he becomes so hysterical that Renato slaps him, showing that Renato really cares for Zaza enough to strike him. Zaza's suspicions then appear justified when we see the young man, Laurent, come to visit Renato while Zaza is onstage.

The way Laurent is introduced lays a trap for the prejudiced audience which assumes a homosexual liaison between the aging

Renato and this young, attractive boy. Renato applies makeup before Laurent arrives, and carefully turns off enough lights to give a romantic ambience to the apartment. Renato says that Zaza is onstage for the next few hours, and Jacob the "maid" has the night off, so the two of them will not be disturbed. Their embraces are truly warm, they compliment each other on their looks, and Renato seems childishly flattered when Laurent says that Renato still looks young for his age. When Laurent informs Renato that he plans to marry, we finally learn that Laurent is Renato's son. Suddenly the embraces, the preparations, and the concern all seem "natural"—an appealing expression of paternal affection rather than the somewhat ludicrous attempts of an older man to captivate a young lover. It seems that the filmmakers are leading the audience to realize that such affection should be acknowledged as legitimate, regardless of who feels it for whom.

Because the film plays with prejudicial notions, contradicting some and fulfilling others, it runs the risk of reinforcing stereotypes. David Ansen, in his *Newsweek* review of *Cage,* comments: "The clockwork formula—and the image of homosexuals as swishy queens—are old-fashioned, but Tognazzi and Serrault manage to invest their parts with great comic zest and delicate pathos."[42] Richard Schickel is more generous in his assessment of the film's characterization: "Though the gays must make eccentric adjustments to the exigencies of living, their behavior is viewed as no more unusual than the quirks everyone develops to get through the day as pleasantly as possible."[43] Certainly the potential for exploitation is apparent, as indicated by the speed with which *Grease* producer Allan Carr snapped up the rights for a Hollywood remake.

Cage II (1980), a successful attempt to cash in on the original's popularity, did well enough in Paris to merit its release in New York, where it made a strong $133,426 in its first week's run.[44] A comparison between the two films indicates that the "clockwork formula" of the original was perhaps one of its virtues. A number of critics noted with some regret that *Cage II* does not offer the same integrity of plot and characters, one of the strong points of *La Cage aux folles.* In *Cage II,* Renato and Albin find themselves unwitting participants in a cloak-and-dagger plot. This places them out of their natural element, but the far-fetched situations are excuses for delightful variations in costumes and comic set-ups. Albin does a disguise as an Italian peasant woman that reveals to him the fact that "it's no fun being a woman in this country," where he/she is expected to work all day long and eat apart from the men. Albin even tries his hand at being a woman who must pretend to be a man, a situation that ribs traditional masculinity as thoroughly as it does homosexual and feminine mannerisms. The admitted homosexuality of the buffoons is remarkably daring in comparison with popular comedies even as recent as a decade earlier. The appearance of these same characters in a second film prompted many critics to observe that both films avoid even a single platonic kiss between the two lovers, an omission that went unnoticed in the well-constructed narrative of the original. Although critics may begrudge the films their tameness, obviously the filmmakers calculated very accurately the level of intimacy that general audiences were ready to respond to favorably. The original *La Cage aux folles* and perhaps the sequel may be well on their way to becoming cult favorites, movies that quietly draw box-office returns for years from faithful followers and newly won devotees.

The Ultimate Cult Film: *Rocky Horror*

In the past twenty years, the American film industry has undergone an economic renaissance. After what many consider the dark ages of the fifties, American filmmakers began to recapture their audiences from television, and they did this through effective marketing to youth audiences. During the late sixties and early seventies Stanley Kubrick's *2001: A Space Odyssey* and Walt Disney's freshly popular *Fantasia* were sure to fill theaters with people using LSD or marijuana, and often the viewers had seen the film five or ten times. With the seventies came the deliberate selling to a younger audience of such highly commercialized films as *Jaws, King Kong, Close Encounters of the Third Kind, Grease, Raiders of the Lost Ark, E.T.,* and the *Star Wars* and *Superman* series. Although cult films occasionally have audience participation in the form of shrieks, T-shirts, special glasses, or ingestion of chemical enhancers, few include the paraphernalia, memory, and devoted viewing of Lou Adler's *The Rocky Horror Picture Show.*

Whereas *Star Wars* production costs were $12 million and *2001: A Space Odyssey* costs were about $18 million, *Rocky Horror* cost about $1 million, a relatively low budget. Within four years of its release in 1975, the film had gained devoted fans and grossed $26 million, partly because of a carefully engineered word-of-mouth advertising campaign, but also due to a serendipitous meshing of the film's eccentric theme and its audience's hungry appreciation of the theme and format.[45]

Rocky Horror represents a small but significant group of films that serve as a locus for social ritual. During the silent period, film attendance often had a communal quality, as Handel and Mayer observe in *Hollywood Looks at Its Audience:*

> During the silent era it was considered acceptable for members of the audience to express audibly their views about the action on the screen. Sometimes this might cause disruption or annoyance, but it also had a potential for forging a rapport of shared responses, a sense of community with surrounding strangers. . . . With talkies, however, people who talked aloud were peremptorily hushed by others in the audience who didn't want to miss any spoken dialogue.[46]

Although film continued to have a profound social influence after the advent of sound, much of the sense of immediate, shared experience was lost when audiences grew so sophisticated that they wouldn't applaud the hero's victory at the end of the film. Toward the end of the sixties, film audiences became more expressive again; a case in point is the spontaneous applause which greeted the finish of *The Graduate* (1967) in theaters throughout the nation. David Thompson points out the paradox of "audience participation" in an essentially passive viewing situation: "we all recognize something unsociable about cinema and unwittingly struggle with the contradiction of a medium concerned with 'being seen' where we are encouraged to think ourselves protected spies."[47] Through the seventies, with the opening of subject matter in film, viewers lost their status of "protected spies" simply by attending certain types of films designed for a particular interest or age group. With no film is this more true than it is with *Rocky Horror,* a viewing experience that even sorts out the "virgins" (who have not seen the film before) from the initiated viewers who come prepared with props and memorized responses.

Before the film begins, audience members prepare hats made out of newspapers, and soon a chant of "Lips, lips!" begins. The opening sequence delivers the requested lips, singing a paean to the "late night double-feature picture show." In an abrupt shift from the lascivious red lips, set against a black background, the story begins with one of the most codified American institutions, the wedding ceremony. Experienced viewers know that the seeds of chaos nestle even in this seemingly wholesome setting, for they recognize the minister and attendants as Tim Curry and the other actors and actresses who populate the realm of Dr. Frank-N-Furter, "a sweet transvestite from transsexual Transylvania." Brad and Janet, a straight young couple from Denton, "Home of Happiness," become engaged and then leave the wedding. They soon find themselves stranded on the road, forced to seek help at the house of Frank-N-Furter, who is in the midst of giving a party to celebrate the unveiling of his latest creation, Rocky. This well-tanned hunk of muscles is based on the Charles Atlas model. The party is momentarily interrupted by the arrival of the older, failed version of the perfect man, played by the rock singer Meatloaf; the character is eventually carted off to become exactly that—meatloaf. After the party, Frank-N-Furter seduces Janet (Susan Sarandon) and still has enough energy left over to seduce Brad (Barry Bostwick).

The satire is presented in such a way that the audience ends up liking Frank, despite his flouting of convention in every way imaginable. The character, brilliantly portrayed by Tim Curry in his film debut, is the ultimate in vibrant androgynous sex appeal. Curry's lusty Mae West voice, masculinized Joan Crawford face, and almost carnivorous leers at males and females alike all combine to create a figure whose allure crosses gender lines. Though he reveals himself to be a sadistic killer, the character is more magnetic than any of the others in the film because of his vitality.

The film is outrageous, a word that contains the word "rage" but also suggests taking some pleasure in trying to enrage the established order. It is designed to shock the audience out of its acceptance of standard views on marriage, adultery, homosexuality, and transvestism, or it is intended to support an already liberated audience in its nonconventional views. The characters in the film are converted to Frank's point of view in the floor show, in which Brad, Janet, Rocky, Columbia, and even Dr. Scott, a college professor, do a chorus-line number wearing black corsets, fishnet stockings, and stiletto heels. The climax of this number takes place in the swimming pool, with all of them kissing and fondling indiscriminately to the lyrics, "Don't dream it; be it." At this point, even Brad, who has sung, "Help me, Mommy; I feel sexy," is liberated enough to luxuriate in the sensuality of a group embrace. The appearance of the incestuous Riff Raff and Magenta, who tell Frank, "Your lifestyle's too extreme," signals the end of Frank's antics on earth. Like Dr. Frankenstein, Frank-N-Furter is destroyed by the creatures he thought he ruled, an association suggested by Magenta's *Bride of Frankenstein* hairdo. By the end of the film, the audience is touched by Frank's poignant rendition of the homecoming song. The straight characters remain after the extraterrestrials have disappeared, but their concepts of marriage, fidelity, and sexuality will never be the same.

The success of each showing depends to a large degree on the devotion of its audiences and live performers. Throughout the film, the in-group recites questions and comments on the action and dialogue. Visual and verbal puns are made concrete as the audience throws rice during the wedding scene, shoots water pistols during the rainstorm, throws pieces of toast when a toast is proposed, and lights matches when the heroine sings, "There's a light in the darkness of everybody's life." What sounds like random noise turns out to be codified formulas that the audience chants at the appearance of each character. This orchestrated chaos is most effective when there is a healthy balance of novices and initiated members, for the laughter of surprise from the innocents is a reward to those who are performing. In most major cities, a number of regulars attend showings dressed as one of the characters in the film, and during the dance numbers these "actors" stand in front of the screen and perform along with the movie characters. During Janet's song, "Touch-a Touch-a Touch-a Touch Me," audience members leap up to touch the screen, much to the dismay but little to the surprise of theater owners. This anarchic behavior serves two opposing functions; it expresses rage and rebellion against the prevailing social order while it creates its own brand of conformity.

Although the theme of the film is an important element in its popularity, the live participation seems to be the key factor in its continued box-office returns. In the *Rocky Horror Picture Show Book* Bill Henkin chronicles the experience of one of the repertory groups that developed around the film:

> The group approached the theater management and explained that they wanted to return to the Village. During the six months they had not been performing, *Rocky Horror* had received no New York media attention, but the night they returned reporters from several publications were present. On their tour, theaters found they were selling out within three weeks of the group's first appearance. The Eighth Street management agreed to let them in, and they have been based there ever since.[48]

Both organized and spontaneous participation often seem to grow out of the individual's desire to exhibit the unconventional traits of characters within the film. A female member of a group named "Double Feature" comments on the excitement of playing Frank-N-Furter and the challenge of being a female who impersonates a female impersonator:

> The one thing I wanted was to get to the point where people would not be sure which I was. I am intrigued by the fact that there is a masculine element in me, and I enjoy being able to bring it out. Women's lib aside, we still believe femininity is soft and passive. As Frank, I have a chance to be on top of things, to be a faggot Clint Eastwood. Frank-N-Furter may wear Joan Crawford makeup and high heels, but he's still so masculine there's no way you could mistake him for a woman.[49]

To a greater or lesser degree, any viewer of *Rocky Horror* is called on to determine his or her role in the microcosm of the film. Whatever role one chooses, the individual is assured of eventual acceptance in a group embrace. This happens within the film, and at most successful showings the spirit of camaraderie carries over to the interaction of audience members; complete strangers begin talking to each other and forming a cohesive social unit for a time.

Rocky Horror didn't just happen to become a cult film; its producers and promoters were well aware of how to appeal to a set of alienated subcultures. After observing the kinds of preview audiences that liked the film, Tim Deegan made these suggestions on how Twentieth-Century Fox should place the film in its initial stages:

> Like so many so-called "cult" movies ROCKY has always succeeded when placed in an accessible but not obviously commercial or super-trendy venue. This allows its supporters initial access and the size of the venue allows a long run to enable its audience to spread to a general public proportion.[50]

The techniques suggested by Deegan, the company's youngest promoter, worked throughout the country, and the film achieved an unprecedented cult status.

At the same time, the film seems to have had effects on audiences that go beyond the immediate experience of the film. Teenage viewers, trained in the *Rocky Horror* response pattern, carry this vocalizing behavior over to other films as well. Older movie patrons may have noticed, with some irritation, the willingness of younger audiences to speak out in answer to dialogue or to criticize or cheer the action on screen. Adults may also find themselves outraged at the readiness of young audiences to laugh at scenes of overt violence or sexuality. Much of this apparently disorderly behavior may be started by those who first indulged in rowdy response while watching *Rocky Horror.*

The live participation is an important element of its success as a cult film, but the content of the piece is integral to its status as well. The sexual reversals and the humor have a particular appeal for youthful viewers, whose sexual identity may be a source of confusion and anxiety. By their very nature, role reversals are a discordant note, an exception to the rules. The popularity of *Rocky Horror* both signals and furthers a change in the relative status of the traditional male and the unconventional male who imitates women. Although the film seems to offer liberation from inhibitions, it is difficult to say what the ultimate effect on audience opinions may be.

Interpreting the nature of the rage expressed and the order established by the ritual of *Rocky Horror* does not result in clear-cut conclusions. Some who witness the phenomenon have seen it as an expression of Dionysian revelry, a release and flowering of individual impulses, both joyous and hostile. Others, who may have been somewhat unwillingly dragged to the event by their enthusiastic offspring, have been shocked by the almost fascist quality of the audience responses, describing the youths as "little automatons" or "mindless robots." Other observers have pointed out the insidiousness of a ritual that tidily contains rebellious impulses in such a set, restrictive environment as the peer group's compulsive weekly gathering at the "late-night picture show," as the title song calls the film. Certainly all these observations touch on some aspect of the truth, for *Rocky Horror* fulfills all these functions, depending on the particular location, time (usually midnight), and audience for each showing. No one screening is like another, a phenomenon that might be used to argue against viewing the film's ritual as essentially constrictive. There are, however, identifiable patterns that can be compared to the stages of development of practically any ritual.

In its inception, behavior that is to become ritualized is spontaneous, demonstrating the same kind of creativity that characterizes artistic production. The participants tend to perceive themselves as rejecting the old order, taking a new direction that opposes the established model. At the same time that they view themselves as iconoclasts, they seek converts, and if the cult has some intrinsic appeal, it carries within it the seeds of its own destruction. A cult, by its very nature, suggests something relatively small, outré, and unappealing to the larger population. Perhaps the most outstanding example of a cult following in western civilization is the early Christian church, in which the number of followers was small and their attitudes were almost totally inimical to the ruling powers.

For this small cult, an activity like the Last Supper was weighted with significance only in retrospect; at its inception, it was spontaneous. As the church gathered followers, communion became a ritual, but in its early phases, it still carried the powerful emotional quality of improvisation it had carried on that first occasion. Participants felt the emotions and clearly experienced the connection between ritual actions and their allusive source. As the mass grew up around the sharing of communion, it developed into its hieratic phase, the Eucharist becoming one of the seven sacraments that had to be administered by a highly trained elite. Attention to detail abounded, and soon every aspect was governed by rules, even down to the direction the priest would face during various phases of the ceremony. This focus on adherence to regulations tends to lead the participants away from the emotional origins of the ritual.[51] Finally, in what some might view as a deterioration of the ritual, participants in the decadent phase have forgotten not only the origins but the proper performance as well, and we see people eating Ritz crackers and drinking Welch's grape juice, hearing someone tell them this is Christ's body and blood, and wondering if it would be impolite to take seconds. As the ritual is handed down over the ages, sense and pattern are ultimately obscured, almost beyond recognition.

This same progression manifests itself in the more trivial kinds of social rituals created by popular culture. *Rocky Horror* began as a musical, originally entitled "They Came From Denton High," and it was a satirical spoof on the B-movies that the author, Richard O'Brien, had enjoyed all through his childhood and adolescence. When producer/director Michael White took the first production to the Royal Court's experimental Theatre Upstairs in June 1973, the show was so popular that they moved it from the sixty-seat facility to the five-hundred-seat King's Road Theatre. After almost a year's successful run, Lou Adler saw the musical and got backing for it from Twentieth-Century Fox. The stage version included some built-in audience responses, but no one guessed that the film rendition would also attract performers in the audience. The original audiences for the film were responsible for its popularity as an underground cult favorite, and the studio's observations on its growth in popularity molded the style of publicity the film was to receive. Whereas the standard method of selling a movie is through short-term bombardment with heavy-selling promotion, the strategy for *Rocky Horror* grew out of the fact that people who go to cult films don't want to feel as if they are being sold something. The promotion advice that goes out to theater managers includes this observation:

> Like all late shows, the key to RHPS is its appeal to an entirely different movie-going audience. Generally, this audience consists

of people between the ages of 17 and 35 who are seeking off-beat, unusual and imaginative entertainment. . . . Promotion should be relatively subtle. The audience should feel they are *discovering* something rather than being hyped or sold.[52]

These observations, made in 1975, were accurate at the time, but gradually the major audience for the show shifted to a younger group. The ritual entered its hieratic phase, manifested by groups and individuals who attended the film religiously equipped with every prop, in costumes exactly replicating those of on-screen characters. These participants had entered the realm of high art and high camp, but in so doing, they had lost the spontaneity and nonconformity that marked the earlier followers. In taking on a uniform, they joined the ranks of any young people who want to identify with a group, be it the Boy Scouts or the Hitler Jugend. Indeed, the phenomenon of transvestism was commonplace in such highly organized cadres as the soldiers of the Prussian army, and in the military and civilian population of the Third Reich both male and female impersonation were quite in vogue.

Many of the *Rocky Horror* viewers of today are high school and even junior high school children. At this stage in the ritual, one is no longer assured that the participants are familiar with the ritual actions, much less with the original spirit. Hence, audiences are aware that they are supposed to be noisy, but instead of yelling out lines supporting the acceptability of homosexuality or bisexuality, some members of the audience may simply scream "Faggot!" each time Frank-N-Furter appears on screen. Such naïve viewers have lost touch with both the spirit and the substance of the ritual, and they seem to attend the film because they have been pressured to do so by their peers, not because they share a common set of values. Individuals bring their own prejudices to the interpretation of the film, and for the viewer who fears or dislikes homosexuality, the film may reinforce these negative feelings or encourage more rigid views or more vocal expression of them. Even if the decadent version of audience participation fails to create the unconventional unity it once did, the film still offers a mixture of experiences. Devoted participants may be submitting to peer pressure, but they nevertheless engage in the deviant behavior of defying society's dress and behavior codes. The film shows that rebellion can be pleasurable, and it has cemented the image of the drag queen in the minds of a generation of viewers who, ten years earlier, had no such character in their repertoire of movie personalities.

Dressed to Kill: Satire or Sexism?

Much like *Rocky Horror,* Brian De Palma's *Dressed to Kill* (1980) prompted much controversy over the effects of film content on audience attitudes and behavior. The focus of discussion has been on the rape fantasies presented in the opening and closing sequences, but the entire film raises questions on the degree to which De Palma has satirized or celebrated misogynist attitudes. Both sides of the argument are amenable to substantiation, but it seems that some of the critics who have been most vehement in attacking the film as antifeminist would have pounced on Jonathan Swift's *A Modest Proposal* as cannibalistic. De Palma satirizes the society and values that create bored housewives and their less respectable counterparts, prostitutes. At the same time, *Dressed to Kill* expresses some misogynist impulses in a more subtle way than many of the film's critics have imagined. The film's detractors have, for the most part, examined the surface content of the film, but few have commented that the film is charged with intentional irony and self-conscious parody.[53]

Dressed to Kill is described in *Newsweek*'s review as "sexy Hitchcock," and the film resonates with *Psycho* images, from the shower scenes to the rather flip explanation of the psychology of a killer who dresses as a woman in order to kill women who arouse masculine desire. De Palma is never totally serious, and the film abounds with sexual innuendo, such as the call girl's statement, "I'll miss having you on my tail." De Palma demonstrates a keen sensitivity to the significance of gesture in the museum sequence, in which Angie Dickinson alternately chases and tries to escape a dark stranger. In distinct contrast, the cross-dressing scenes reveal nothing about what constitutes femininity in terms of gesture or mannerism. At one level, females appear to be passive victims, but closer analysis reveals a fantasy common to the majority of De Palma's films: woman as controller, destroyer, and survivor, a figure to be feared and admired.

The title and plot structure of *Dressed to Kill* reveal much about woman's place in De Palma's fantasy world. The play on the popular expression, "dressed to kill," suggests that females are the true victimizers when they use the tricks of clothing and makeup to render powerless those men who succumb to feminine trappings. The killer psychiatrist (played by Michael Caine) must be dressed in women's clothing in order for the destructive, female half of his psyche to murder. However, the supposedly feminine disguise and psyche seem to be the scapegoat for essentially masculine misogynist impulses. The two women in the film are represented as deserving and almost desiring the violence aimed at them, for it is their fantasy, be it sexual daydream or nightmare, that shows the male attacking the female. The mother behaves like a "whore" in first propositioning her psychiatrist and in later participating in the rather sordid sexual encounter with a complete stranger in a taxicab. She is appropriately punished for her aggressive wantonness, slashed to death by the mysterious female impersonator. Whether or not the audience has been clued in to his gender by advance publicity, few people would be convinced by his feminine attire—a blond wig, sunglasses, and a black trench coat. Only the call girl is fooled by her momentary glimpse of the killer, and she in turn takes the place of Angie Dickinson as the murderer's next potential victim, deserving punishment not so much for being a witness but for arousing the masculine desires of the killer.

The son in the film seems to come closest to the filmmaker's own idealized vision of himself. He is sexually naïve, interested only in gadgets until he is pulled into the world of threatening sexuality by his mother's murder. He then becomes voyeur and listener, who discovers through his bugging device his mother's sexual activities on the day of her death. The situation resonates with Oedipal fantasies, but all the boy's actions are one step removed by the fact that his father is already dead and his mother killed before he has a chance to rescue her. He saves the call girl's life, paralleling what he would wish to have done for his mother.

The film depicts women as aggressive controllers rather than defenseless victims to be protected by men. With the most sympathetic female of the film neatly out of the way, the call girl serves as De Palma's representative for womankind. She is a mercenary creature who, even in the midst of a struggle for survival, coolly takes time out to call her stockbroker while she arranges for the tricks it will take to pay for more stocks. Curiosity rather than sympathy prompts the audience to wonder whether she will be killed. Although the son proposes to use her to get the psychiatrist's appointment book, the arrangement obviously profits her as much as it does him. He must remind her of the fact that he saved her life, a bargain she is capable of appreciating and honoring. The other two females in the film share in her coolness and almost masculine control of the situation, but once again, they seem to be not so much women as a paranoid male fantasy of the emotionless controller. The policewoman who follows the call girl and eventually kills the psychiatrist is expressionless, perfect for the part of a female impersonator because she herself is masculine in her manner and carriage, despite her feminine gender and attire. The nurse in the final dream sequence is not really a character, but through her position she is controlling agent and arousing seductress. A gallery of male patients cheers as the psychiatrist strangles her, a scene that draws on the film tradition of portraying nurses as the sadistic managers of helpless victims.

The film's happy ending is the fulfillment of the son's (and very possibly the filmmaker's) fondest dreams. After all the slashing, almost lyrical violence, in which blood looks like red paint and time seems to slow down, De Palma's innocent boy tells the call girl (and the audience) that this final murder attempt, an echo of *Psycho* and the opening fantasy scene, is only a dream. If we view the mother and the call girl as the Madonna/whore of De Palma's fantasy subtext, then the psychiatrist and the son may represent the duality of impulses in a single psyche. The film allows the boy to rescue the Mom of his dreams from her nightmare, and in so doing he can absolve himself of guilt over the desire to destroy the all-powerful female. The rescue fantasy is the counterpart to the pathological desire to slash instead of caress, to destroy rather than to desire. The unattainable mother is replaced by the very available call girl, and the murderous, sexually disoriented psychiatrist is replaced by the gentle boy, who is about to receive his initiation into the joys of sex.

De Palma is a sophisticated, psychologically and politically aware filmmaker. If his private fantasies include fear, awe, and even hatred of women, he couches these feelings in layers of irony that make it difficult to sort out which sentiments are genuine and which are being ridiculed or subverted. Much of his power as a filmmaker resides in this ambiguity, for he creates a strong case for a wide range of emotions and attitudes, thus providing a multitude of possibilities for audience identification. As with Josef von Sternberg's films, De Palma's works leave critics wondering whether he worships or despises women, and certainly the two emotions are not mutually exclusive. Whether a film like *Dressed to Kill* incited rape or misogyny is a moot point, but the very fact that the film has elicited such vigorous controversy demonstrates a healthy public awareness of film images of women, a concern that has become prevalent only over the past two decades.

CHAPTER FIVE

1960–1985:
OTHER SCREENS, OTHER VOICES

TVTV: Transvestite Television

THE FASHION INDUSTRY has always maintained a close symbiotic relationship with film, a connection that has been brilliantly elucidated in Charles Eckert's work on the mutually profitable arrangement between film and product advertising.[1] A similar cooperation developed between television and film during the sixties and seventies, with film successes becoming television series, and television providing publicity for movies and their stars. The development of television treatments of cross-dressing follows a pattern similar to the course of film treatments, albeit in conservative, telescoped form. Early comedy programs of the fifties made frequent use of male and female impersonation, demonstrating the same kind of imaginative range found in silent films. Lucille Ball appeared in male disguises in various *I Love Lucy* episodes, and vaudeville-style drag acts were a recurrent feature of Milton Berle's comedy routines. Red Skelton appeared *en femme* in numerous skits, and one of his most famous and frequently imitated routines was one in which he dances with himself, with one half of his body made up and dressed in feminine and the other half in masculine attire. This period of play-ful, farcical treatments was followed by a decline in the appearance of female impersonation, a self-censorship probably created by the growing awareness of homosexual overtones in such routines.

During the late sixties and seventies, the topics of female impersonation and sex change operations reemerge in talk shows and programs like *Real People,* introducing real transvestites, ho-mosexual drag artists, and transsexuals in relatively serious dis-cussions. Meanwhile, comedy treatments had become more risqué, and the connections between female impersonation and homosexuality were more directly articulated. *M*A*S*H* fea-tured Corporal Klinger, the character who wears women's clothes in order to get out of the army. Although he is identified as a heterosexual, he demonstrates a real love for feminine fashions, and transvestism is touted as a family tradition. The British im-ports *Monty Python's Flying Circus* and *The Benny Hill Show* pre-sented drag acts in almost every episode. Flip Wilson's Geraldine was younger and more sexually aggressive than the British or vaudeville matrons, and in *Saturday Night Live* drag routines, female impersonations were openly suggestive of homosexuality. One episode played on the word "drag," featuring "drag racing," in which men dressed in black corsets and stockings ran a race, and "Dragnet," in which policemen dressed as women while they worked the police beat. The program *Bosom Buddies* has Tom Hanks and Peter Scolari playing two men who disguise them-selves as women in order to live in the Susan B. Anthony women's hotel. Although the two characters are nominally heterosexual, the scripts contain frequent double-entendres and patently homo-sexual in-jokes, creating a surface text that is acceptable to a popular audience and a subtext aimed at a very different one. The lyrics of the theme song by Billy Joel, "I never claimed to be a victim of circumstance. . . . Go ahead with your own life and leave me alone," suggest that beneath the veneer of circumstan-tially enforced cross-dressing are two men who have willingly chosen to dress as women and remain "bosom buddies." Another popular comedy program, *Mork and Mindy,* featured Robin Williams in a number of disguises, including that of a little old lady and as Mindy herself. Williams demonstrates a particular interest in role reversals in his stand-up comedy routines, often borrowing a piece of feminine clothing from an audience member, and in choosing to play the lead in *The World According to Garp,* considered by some to be a feminist film.

Going Beyond Clothing: *The World According to Garp* and *Come Back to the 5 & Dime, Jimmy Dean, Jimmy Dean*

George Roy Hill's film version of *The World According to Garp* stirred up as much controversy as John Irving's novel did, but the assessments of the movie tend to be more negative. The story, as told in the film version, looks a lot like a screwball Hollywood romance, except for the random violence that peppers the plot. The movie opens with slow motion shots of a baby being tossed high into the air, an image to be repeated, for fearful symmetry, at the close of the film. This is only the beginning of the movie's attempts to symmetrize, sweeten, and conventionalize its source. Leaving out several essential ideas, the filmmakers have created a film that fails to cohere in the way the novel does. By deemphasizing the concept of what Garp's son calls the "Under Toad"—what Garp identifies with death, fate, the seamy underbelly of life—and by practically eliminating references to rape (except for Garp hearing a brief account of the rape of Ellen James and immediately attacking the feminist cult that arose in her memory as perverted extremists), the screenplay lacks thematic unity and tries to substitute for it the emotionalism of Hollywood. Relationships are considerably altered by the Hollywood version, showing Garp and his mother as a slightly eccentric yet basically normal pair. Instead of portraying a woman who dislikes men enough to slash them with a knife if they get too familiar, a woman who will only become pregnant by a man who is a vegetable with a semen pump, and a son who never even questions the absence of a man in the household, the film shows a rather ordinary woman who manages (bravely, but not necessarily by choice) to raise a son without a husband, while her son fantasizes almost obsessively about his departed father.

Another example of the film normalizing the bizarre is in the portrayal of the relationship between Garp and Helen, in the book a fairly unromantic joining of equal if different minds. In the hands of Tesich and Hill, Garp becomes a hero who charms his way into Helen's heart, even lecturing her on James Joyce while she listens, rapt. This would not seem so odd if she were not supposed to be the Ph.D. in literature and he, the wrestling coach. Granted, he is an author, but even in the scene where he shows Helen his first book, the stuff of the novel is transformed. Instead of giving Garp the novel's measured response that his first story "shows promise," the movie's Helen gushes as she cradles the manuscript against her breasts and looks up at Garp adoringly. We see the same kind of careful selection going on in the treatment of each partner's adultery. The book's rather disturbing description of Garp's habitual seduction of baby-sitters is changed to one brief incident, while Helen's long-term affair with her student becomes the apparent sole cause of the horrible accident in which their son is killed and her lover mutilated. Garp's philanderings, foolishness, and his own acknowledgment of partial responsibility are all eliminated, leaving the woman holding the guilt bag.

The film received mixed reviews, many pointing out the problems inherent in adapting so singularly literary a work. The adaptations made by George Roy Hill and Steve Tesich take some of the bitterness from Irving's vision, eliminating some of the violent details, but they do nothing to improve the status of women; according to John T. Hartzog's assessment, Tesich and Hill "have emasculated a feminist novel."[2] Michael Sragow sees the omissions of Irving's concern with rape, overprotective parenting, etc. as reasonable choices that do not destroy the novel's original intent. *Newsweek's* David Ansen finds the film less satisfying, and he argues that the depiction on screen of the rabid feminists who cut out their tongues in protest over the rape of the young Ellen James reveals the misogynist substructure in what many have perceived to be a feminist novel. Ansen observes: "One is meant to be appalled by their perversion of feminism, but their appearance on screen boomerangs: I was more appalled by the imagination that conceived them, that gleefully dreamed up the relentless horrors that befall everyone thereafter."[3] Marilyn French makes a similar observation about the book and the film, stating that Irving chooses a recurring option: "When men em-

body 'feminine' qualities—are affectionate, nutritive, spontaneous, non-dominating, and fun—they push women into opposite
qualities, seeing or showing them to be practical, realistic (about
small things), calculating, or purely sexual, or subhuman."[4] In
Garp the violent men are eliminated, with the two male assassins
who make attempts on Jenny's life never pictured, while Garp's
female slayer receives devoted closeups. Sex role exchanges don't
appear in the family arrangements, aside from a few superficial
features, such as Garp making meals while his wife teaches,
hardly a drastically unconventional situation.

The most interesting insights to be gained from the sexual
reversal in the film come from John Lithgow's comments on what
it felt like to play the part of Roberta Muldoon, who has undergone a transformation from tight end for the Philadelphia Eagles
to one of the largest women to be taken under the wing of Garp's
mother Jenny. One of the first observations Lithgow made as he
encountered the film crew was his reaction to the whistles and
catcalls: "I begin to hear a faint, female voice deep inside me
muttering an angry and unfamiliar phrase, almost shocking in its
vehemence: 'Christ, I hate men!'"[5] He notes that one of the
reasons he was drawn to this role, despite his heterosexual non-
transvestite status in daily life, was the fact that he preferred
women because they seemed to be more "generous and empathic." The experience proves arousing as well as enlightening:
"I had the feeling that I was conducting a prolonged, illicit love
affair with myself. Sitting alone in my trailer, all dressed up in
drag, I would run my hands over the strange, artificial curves of
my body, look at myself in the mirror, smile and wink. Boy-John
and girl-John were sharing a secret, sexy joke that no one else was
in on."[6] Lithgow discusses how the male crew and cast members
react to his presence with raucous humor and crude jokes,
whereas the females seem to accept him with warmth and ease,
perhaps because the women see his imitation as an attempt to be
less strange while the men see it as a kind of betrayal. Lithgow's
performance receives praise from *Rolling Stone* reviewer Michael
Sragow: "Nearly everything Lithgow does is funny—the slight
hip-swaying roll he adds to his big-lug walk, the way his round
face puckers when he's worried—and his humor has resonance.
The generosity of his concern for Garp and Jenny, and the authen-

ticity of his pain, give the film its greatest depth."[7] Lithgow's performance receives plaudits from David Ansen, who describes his character, Roberta, as the film's "spiritual heart, the balm at the center of the storm."[8] In several cases, Lithgow's transsexual is the only part of the film that receives any praise. Richard Grenier's assessment of the film places the blame for its failure on Irving, again commenting that Lithgow's performance is "an absolutely first-class drag act, and is about the only thing I enjoyed in the movie."[9]

Ansen is on the mark in selecting Roberta as the psychic center of the film, if it has one. Lithgow's performance is not really a drag act, though, but a good transvestite routine, for he shows none of the campy glamor, the sarcastic wit, or the threatening sexual aggressiveness of the queen. He demonstrates all the appealing elements of the androgynous figure, without making the audience uneasy by displaying blatantly sexual features. The filmmakers underestimate the level of tolerance for variation from the norm, however, in every other part of the film, and most critics and audiences find Garp's caveman response to Helen's infidelity and the ludicrous imitation of a woman when he attends his mother's funeral in drag to be somehow behind the times. Despite the film's inadequacies, it achieves just the right balance in its depiction of the transsexual, a success that may be attributed in part to Lithgow's ability to identify with the female role and in part to the fact that the audience of 1982 was predisposed to admire the androgynous figure as a source of compassion and moral strength.

Robert Altman's *Come Back to the 5 & Dime Jimmy Dean, Jimmy Dean* (1982) is another film with a transsexual at the center of the action, but it differs drastically in that Altman has chosen a woman to play the part of the male who has become female. Also, rather than being an expensive Hollywood-style production designed for popular audiences, *Jimmy Dean* has all the makings of a cult film. It was reviewed by very few of the popular magazines, partly because it was an extremely low-budget film. After directing the Broadway production of Ed Graczyk's play, which was generally panned by critics, Altman made a Super 16-millimeter version that cost only $900,000, with the rights for cable distribution going to Viacom Showtime and the blown-up 35-millimeter version going out to movie houses catering to the intelligentsia.

Every critic agrees that Altman's film rises above its source material. *Newsweek's* David Ansen describes it in a single paragraph, stating that "the wonder of Robert Altman's film version is that through some deft trimming, graceful camera work and several fine performances, some behavioral truth emerges from this wheezy work."[10] Lawrence O'Toole similarly remarks on Altman's brilliance and the original play's lack of it: "The technique Altman applies to *Jimmy Dean, Jimmy Dean* oils all its rusty cogs and takes all the onerousness out of its labored parts."[11] Pauline Kael goes into much greater detail in describing the merits of the film, but she also finds fault with the basic material, giving credit for the film's quality to Altman's use of the camera and the performances delivered by the leads. The combined facts that so few critics reviewed the film and that that handful lavished such praise on it lend the work the cachet necessary to make it survive as an arthouse return. However, the basic material, which critics view as the film's weakest component, is probably exactly the source of its appeal. The stagey, glittery, sentimental aura that surrounds the plot is precisely the element that draws an audience looking for something different, a world view at odds with the dominant culture. None of the critics use the adjective "campy," but that is the term that captures the film's charm most closely.

Like *Three Women*, *Jimmy Dean, Jimmy Dean* is a movie about women caught between adolescent fantasies of the past and the glaring realities that overwhelm them as the action progresses. The irony rests in the fact that the women have built their lives and their dreams around men, how to attract them, how to keep them, how to bring them back, while the only man in the film has spent his life learning how to be a woman. The group comes together in a reunion of the Jimmy Dean fan club, formed in a Texas town whose only claim to fame is its use as a location for the 1955 filming of *Giant*. The setting is crucial to the film's capture of a make-believe time warp, with its hot, rosy yellow light filtering into the cool interior of a tiny five-and-dime store, an anachronism complete with a vintage array of Dell comic books, pink spooly curlers, and syrup candy in wax molded to look like miniature bottles. Altman's camera unobtrusively glides through the store, highlighting the tinsel sign that reads "Disciples of Jimmy Dean," the dusty shelves that look as if they haven't been restocked since 1955, and the old-fashioned soda fountain with red stools and a mirror running the length of the bar.

Through gradual exposition the film reveals the deceptions of each of its main characters, as they gather to celebrate their twentieth reunion. Mona, played with the perfect touch of veiled hysteria by Sandy Dennis, describes how Jimmy Dean seduced her on the last night of filming, producing the slightly retarded son she named Jimmy Dean. The audience doesn't believe her, nor, as we eventually learn, do her companions, but her determination to maintain the illusion has been so strong that no one dared challenge her account. She has remained in the town, almost virginal after her only fling, keeping her story intact, defying anyone to claim that her child was any but the son of James Dean.

In distinct contrast to the prudish Mona we have Sissie (played by Cher), who proudly describes the charm she has exercised over the variety of men she has had in a variety of places, including a graveyard. She attributes her attractiveness to her "knockers," which she displays with a flirtatious arch of her back, asking her companions if her breasts still look as big as they did when she was younger. Cher plays the role with all the swaggering confidence and tenderness of a good old girl from Texas, and when Sissie finally confesses that Buck, the man she had been counting on to marry her, has left and that her famous breasts are really made of foam rubber, the audience is touched by her essential sadness, the nagging self-doubt that makes her latch onto the one thing that isn't even real as her most important asset.

Other characters also have their delusions, which are gradually stripped away. Juanita, played by Sudie Bond, is the hypocritical Bible-thumper who runs the five and dime, maintaining her lies about her dead husband, an alcoholic whose affliction she would never acknowledge because she wanted to maintain appearances. Two other women come to the reunion: Edna Louise (played by Marta Heflin), a meek breeder who is pregnant with her sixth child, and her rowdy companion, Stella Mae (Kathy Bates), who wears a cowboy hat and demonstrates a compulsive desire to drink and to boss Edna Louise. These two are the only characters who do not reveal a major secret within the course of the film, and the contrast between these minor figures and the three major ones makes the audience consider which is preferable: having delusions, having shattered delusions, or having neither.

The centerpiece of the film is Karen Black as Joanne, the transsexual who was once Joe, the only male member of the fan club. The one with the most to hide, she is willing to reveal the most, and her frankness is the catalyst that makes the others gradually strip themselves of lies they have been hiding behind. At first, no one knows who the sophisticated stranger is, as Joanne hops out of her red sports car and strolls in wearing a white suit, looking like a successful career woman. Karen Black's cynical smile, touched with a bittersweet remorse, takes on new meaning when the group learns that this woman was once their companion, Joe. Their first response of horrified disgust is gradually overtaken by friendly curiosity, with Sissie being the first to ask the kinds of questions most people are too polite to ask about transsexuals. The mirror comes into play as the action flashes back and forth between 1975 and 1955, showing the girls and Joe doing a torchy rendition of "Sincerely" by the jukebox. Altman makes no attempt at realism, using an impressionistic style that creates a sense of the past by changing the lighting, shooting through a gauzy filter, showing the action reflected in the mirror, adding a slight change of costume, and playing songs from the fifties. A young man (played by Mark Patton) with very little resemblance to Karen Black plays the role of Joe before his sex-change operation. This technique of having the actors and actresses change clothes is similar to the transformation in *Three Women*, and is the kind of sartorial symbolism that makes Altman's films appeal to an audience sensitive to the nuances of dress and social role-playing. The film does not pretend to offer any realism in its production values, but it lays claim to some kind of affective authenticity, and the women playing the rather stock characters manage to make the situation convincing. Pauline Kael comments: "But there's still the puzzle—it's not just the actors who have swallowed Graczyk's big, windy ironies—Altman bit on them, too."[12] Although all the reviewers have identified Graczyk's premise as hokey, with only the acting and Altman's direction saving the film from disaster, perhaps it is, at least in part, the basic material that touches some chord in the audience, an empathic response of nostalgia for lost dreams.

Actors Will Be Actresses: *Tootsie*

Tootsie is a movie dominated by a single actor, regardless of how much it is influenced by director Sydney Pollack or a dynamic supporting cast. Indeed, Dustin Hoffman is responsible for bringing the film to the producer's attention, and the project dovetails with his previous interests. In *Little Big Man* and *Kramer vs. Kramer* we see the beginnings of Hoffman's concern with the notion of gender. The well-meaning egotist that actors often are, Hoffman wants to show that not only can he play the best Ratso, the best graduate, and the best male mother, but he can also show women a thing or two about how to act like women.

Tootsie has become famous for its multiple revisions, writers, directors, titles, and producers, and it promises to become a movie standard and favorite for future audiences. The film follows the struggles of a jobless actor (an ever-popular topic for movies) who is so desperate that he decides to impersonate a woman to try out for a part in a soap opera. His friend Sandy, played by Teri Garr, has tried out for the same role, but Dorothy Michaels (alias Michael Dorsey) is so aggressive that she gets the part of the tough hospital supervisor. The film makes effective comedy out of such scenes as Sandy discovering Michael about to try on one of her dresses, after which he makes love to her in order to have an excuse for being in her bedroom in his underwear. Michael (as Dorothy) is thrust into a dressing room with a beautiful seminude actress, whose hand he must shake with all the aplomb Dorothy can muster. When Dorothy falls in love with the soap opera co-star Julie Nichols, played by Jessica Lange, and Julie's father (Charles Durning) courts Dorothy, even more gender-based jokes draw laughs from the audience.

Much of the humor derives from situations that are essentially cruel. Michael's making love to a woman in order to avoid being caught in his scheme results in suffering, and Julie's inadvertent temptation of Dorsey/Dorothy resembles a situation that many homosexual women and men must encounter in a society that rarely allows the kind of open expression of their proclivities that would eliminate such misunderstandings. While the transvestite is not ridiculed, the women in the film are often victims of the deception; the other characters who come in for their share of barbs are those older men who find the transvestite attractive. Pauline Kael observes: "It would be easy to say that the movie was itself being condescending to women—that it was suggesting that it took a man to be tough and forthright enough to speak up for women's rights."[13] She does not view the film in this light, however, because she sees integrity in the Chinese box of Hoffman's portrayals of Michael Dorsey, Dorothy Michaels, and hospital supervisor Emily Kimberley. A number of feminist critics have been less enraptured with the notion of actors like Hoffman taking on women's roles, not only because they find such characterizations condescending, but because there are already few enough roles for actresses in Hollywood without male actors taking over women's roles as well.

All films that employ role-reversal and transvestism may be interpreted by some viewers as presenting a negative image of women, for in order to accomplish imitation, the actor must focus on precisely those elements of female anatomy, dress, and makeup that seem the most superficial, the most governed by restrictions and dictates of society. Hoffman makes the observation that although he tried to be as attractive a woman as possible, he did not measure up to his own standards for judging women: "I found I would turn myself down; that if I met Dorothy, me as a woman, at a party, I'd turn me down."[14] This confession sheds little light on a fact of life that most males and females, attractive and unattractive, become aware of as soon as they take their first steps toward mating. It reveals more about the actor's relationship to the role; his imagining making love to himself as a woman is blatantly narcissistic, even if he does decide to turn himself down.

As with John Lithgow's playing of Roberta in *Garp*, it is the degree to which Hoffman is enamored of himself as a woman that saves the character from being the kind of ludicrous caricature that many earlier female impersonations are. One can see the

degree of identification in Michael's statement that he knows
what it is to be a woman because he is an actor: "An actor waits
by the phone; he has no power when he gets a job," a sentiment
that several reviewers have seen as coming as much from Hoffman
as from his character in the film. Colin Westerbeck observes that
the original film script was much improved when the central
character was changed from a tennis pro to an actor, because the
tennis pro "role wouldn't have allowed Dustin Hoffman to draw
upon who he really is, an actor, the way subsequent script by
Larry Gelbart does."[15] One could list ad infinitum the similarities between the role of woman and the role of actor (or
actress) in our society. Perhaps the most salient link is the notion
of relying on appearances, on playing a role in which one is
almost wholly dependent on others for a sense of self-worth. It is
no coincidence that the vast majority of film tales of female
impersonations occur within the context of the performing arts.

The idea of the double is cleverly explored in *Tootsie,* no doubt
because the actors, writer, and director could bring to bear a
personal connection with the theme. In a scene almost reminiscent of "The Secret Sharer" Michael's admiration for his other self
surfaces, as he tells his roommate Jeff (Bill Murray), "I think
Dorothy's smarter than I am." Michael isn't the only one half
convinced of Dorothy's existence as a separate entity. In a comic
follow-up Jeff calls Dorothy a slut for supposedly leading on her
co-star in the soap opera. Michael looks to Dorothy as a representative of his better self hidden within, and as long as he maintains
his secrets, it's a wonderful life.

Michael learns that honesty is no guarantee of success, either in
geting jobs or in getting along. As an actor Michael is so honest
that he loses his job as a tomato in a television commercial
because he refuses to sit; he doesn't feel it would be true to the
character. He is not so honest that he feels any qualms about
pretending to be a woman, which tells us something about the
code of honesty employed by the character. Once Dorsey has
become Dorothy and landed the job, candor strikes again, and
she ad-libs her own lines, which she feels would be more fitting
than the simpering drivel created for her. It turns out that her
fans love what she says, and she manages to keep her job by
speaking for the thousands of women who have no voices of their

own. Truth doesn't always work, though, and knowing what is true doesn't necessarily make people any better. Michael treats Sandy as shabbily as Julie's boyfriend treats her, and Michael's cognizance of the situation does nothing to alter it. Julie claims to want honesty from a man, but when Michael (as a man) tries the line she recommends ("I find you interesting. I'd like to make love with you.") when he sees her at a party, Julie throws a drink in his face. When he reveals before the live cameras his true gender, he loses his job, Julie stops speaking to him, and her father threatens to kill him.

Honesty doesn't even seem to work at the level of filmmaking, for many critics, despite their sophistication, seem to prefer that the aspect of homosexuality not be addressed. Kauffmann declares that the subject of *Tootsie* "is sexuality, not homosexuality, which it was in Blake Edwards's polished farce, *Victor/Victoria*, when the old queen played by Robert Preston was the Rosetta stone of the tangle."[16] Indeed, there is a difference in emphasis, but Kauffmann's attempt to delineate so clearly between homosexuality and sexuality points to a possible reason for the difference in critical response to the two films. As much as critics protest that it is the flipness of the treatment of homosexuality that disturbs them in *Victor/Victoria*, it would really seem to be the subject itself. *Tootsie* remains safe, with all characters stringently heterosexual, occasional hints at anything otherwise (like Sandy thinking Michael is gay or Julie thinking Dorothy is a lesbian) carefully whisked away, the moral being that it's all right for men to empathize with women, to locate the woman in themselves, as long as they themselves still have the healthy red-blooded desire to make love to pretty women. John Simon puts his finger on those sections of the film that skirt too closely the kind of implications that *Victor/Victoria* plays with more directly: "The imposture turns oppressive when Les, Julie's father and a good-natured farmer, becomes enamored of Dorothy and wants to marry her." His choice of the word "oppressive" and his later statement, "One wishes he wouldn't go around giving interviews about how playing Dorothy has changed his life (even if it's true). . ."[17] represent an honest reaction against the subject matter of either homosexuality or feminist issues. Westerbeck makes a similar statement: "If you listened to what Pollack and Hoffman have been saying about *Tootsie,* you'd never go to see it. They think they've made a movie about Feminism."[18] The implication that audiences will avoid any movie that smacks of intellectualism only thinly veils the underlying belief that audiences will respond just as negatively to a feminist film. It is clear, however, from the generally positive response of most critics, that *Tootsie* avoided offending seriously in any direction.

While the film steers clear of troubled waters that might make some viewers a bit seasick, it does satisfy the curiosity by giving an authentic, if not totally honest, impersonation. *Tootsie* contrasts with the vast majority of cross-dressing films in its richness of detail and the seriousness of Hoffman's impersonation. Kauffmann applauds him for the completeness of "the transformation—of movement, voice, and sensibility—without any trace of swishing."[19] (I suppose Kauffmann, along with a number of other critics, would rather see true female impersonation than a drag act that stuns the viewer with the campy brand of homosexuality.) The audience is privileged to see the actor in the in-between stages, with part of his makeup on, with a wig of rollers on his head, and then in the scene of final revelation, with the illusion of femininity shattered as he speaks in his own voice and reveals the matted masculine haircut beneath the fluffy red wig. Viewers cheer when Dorothy tells off her male chauvinist boss, but what is most touching is seeing the actor unveil himself in both his delicacy and his homeliness. Seeing both sides of Michael's complicated physical and mental transformation highlights the tension between surface and hidden selves, a conflict that both male and female audience members can recognize as legitimate and moving.

What Ever Happened to Male Impersonation?

During the sixties and seventies actual male impersonation practically vanished from the screen, while imitation of masculine clothing created multi-million-dollar fashion trends. Various "looks" are popularized by films, and fashion-conscious women across the country begin one season wearing ties, hats, and baggy pants, like Diane Keaton in *Annie Hall* (1977), finish another season sporting boxing shorts and tank tops, like Barbra Streisand in *The Main Event* (1979), and open yet another in tight blue jeans and high-heeled leather boots, like Jane Fonda in *Electric Horseman* (1979). During the seventies, an increasing number of films dealing with masculine heroines or women in traditionally masculine roles were made-for-television movies. These works typically present an offbeat situation that is eventually resolved in a reconciliation between the outcast heroine and the social group, a resolution that calls for compromises on both parts. Although such films attack certain stereotypes as unjust, they often carry a message that supports the status quo. A typical example is *Fast Break,* which, although it is not a television movie, is remarkably similar to its television siblings. The similarities suggest that profit-conscious filmmakers of the seventies no longer imitate life, but attempt to imitate television in their bid for assured audience approval.

In keeping with the move toward transplanting television personalities to film in the hope of capturing juvenile audiences, *Fast Break* shows us that even basketball players make better actors than the majority of television regulars. Gabe Kaplan, former star of *Welcome Back Kotter,* the popular fun-in-the-slums situation comedy, stars in *Fast Break* as a coach looking for a team. A few expletives and one or two shots might have been eliminated for television airing, but otherwise the film is closely in line with the television mentality of the late seventies. *Fast Break* touches lightly on several real issues, including the difficulties of uneducated ghetto blacks, women athletes, and homosexuals, but the "fast break" could easily describe what the film does when it gets anywhere close to an unconventional solution to these problems.

The story begins with Gabe Kaplan receiving the news from Cadwallader College that they are willing to hire him as their coach with a guaranteed three-year contract if he can create a basketball team to beat Nevada State. Kaplan rounds up three enormous black players who are ready to go with him to escape the law and a paternity suit (in the form of a father with a gun). The next player is "Bobby," and Kaplan is as eager to recruit him as he is curious to know why no one else has snapped him up. As Bobby emerges from the locker room in a dress, Kaplan assumes that Bobby is a drag queen until he is introduced to Roberta, who is actually a girl. Because she can get only an academic and not an athletic scholarship as a girl, she decides to accept Kaplan's offer of a basketball scholarship if she maintains a masculine disguise.

"Swish," as Bobby comes to be called, loses status in her male disguise, because she is not totally successful at assuming masculine mannerisms, a failure that stigmatizes her/him as a homosexual. When the other team members first see Bobby, they notice the effeminate walk, and they all protest that they don't want to ride all the way to Nevada with "one of those." D.C. (who can imagine the significance of a name that is one-half of AC/DC?), the biggest, toughest player on the team, resents Swish more than the others do, backing away in disgust every time Swish comes near. When D.C. has trouble passing English, Kaplan suggests that Swish help him, since Swish is a top student. D.C.'s response is a disgusted, "It figures," which makes the common connection between the images of the homosexual and the effeminate intellectual. When D.C. passes his English exam, Swish runs to hug him in a burst of affection, a response that causes D.C. to push him away in horror.

When Swish shows that his feelings are hurt, D.C. feels guilty and tries to comfort him in a bullying way, talking about how Swish goes around walking, talking, and acting like a girl. Swish starts to cry, and D.C. says, "You even have emotions like a girl" and reaches to touch Swish. At that moment a passerby startles D.C. into jumping up, holding his hands above his head to show that the two of them weren't touching. This incident drives D.C. to leave rather than confront the ambivalent, confusing emotions he experiences around Swish. Kaplan asks him why he wants to leave, and D.C. says that he is turning into a "faggot." Kaplan begins describing D.C.'s feelings of lust and protectiveness as "normal," and D.C. is momentarily convinced that Kaplan is also gay until Kaplan explains that Swish is actually a girl. In the next scene, D.C. comes into Swish's room and starts to make a play for the boy he now secretly knows is a girl. Swish resists at first, but when D.C. presses up against her, there is a moment of desire and surrender, a titillating split second in which Swish doesn't care if D.C. thinks she's a boy or a girl. This moment of almost adrogynous sexual excitement is brought to its purely heterosexual end when D.C. calls her "Roberta," making his advance and her acceptance "normal."

A few more gender-related gags are tossed around, including a scene in which D.C. and Swish are caught kissing by the team manager. During the final game, D.C. almost trounces an opponent who overzealously guards Swish, thus giving us an example of how a woman's status as female automatically brings out the male's protectiveness. All the jokes that play on gender distinctions, homosexuality, and sexual roles are designed to support the status quo. D.C.'s fears about his own feelings for Swish are shown to be ridiculous, not because he shouldn't find homosexuality loathsome but because Swish is a girl. The film even goes so far as to suggest that a female's true gender shines through, despite the masculine disguise, a dubious proposition as regards the very masculine actress who plays the part of Roberta. The film is more explicit than earlier films in showing exactly how Bobby disguises herself, for we see her binding her breasts, a subtle touch that prepares the audience for the final scene in which Roberta comes out onto the basketball court, breasts unbound, to make the winning shot as a woman.

This would seem to be a strong statement for women and minority rights, but in fact the film glosses over these issues in the end. In the 1945 *National Velvet,* we learn that Velvet must forfeit her prize because she is female, but *Fast Break* doesn't make the audience confront such sordid details. It allows us to believe that the team will be able to keep its winning title, just as it lets us believe that the New York police will simply put D.C. on probation. Kaplan's estranged wife follows him to Nevada, taking on the subservient role of the woman behind the man, and the film doesn't worry us with what is to become of the basketball career Bobby has suffered so much to create. Just as Bobby's breasts pop out in the end, so does the conventional resolution of the issues. The film teaches us once again that the place for women is behind their men, and the place for homosexuals is in jokes.

Not all male imitation films of the last twenty years support conventional values the way *Fast Break* does. In Sydney Pollack's *Electric Horseman* (1979), Jane Fonda plays a television reporter who falls in love with Sonny Steele (Robert Redford), the exploited rodeo star she follows into the wilderness, where he is hiding out with a stolen horse. After the initial hatred, misconceptions, deceptions, and revelations, the two characters find camaraderie and love, but they each go their separate ways in the end. Colin Higgins' *Nine to Five* (1980) offers the central fantasy sequence in which the three dissatisfied office workers (played by Dolly Parton, Jane Fonda, and Lily Tomlin) all imagine their versions of revenge on their male chauvinist boss. Dolly pictures herself in a cowgirl outfit, roping, tying, and even ogling and pinching her humiliated victim, while Jane Fonda imagines herself dressed in big game hunting gear, shooting the boss and mounting his head as a trophy. Although some feminist critics have accused the film of subtly demeaning women and undermining its own revolutionary aspects by resorting to exaggerations and pat conclusions, it has been an enormous box office success, particularly among office workers. The solutions are in part an attempt to reconcile the workers to their places in the system, but the film does show women rejecting subordinate positions and demanding alternatives to the traditional hierarchies.

In Howard Zieff's *Private Benjamin* (1980), Goldie Hawn (who is also executive producer for the film) plays a Jewish woman who has been passed from her father to one husband to another, and who, in the words of her father, " has never been trained to do anything." After the death of her second husband, in desperation she joins the army, and after a rocky beginning, decides to take her life into her own hands and really try to succeed at something. She is so successful that she is assigned to become the first female "Thornbird," member of an exclusive paratroop company. After the commanding colonel attempts a seduction/rape, she blackmails him into assigning her to Europe, where she becomes engaged to a French doctor who soon begins to treat her with the same contempt that her father and former husband showed her. She finally decides at the altar that she doesn't want to marry the Frenchman, and when he calls her "stupid," she punches him in the mouth and delivers her final words of the film: "Henri, don't ever call me stupid again."

Although the film is a comedy, the underlying message is serious: women like Goldie Hawn and the character she plays are tired of being called stupid and they will no longer remain in confining stereotypes. The film is not exactly arguing that women have to put on uniforms and let the army "make a man" out of them, but it suggests that the army is preferable to the traditional role of child-wife. The film offers a role model for women who wish to choose something other than marriage and domesticity. Like *Electric Horseman, Private Benjamin* presents a central female character who goes her own way alone rather than follow in the footsteps of her domesticated predecessors. One similarity between *Private Benjamin* and the more conservative made-for-television products is the fact that it, too, became a network series, with each incarnation creating a market and public recognition for the other.

Alien: A Different Breed

Television helped create a growing market for science fiction, with the success of series such as *Star Trek* and *The Outer Limits.* Critics and audience responses to science fiction films of the last two decades have been mixed. It is a psychological commonplace that people can almost always tell whether they like something or not and can almost never fully explain why they feel as they do. Analysis of critical reactions to role-reversal films through the decades suggests that when critics dislike something they almost always find a reason that is only peripherally related at best, and at worst totally unconnected. The critics who responded almost *en masse* in condemning Ridley Scott's *Alien* are no exception, and the wide and often contradictory range of their justifications bears witness. Some describe it as too much like earlier science fiction films, while others have said it revels in the horrible in a way that previous films tastefully refrained from doing. None of the reviewers believe that *Alien* is valuable as one of the first science fiction films to offer woman as a true heroine and survivor. It is worthwhile to look at *Alien* and its critics in some depth in order to discover how true role reversal may be greeted.

The science fiction film, more than any other genre, has served to reinforce stereotypical notions of masculinity and femininity; it is a subspecies even more thoroughly dominated by males than is the western. Most science fiction and fantasy films depict woman as the helpmate to man, and she is more often than not a hindrance at the crucial moment when the protagonist is trying to escape from or defeat the villains and monsters. How many times have we seen the heroine trip and fall as the couple run from their pursuers, and how many times has the hero been forced to go back and help her to her feet to carry her quite literally from danger? Writers Dan O'Bannon and Ronald Shusett have created in *Alien* a heroine who is so foreign as to be unrecognizable to most popular critics. *National Review* offers one of the few critiques with the insight to address a rather obvious question, pointing out that what is curious is the film's "hostile critical reception, despite the excellent visual values, direction that is no more hokey than usual in such films, dialogue that (when it is decipherable) is par for the course, and acting that is generally superior."[20] The reviewer goes on to suggest that perhaps it is the fact that the horror is too horrible, the "loathsomeness . . . basically unfudged." This may explain part of the revulsion that critics feel for the film, but perhaps what truly discomfits critics is that Scott has actually succeeded in creating something alien: not only a monster, but a heroine and a social system that bear little resemblance to what we have come to expect from science fiction films.

The character played by Sigourney Weaver offers a prototype for a new female lead that differs profoundly from the typical science fiction and fantasy film heroine. Like the alien, half mechanical and half organic, Weaver's character is also alien to our expectations for the genre because she is not stunning, stunned, or simpering. Reversals abound, in the female computer named "Mother" (MU/TH/UR 60000) with a seductive feminine voice, in John Hurt's character giving birth to the hideous offspring of the monster, and in the ending, in which the female protagonist survives alone, not as a result of the rescue efforts of a man but because of her own ingenuity, level-headedness, and humanity. Even more threatening than the unexpectedness of these reversals is the fact that many of the elements of strangeness connect somehow with that most fundamental element of vulnerability—human sexuality. The attack of this alien carries the idea of sexual violation; and what is worse, the penetration happens not to a woman, the usual victim of such attacks, but to a man.

To add to the horror, the viewer, to escape with a living model for emulation, must relate to and identify with a female character whether the viewer is male or female. Women viewers have long been accustomed to the rather confusing situation of having to cross gender lines to identify with a heroic character or else relate to the victims who fall down, are mauled by the monster (e.g., King Kong's simian-fingered probing of Fay Wray), and are finally rescued by the masculine hero. However, male viewers have seldom been called upon to identify with the opposite gender in order to put themselves in the role of defender. Most critics of *Alien* have failed to recognize what is taking place, and if they do mention the reversals, the disparaging condescension is designed to undercut any statement being made by the film. Stanley Kauffmann, in withering tones, states that "the crew, just to keep things au courant, includes two women and a black," and just to show how hopelessly non–au courant he is, goes on to object to the profanities (after all, a crew on a cargo ship wouldn't use vulgar language, would they?) and to describe Sigourney Weaver as "pleasant to look at and pleasant to listen to."[21] Another critic argues that "the mixed male-female, black-white crew is just the latest version of the old bickering spaceship from the fifties," and then describes Weaver's reaction to the monster as follows: "She puts up her hair, presses her lips together, and then swears."[22] Both critics, whether they realize it or not, seem to find one of the noteworthy horrors of the film to be a woman swearing.

Martin Jackson, in *USA Today,* sees no ingenuity, courage, or survival ability in the character, but along similar lines comments that "Ms. Weaver, who is attractive and probably talented, gets to sweat, breathe heavily, and react with terror."[23] Lawrence O'Toole at least recognizes the character as "steely modern woman,"[24] although he's clearly "agin it," and only Arthur Schlesinger is able to see that the crew, seedy and unkempt, is anything but a remake of earlier science fiction crews, and that there are two distinct female characters, "one who is jittery and inclined to hysteria, the other one controlled, earnest, and intelligent."[25] He is the only critic who mentions heroic rather than anatomical virtues in the female lead. A number of the reviewers refer to Weaver as Ms. Weaver, and one can only speculate on why they do not maintain a parallel formality by referring to "Mr. Hurt" or "Mr. Scott." The most sympathetic review, that of *Newsweek*'s Jack Kroll, misses altogether the fact that the character played by Weaver is not the typical heroine, describing her part as "the classic B-movie woman's role—all the heaving and hysterics of noble women like Fay Wray, Faith Domergue and Julie Adams."[26] Perhaps his failure to perceive the kind of character being offered is one of the reasons for his appreciation.

Such critical reception demonstrates that our perceptions are formed by what we expect to see. When neither Weaver nor the monster nor the crew behaves in a stereotypical fashion, it is an unpleasant shock for some—almost as unpleasant as the gore that spurts during the alien's attack—and for other viewers, the characters and situations of the film are so foreign that they are totally unrecognizable, seen only as poor imitations of the "real thing" that earlier films have brought us to expect. For ideological critics, the film also violates expectations, and they therefore assign certainty to ambiguities in order to make the film fit their conceptions of the Hollywood film.

Much science fiction concerns itself, at least in part, with the confrontation between humanity and the mechanical world. The treatments range from the optimistic *Star Trek* movie vision of the sexual melding of human male and female machine to the Frankenstein-style destruction of the creator by the created in Walt Disney's *The Black Hole,* an ending that suggests a Dantesque eternal union of the scientist and android in a timeless, hellish void. In *Alien* the division between human beings and machines is hazy, for the people behave in a lifeless manner typical of bureaucrats (a lackadaisical attitude intensified by their recent emergence from "hypersleep"), while the machines, including ship's computer Mother, the closet android Ash, and the alien itself, all demonstrate a strong life force. In the case of the alien, which artist John Giger conceives as a product of "biomechanics," the appetite for life, both its own and others', far surpasses the passive, almost machine-like struggle for survival demonstrated by the majority of the human crew members. In its quest for dominance, the alien reveals a frighteningly voracious sexuality, one that makes the crew members appear positively asexual by comparison. The filmmakers describe the alien as a being "whose body is completely incompatible with a human's, but who is compelled to consummate a very strange sort of physical union."[27] It is this sexual feature that many critics seem to find most repulsive.

The visual imagery of the film supports the underlying sexual motif. In the opening of the film we see sleep chambers that look like enormous insect-machine egg cases, cradling humans soon to be awakened by their computer mother. The interior of the ship has different levels, not unlike the segmented nests of the insect world, each designed for a different function, just as each crew member has a specialized role within the micro-community of the ship. The compartments parallel the later appearance of the real egg cases that house the dormant alien. The ship *Nostromo* is designed to bring an enormous load of fuel cargo back to earth, and its crew members are run-of-the-mill workers, like bees whose sole assignment in life is to cart pollen to the colony and depart again for another load.

Once awakened by their maternal computer, the humans groggily perform their tasks and, much like creatures emerging from hibernation, begin to do their jobs before they are fully awake. Only Ash, the science officer, seems fully efficient from the first, a minor detail that proves significant later on in the film. For the time being it fits in with a whole complex of images surrounding the notion of science as cold, mechanical, efficient, and inimical to humanity, albeit an invention of human beings. The slow-moving crew of seven finally pries out of Mother the information that they have not returned to earth but instead have been pulled out of hypersleep to follow a distress signal.

No one is happy about the unexpected delay, but the two engineers, Parker and Brett, mention the possibility of bonuses from the Company, and the economic subtext of the film begins to emerge. Unlike many earlier films of the genre, in which the government or scientific experts are involved in the confrontation with the unknown, *Alien* presents profit-seeking as the very realistic premise for the *Nostromo*'s forays into the mysterious depths of space. The ship's name is more than a coincidental reference to Conrad's novel. Several critics question the connection between *Alien*'s plot and Conrad's major themes, suggesting that they must be tangential at best. A closer look at the situation in the film reveals that greed, commercial exploitation, the baseness of company motives, and the essential aloneness of the individual are underlying themes connecting Scott's vision with that of Conrad in works like *Nostromo, Heart of Darkness,* and *Typhoon.*

At first it apears that even the Company has higher ideals than profit, for it is part of the contract that the commercial tug must answer any transmission indicating distress. Dallas, the captain, stoutly follows his contract, ordering that they land on the inhospitable planetoid. The rescue party of the captain, Lambert (the only woman besides the heroine Ripley), and Kane emerges into the wind-blown wasteland.[28] The visual imagery speaks volumes on the sexual nature of the human encounter with the alien. The most striking symbol they come upon is the discarded body of the Space Jockey who originally sent the signal, his phallic machine still erect alongside the husk-like dead body of its former operator. The useless implement stands as a subtle warning that the alien has laid waste to some rather macho characters. Kane enters the vaginal entrance to a chamber that holds what appear to be egg cases, and after one of them is inadvertently cracked and stroked to life by the light from his flashlight, a toothy, leech-creature explodes from its shell and coils itself over Kane's face, penetrating his face mask and slipping inside the protective suit. This scene could hardly be a more direct pictoralization of Freud's textbook phobia: the vagina with teeth clutches and eats alive the intrusive phallus, rendering it impotent. The interior of the alien chamber exquisitely combines various hues of machine gray with the slick, shiny, rounded concavity that calls to mind the female sexual organs.

Meanwhile, Ripley is skeptical about Ash's report that Mother cannot identify the distress signal, and she takes the initiative of searching through the computer to discover that the signal is actually a warning. She wants to go after the rest of the crew, but Ash convinces her it would be futile. When the party returns with an alien firmly plastered on Kane's head, the ordinarily business-like science officer countermands Ripley's directive that the three remain in quarantine. It appears that Ash's motives are humane. The audience, as in countless viewings of *Alien*'s antecedents, literally cries out in sympathy with Ripley's good common sense, "Don't open that door," but of course they do open the door and the monster gains access to the ship. Strange, isn't it, that the usually cold-hearted science officer should impulsively break the rules to save someone's life? Ripley is immediately suspicious, and the audience knows once again that she is right. At this point the intelligent viewer's bets begin to ride with Ripley, and she becomes the central figure for identification.

The crew must rely on Ash as the closest thing to a doctor to treat Kane's delicate condition. X-rays reveal that the alien has managed its own version of rape by extending part of its body down Kane's throat. The crew speculates on whether some sort of symbiotic feeding might be taking place, since Kane's life functions still look fine. They leave Kane for a time and concentrate on taking off and repairing damage, and the next thing they know, the alien has disappeared. While the reasonable decision would be to turn on the lights during the search, the filmmaker's choice is to leave the characters and the audience in semidarkness, in order to heighten the suspense. In a seat-jumper scene, Ripley, Dallas, and Ash look for the monster, which suddenly drops onto Ripley's shoulder and onto the floor, apparently dead. The camera zooms in as Ash probes the creature's upturned underbelly; the slimy parts look like a distressing combination of reproductive organs and fish innards. Ripley gives the shudder of disgust that the audience feels, furthering the viewer's identification with her. With the one-eyed, snake-tailed claw dead, the crew feels a false sense of security. The recovered Kane and his shipmates have a final pre-sleep feast, and the audience begins to smile and relax along with the crew. The ravenous Kane (little does he know he's eating for two) devours his food and then in the most hideous scene of the film, delivers through a kind of spontaneous Caesarian birth the product of the union between man and alien.

During the filming of this scene, none of the actors knew exactly what to expect, and when a blood-spurting machine squirted a jet of gore into Veronica Cartwright's face, she literally fell backwards, unable to do anything more than scream her way through the entire take. Scott had brought in real viscera to go sailing as the alien emerged, and when the filming was completed, cameraman Derek Vanlint ran off the set and threw up his lunch.[29] (One must admire the professionalism of his timing.) This scene left the crew both shaken and impressed with Scott's directorial skill, but it gave the critics an opportunity to accuse him of tasteless exploitation of the audience's thirst for blood. While this accusation contains some truth, the charge ignores the more important fact that this scene is pivotal, not only in its shock value and placement as a kind of horrific centerpiece, but also insofar as it crystallizes for the characters and the audience the sexual nature of the creature's otherness. The creature's unnatural desire to mate with a man brings forth echoes of *Invasion of the Body Snatchers,* but the notion of raping and forcing involuntary motherhood on a human male makes the foreign inhabitation of *Body Snatchers* appear benign by comparison.

As in the scenes on the planetoid, the sets again parallel the action as the chase begins. Moving from the womb-like atmosphere of the mess hall, aglow with food, camaraderie, and comfort, the camera witnesses the horrible birth of the alien and follows the crew as they emerge for adult aggressive action. The crew heads to the computer-dominated section of the ship to determine their plan of action, and they agree on trying to trap the creature in a net and then eject it from the ship through the airlock. Earlier attempts at cutting the creature off of Kane's face had taught them that the creature's "blood" is universal solvent that could destroy the ship. Throughout the decision-making process Ripley participates with the men, and not once does she have to be carried as they hunt down the alien, nor does she scream hysterically and have to be slapped. Lambert serves as a foil by behaving in a more stereotypical feminine mode, but then the group has already been rather neatly balanced out in the ultimate reversal of motherhood for the somewhat delicate John Hurt/Kane character. As the action progresses, the film refuses to divide the ship into the women's domain and a grimier world. Ripley sweats and gets dirty along with the men, and her calm logic, combined with intuitions that the audience automatically recognizes as accurate, makes her the natural leader, even before the official captain Dallas meets his doom.

The crew members are picked off in a pattern that does not differ significantly from the standard *Cat and the Canary* design. Each time a search is made and someone is alone, the creature attacks, in this case not killing but storing the bodies for future use, perhaps as incubators. The most interesting reversal after the shock of Kane's alienbirth occurs when Ripley communicates with Mother and discovers that Ash is a traitor. Just as she learns this he comes in and attacks her. Ash gets Ripley down on the console and attempts to kill her by stuffing a rolled-up magazine down her throat, an action that parallels the creature's earlier oral rape of Kane.[30] However, the symbolic attack fails when Lambert and Parker, the only others remaining, arrive in time to rescue Ripley. They knock Ash's head off, revealing a set of wires rather than the expected blood. The undaunted android gets up to look for its head, but Ripley manages to poke it with a prod designed to trap the alien, and the electrical shock short-circuits Ash's system. They hook up Ash's head long enough for him to reveal his motives in protecting the alien. The eerie separation of head from body creates a grotesque effect and also makes a subtle comment on the problem with science and technology, i.e., too much distance between the head and the heart. It seems that the Company had programmed Ash to reprogram Mother to bring back this alien life form, if necessary at the cost of the entire crew. The Company had been fully aware that the call was a warning rather than a distress signal, but it had counted on the crew's ignorance to help import an illegal, dangerous life form that it hoped to turn to its own profit as an ultimate weapon.

With this crucial information disclosed, the film suddenly takes on added resonance. It is no longer, as one critic suggests, "the usual warning against the evils of heartless technology,"[31] nor is the comment by Martin Jackson justified, suggesting that "there isn't very much in 'Alien' that makes sense either as drama or social comment."[32] So rarely does the American film industry attack commercial greed that the idea is an unrecognizable alien when it occurs. The film does suggest, particularly in the initial stage of the plot, that the technology is heartless and that the alien evil is inexplicable. However, it becomes apparent that the real source of evil lies in the Company's unmitigated greed, its willingness to sacrifice human beings and pervert technology at the hint of a new resource to exploit. The alien has its place in this scheme as well, for it is a perfect model of what economic exploiters admire most, pure efficiency.

The film calls into question the validity of efficiency as an ideal by taking the concept to its logical extreme. As Ash points out, if one's judgments are based solely on survival value, the creature is superior to human beings. A closer look at this efficiency model also reveals an interesting paradox, one central to the capitalist system. The ideal is efficiency, and yet the purpose of that conservation is to create a better waster of goods. The ship *Nostromo* is on a mission to return fuel to the earth for consumption; the crew members are expendable, i.e., consumable; and the alien itself does nothing more than live to consume and consume to live. Like the Companies of the world, it grows exponentially with the absorption of each new victim. Like the companies in Conrad's novels, the Company in *Alien* doesn't concern itself with the bodies of the little people left in its wake.

A look at who survives, why and how she survives, shows that this film is less pessimistic than its novelist predecessor or than film siblings like *Phantasm, Nightwing,* or *Prophecy,* all of which feature a fanged, clawed creature of single-minded (if we can call them minds) voracity. In *Alien,* Weaver's character prevails, in part because she is tough-minded and sensible in the face of danger, but also because she has a certain sentimental, illogical attachment to Jones the cat, a creature with no apparent function other than providing homey companionship and mindless amusement for the crew members during their few waking hours. Its presence is never really explained; if it were on board to get rid of rats, they wouldn't put it into hypersleep. During one of their early attempts to capture the alien, they succeed in capturing Jones instead, and at this point it seems that the cat is in the story to provide false scares for crew and audience. However, as the film progresses, the cat takes on more importance. When only Ripley, Lambert, and Parker remain alive, Ripley insists on going off to find Jones before they take off in the space shuttle. Lambert and Parker, who selfishly and practically state that searching for the animal is foolish, remain behind to become the alien's next victims. Once Ripley realizes that they are dead, she takes off with Jones in the space shuttle, believing that she has escaped the alien. Only after her final ejection of the alien from the ship is she left to stroke her cat and fall asleep in peace. In the original screenplay, Jones the cat was to play a more crucial role at the end. Relying on animal instincts, Jones screeches at the creature lurking in the shadows, and in so doing alarms Ripley and inadvertently saves her life once again. In the version shown to preview audiences, Ripley leaves Lambert and Parker and comes upon Dallas, who begs her to kill him rather than leave him as he is, half-dead, his body already partially consumed by the alien. Ripley performs the mercy killing, but preview audiences responded negatively to this action, perhaps feeling that it violated too profoundly their expectations for her as life-giver and comforter. As the film stands, were it not for Ripley's inefficient, maternal attachment to a nonutilitarian, nonhuman animal, she too would have been destroyed by the alien.

Perhaps the statement that self-interest should not be the end of our existence is a bit simple, but it seems to be one that the critics, for a variety of reasons, failed to notice. This is not the fault of the film, which makes its point in an understated yet clear way. Rather this failure to recognize the message results from several preconceptions on the part of the critics: (1) Science fiction films make comments on technology, not on economics; (2) their heroines are valuable for providing love interest and appropriate rescue objects that scream and heighten the suspense; (3) science fiction takes us to worlds whose problems are more dramatic and exciting than our own, whose characters are flashy, glamorous, and exotic. For many viewers a female heroine, particularly a no-nonsense, no-screaming, no-sex character like Ripley, can be no match for a masculine hero, whose daring and sexual prowess provide countless vicarious thrills. *Time's* Frank Rich comments that the "all-knowing computer called Mother is . . . no match for Hal in *2001*."[33] It isn't meant to be, nor is Weaver's character meant to fulfill our stereotyped notions of the science fiction heroine or hero. The world of *Alien* is not the slick, glossy future of *2001*. It doesn't deal with man's glorious quest for self-knowledge or understanding of the unknown. It treats the Company's grimy search for profit at any cost. Mother pretends concern for human life, just as does the science officer, while both are programmed to seek out a potentially deadly alien force, not for the sake of scientific knowledge but for economic possibilities.

The characters aren't military experts or important government workers, nor are they even particularly competent compared with the brainy scientists of earlier science fiction films.

They are everyday working people, tied to a company that cares nothing for their welfare, only for their ability to produce greater profits. The language of these people is profane, rough, and minimal, much like that of real workers in similar jobs. They are not excited about their work, nor do they possess the imagination or education to be particularly articulate. The ship itself is not beautiful, only functional, and this too is one of the film's comments on the direction our civilization is taking: caring more for function than for aesthetics, more for money than for our environment. What makes us more human, more worthy of survival, than the alien?

Charles Nicol argues that science fiction is concerned with "the limitations of the rational mind and the confrontation with the Alien, the incomprehensible stranger who dwells within us."[34] Perhaps what some critics loathe is that the confrontation tells the audience something rather unpleasant about society. The alien has more energy than the lifeless crew members do, and were it not for its appearance viewers might find it easier to identify with than the dull humans of the film. Only Ripley, alas a woman, stands out as having a bit more gumption. Samuel Delany observes that despite the ostensibly feminist elements of the plot, the subtext of the film suggests the kind of second-class status that women have encountered for centuries.[35] At several crucial points, when Ripley gives an order, it is ignored or countermanded; no one pays attention to her advice, despite the fact that it is right in every case. Delany's observation is sound, but this kind of situation is not limited to female characters in science fiction films (consider Kevin McCarthy's futile warnings in *Invasion of the Body Snatchers*), nor does the injustice of the situation escape the viewers. Rather, the holdover of inequality in an apparently egalitarian future world makes the film speak to today's concerns.

In an ideological analysis of the film in *Science Fiction Studies,* Peter Fitting argues that "the crew of the *Nostromo* might be seen as the model for a renewed and enlightened capitalism, while the Alien suggests the threats which an increasingly militant Third World is seen as posing,"[36] and he maintains that the film does not criticize the Company. Judith Newton, along similar lines, views the ending of the film as a happy ending for capitalism:

"Despite the Company's betrayal of herself and of the entire crew, Ripley disposes of the Alien only to sit down and complete her captain's log: 'Crew—and cargo—destroyed.' . . . Unallied with minorities, with working class, or with other women, she is also—and in contrast to Conrad's *Nostromo*—a Company Woman to the last"[37] Although these critics perceive a number of points that mainstream critics fail to recognize, it seems that their conclusions rest not on solid evidence from the film but on their preconceptions: the film will tap into the ideology of its audience and financial backers, "as we might expect from a director who is the veteran of several thousand commercials."[38] Audiences are not monolithic, however, and not all viewers will see the ambiguity of Ripley's terse report as obeisance to the Company, just as not all viewers will make the supposedly automatic connection between the Alien and Third World aliens.

Critics who are sensitive to possible sexist overtones notice the final sequence in which Weaver removes her clothes, "a strip-tease sequence near the end, . . . subjecting its viewers to the hackneyed scenario of the white woman's flesh being exposed to the non-white rapist's salivating visage, . . . a titillating, sensationalist exploitation of rape."[39] Ernest Larsen states that the film offers the "lonely bitter triumph of an individual American. . . . but not before an exploitative scene in which Ripley strips before the alien."[40] The viewers who see this scene as sexist do not comment on the parallel opening scene, in which we see Kane emerging from hypersleep in a similar state of seminudity. The two scenes are a framing device that creates suspense; the roving camera gives the audience the idea that the characters are not alone, and the nudity creates a greater sense of vulnerability. It may be argued that the film's manipulation of emotional response is exploitation in itself, but the inspiration of fear and pity seems even-handed in terms of the sexes, and it is justified in terms of structure and plot.

In a more optimistic vein, the film may be viewed as a parable of confrontation between two of evolution's experiments. The story is similar to A. E. Van Vogt's *Voyage of the Space Beagle* (*Beagle* being the name of Darwin's ship), which explores the question of evolutionary superiority. Peter Fitting remarks on this theme, identifying Ripley as "the synthesis of the human and the animal:

not only in her designation as the owner of the cat and the familiar (sexist) coding of female sexuality in terms of the feline and more generally in terms of the instinctive, but more importantly, in terms of her single-handed victory as the return to an earlier Social-Darwinistic model of the survival of the fittest."[41] What is unfamiliar and perhaps nonsexist about Ripley's identification with the cat is that it is a positive depiction of both cat and female, a contrast to numerous filmic predecessors. Likewise, the Darwinism of the film is distinct from social Darwinism in that the alien is truly of another species, not simply a less successful human. In fact, if the creature is allied with any parallel social group, it should be with the voracious, all-consuming Company. *Alien* suggests that a creature of boundless rapacity is an evolutionary deadend, despite its apparent invulnerability. Ripley's ultimate survival is a subtle hurrah for the human race, and for womankind at that. Perhaps the possibility of future action against the Company, rather than the idea that American capitalism has triumphed, makes more enlightened audiences appreciate the film. The decision to make the hero a woman, even if producer Alan Ladd, Jr.'s choice was as cynically for profit as *Jump Cut*'s reviewer suggests, indicates a healthy shift in tastes, one that bodes well for women.

Most critics did not like what they saw in *Alien*, whatever it was they saw, whereas audiences flocked to the film. Part of this must be attributed to the $6 million advertising campaign, which shot a $9 million film to over $12 million in box-office gross in just six weeks; however, such campaigns do not necessarily guarantee success. The other undeniable factor that advertisers and word-of-mouth revealed was the gory violence, which drew viewers like a magnet. *Saturday Review* asks, "Aren't we justified in being alarmed by audiences who can be manipulated into howling for blood? Surely the purpose of art, whether it's created for the few or the many, should be to make us more human, not less."[42] At the risk of sounding gruesome and amoral, some may argue that people are never more human than when they are struggling for survival or when they are experiencing that struggle through the filmmaker's medium. It may be that audiences don't need to be manipulated into "howling for blood," that the desire to witness such events in film is a substitute for the adrenalin-pumping confrontations that human beings as a species rarely encounter in everyday civilized existence.

Paul Leggett points out that a common theme of science fiction films is the idea of "monsters unleashed upon humanity by a science gone too far," and he goes on to say that *Alien* is "little more than massive mayhem for its own sake."[43] One could replace one word in his formula, making it "a monster unleashed by a business gone too far," and see more than violence for its own sake. All the unnatural events can be traced to a single source, the Company. *Alien* uses violent action to call on us to become, if not more humane, at least more skeptical of the good will of mega-industries.

The world of *Alien* is atypical of Hollywood films also in its refusal to beautify the characters, the monster, or the set. The multiple levels of the ship underscore social differences between the engineers, who live in a *Hairy Ape* environment that one critic describes as resembling a World War II submarine, and the captain and navigators, whose realm is dominated by high tech, gleaming surfaces, and machine precision. The slow tracking camera forces us to examine details we might rather ignore. The actors and actresses actually sweat, their skin is not flawlessly tanned, their hair looks oily and mussed, their clothing is stained, and there are globs of grease on some of the pipes and equipment. The audience is assaulted with these visual imperfections, and there are also times when we cannot understand the words clearly—the sound is muffled, the actor mumbles, or the words themselves are some kind of technical mumbo-jumbo that people might use on a space craft. The film uses the anamorphic lens, which is, according to Richard Anobile, "so precise and perfect that the images they produce are too clinical and mechanical—they need feeling."[44] Some filmmakers put smoke into the anamorphic lens chamber in order to soften the image, to achieve the kind of hazy look that aging actresses love. Part of the disturbing quality of *Alien* derives from its hard edges, the details that give us indelible impressions of all too realistic human beings and of an alien creature the filmmakers describe as "perverse, obnoxious and disgusting, but absolutely gorgeous."[45]

Alien does derive from its predecessors. As Charles Lippincott, former vice-president of Star Wars corporation, observes, "*Alien* caps the subgenre of the bug-eyed monster movies of the Fifties."[46] The plot is similar to that of the 1958 film *It! The Terror from Beyond Space,* and Howard Hawks' *The Thing from Another World.* As in *2001,* machine intelligence battles against human survival, and as in *The Thing,* the monster appears indestructible and beyond reason. At the same time, however, the vision in *Alien* is slightly different, most notably in its creation of a new kind of science fiction heroine set in a social system that may be too real for the genre. We see her ability to fend for herself as clearly as we see the pores in her skin. What she has lost in beauty, sex appeal, and dependence on others is recompensed by her readiness to stand on her own—without falling down.

Victor/Victoria: Is the New Man Really a New Woman?

Victor/Victoria follows the tradition of farce established by films like *Some Like It Hot* and *La Cage aux folles* in that its tenor is one of acceptance of deviation. Indeed, the straight characters are either forced to accept the legitimacy of homosexuality or turn out to be closet homosexuals themselves. Julie Andrews, the lead who finagles her way into show business by pretending to be a female impersonator, brings with her the screen image of wholesomeness and purity partly because of such roles as Mary Poppins but also because of her own attributes: a lilting lyric voice, an angelic face, a slim virginal body, and a proper British accent. *Victor/Victoria* shows social standards being overturned, innocence lost, and people emerging literally and figuratively from closets.

Andrews plays a coloratura soprano who is starving as long as she remains true to her art and her morals; but as soon as she turns dishonest, pulling the old cockroach-in-my-salad routine to get a full meal and dressing as a man who impersonates women, she is bound for success. Teaming up with Robert Preston, who plays an aging homosexual named Toddy, Andrews soon becomes the toast of the stage as Victor Victoria, Preston's invented European "artiste" who looks so much like a woman that he/she fools wealthy American King Marchand, played by James Garner. Much to his chagrin, Garner discovers that the beautiful woman he has been eyeing at her nightclub performance is supposed to be a female impersonator. Disturbed, and determined to re-establish the validity of his heterosexual instincts, he sneaks into her hotel room in a scene of multiple comic entanglements, and there manages to catch a glimpse of her getting into the bathtub, confirming his suspicions that she isn't a man. Once he has this inside knowledge, he is the one fooling Victoria, and he pulls the usual tricks designed to reveal her gender, such as forcing her to smoke a cigar. (The cigar is so frequently used in gender-based comedies, it is practically a trope, one that surely would have delighted Freud.) When King finally kisses Victoria, he tells her that he doesn't care if she's a man or a woman, and she feels obliged to confess that she is female.

The story is by no means resolved at this point, for there remains the conflict between her desire to continue her successful career and Garner's desire to domesticate her. He grudgingly accepts a role as her homosexual lover, and we see the two of them together at the opera, at the fights, and even dancing together at a gay bar. Here the film defies its period setting of the 1930s by creating a heroine who does not gladly drop her career and fall into the arms of the man. The courageousness of King's willingness to disregard the potential damage of appearances inspires his bodyguard Squash, played by former football player Alex Karras, to reveal that he himself is homosexual, planting a brotherly kiss on the face of his much bemused employer. Now that Squash knows (or thinks he knows) that his boss loves a man (or someone he thinks is a man), he is ready to confess his own preferences, eventually ending up in bed with Toddy, in the kind of neat parallel plot that is *de rigueur* for bedroom farces.

In the end, King is ready to give up his career for love of Victoria, but she reveals her own gender to the public, appearing in the nightclub as the woman she really is and rescuing him from being beat up by the puritanical mobsters who have no tolerance for homosexuals in their ranks. Although this might seem to be the typical "happy ending" in which the woman gives up her career for her man, it also presents the less conventional situation of a man who gives up his career for love as well. The unmasking of disguises hints at a future in which both the male and the female will begin a new life, she without her male disguise (except for a possible jaunt into nostalgia) and he without his mob connections. The finale even suggests a new career for Toddy, who substitutes for Victoria in her Spanish fandango routine, to which the audience responds with a standing ovation. Albeit ludicrous, Preston's imitation is charming slapstick, and the positive response of the audience makes the character admirable rather than simply buffoonish. To quibble with the fact that Andrews and Preston both deliver totally unconvincing performances as the opposite sex here would be as pointless as to wonder why Shakespeare's characters cannot recognize Ganymede as Rosalind. Certain comedies do not claim to create lifelike situations, and therefore the characters need not fulfill all of the expectations and requirements of verisimilitude.

Director Blake Edwards has long been fascinated with the possibilities of role reversals and transvestism, in such films as *High Time* (1960), *What Did You Do in the War, Daddy?* (1966), and *Gunn* (1967), but with *Victor/Victoria* he has gone somewhat beyond stereotyped depictions and created characters whose struggles with identity are more profound and more hilarious. The film is based on Reinhold Schunzel's 1933 *Viktor und Viktoria,* and it captures some of the playful, androgynous spirit of the original, which came into existence at the height of German society's experimentation with sexual reversals. The songs and the language betray the 1930s setting, and the material is considerably updated by its casual references to homosexuality. Indeed, in the original and in the 1935 British remake, *First a Girl,* the man who convinces Victoria to do her routine is definitely heterosexual, despite his potentially misleading occupation of female impersonator. Lawrence O'Toole notes that the "portrayal of a homosexual and a woman having a full-fledged relationship that's primarily warm and goofy is a film rarity."[47] The treatment also distinguishes itself from many earlier comedies in its details, particularly in the degree of explicitness of the jokes on sexuality and the discussions of exactly what happens when one impersonates the opposite sex. Victoria complains about binding her breasts, and she wears neck pieces to conceal her lack of a prominent Adam's apple. These minor touches make up for the anachronisms and the lack of a true sense of Paris in the thirties by replacing one kind of fidelity to detail with another.

Edwards is a master of farce, milking every scene and every sight gag. For example, characters keep coming out of closets, with every pun intended. The first instance occurs after Victoria has spent the night with Toddy. Discovering that her dress has shrunk, she is in the midst of trying on Toddy's ex-lover's clothes when the young man rushes in, whereupon Victoria hides in the armoire, delivering a determined roundhouse to his jaw as he opens the closet door. The next closet scene occurs when King hides in Victoria's bathroom cabinet to watch her getting undressed, at last to confirm his suspicions about his/her true gender. The voyeuristic appeal of this scene, with its intimacy, the steam rising from the luxurious art deco tub, and Victoria leisurely removing each article of clothing in an unwitting strip tease, contrasts with the purely comic follow-up, in which a detective (Sherloque Tanney) seeking to discredit Victor, hides in the bathroom closet to see if the famous impersonator isn't really a woman. Unable to accomplish his mission, the unfortunate detective lurks in the dark, only to have Victoria breeze through and slam the door on his finger, after which she exits and an exquisitely small moan issues from the closet.

Some critics are disturbed by Edwards' unwillingness to take risks, as revealed by jokes that exploit stereotypes and conclusions that come down safely in the realm of what is acceptable to the popular heterosexual audience. Marchand declares his love only after he is assured that Victor is a Victoria, and the homosexual characters serve mainly as comic foils to the hero and heroine in a subplot that sets up gays as underlings playing to groundlings. John Simon argues that despite the "principal aim of cashing in on the new trend of let's-be-sweet-to-homosexuals pictures, in which the idea is to make inversion as nearly indistinguishable as possible from so-called normality," the film "has been created by a non-risk-taking heterosexual and a pious fraud."[48] In *Film Comment*, Carrie Rickey argues that Victoria's comparison of her deception with Marchand's deceptive association with gangsters is tantamount to "linking a commonly accepted sexual preference with a universally abhorrent code of violence."[49] Rickey also states that the film "congests the screen with a gay-straight dichotomy" by having the decor of King's suite be gray and stark, while Toddy and Victoria's is pink and plush, thus fulfilling a stereotype. Although the reviewer's impulse is to defend homosexuality from the assault of prejudice, it seems that she reveals her own biases in her assumptions that

Victoria's argument is Edwards' stand as well, that the pink plushness of Toddy and Victoria's suite is a negative image, whereas the cold starkness of King's environs is somehow positive. Edwards uses clichés effectively, portraying the surroundings and the relationship between Toddy and Victoria as warm and loving, playing on the visual puns of hiding in closets, emphasizing the idea of insiders vs. outsiders by having the camera repeatedly view the action through cracks, doors, and windows. The critic for *Ms.*, Catharine Stimpson, concludes that the film is a "man's movie about the New Man. Victoria is an Old Woman—choosing between being like a man or being with the man she loves."[50] *The Christian Century* reviewer, James M. Wall, while disliking the film, makes the trenchant comment that whether or not the film succeeds "depends on audience tolerance for humor leaning heavily on men dressed as women and women dressed as men."[51]

If Edwards errs, it is not in his depiction of the gay or straight worlds, both of which he smears with intentional tastelessness, but in his casting of the lead roles. Julie Andrews as an ingenue and James Garner as a bachelor who has never found Ms. Right are not convincing; Andrews' voice has none of the huskiness that would make us believe she could pass for a male, and neither star is young enough to fulfill the age requirements of the parts. Robert Preston is charming, but his screen image has been so firmly associated with conventional roles like the Music Man that he has a hard time creating a convincing "aging queen," as the character calls himself.

What the film does have that makes it perfect material for a cult classic is that mysterious quality called "camp"—the combination of nostalgia, absurd humor, exaggeration, sentimentality, outrageousness, glamor, and theatricality—which brings the film under fire from conservative and radical critics alike. While more conventional role-reversal films like *Tootsie* receive acclaim, films like *Victor/Victoria* and *Alien* return at showings designed for a slightly more offbeat crowd. The fact that mainstream critics find objectionable elements in a film indicates that there is something in its content or style that may appeal to a particular subgroup. By its very nature, the cult film must belong to a few; mass approval kills the cult as surely as assimilation co-opts rebellion.

Yentl: A Resurgence of Male Impersonation?

Determining which stars and topics are "mainstream" in American culture is a presumptuous task, but perhaps one of the best gauges of an actress or actor's place in the spectrum is the ability to draw automatic box-office returns. Barbra Streisand is one of the few actresses working today who attracts audiences simply by being in a film. As a producer of her own work, she avoids the problems that many actresses have of choosing vehicles and co-stars sufficiently marketable to ensure producer support for the project. Streisand's choice of Isaac Bashevis Singer's story about Yentl, a young woman who disguises herself as a boy in order to attend yeshiva and learn about the Talmud, is idiosyncratic in that she is her own producer and is therefore less constrained by commercial demands. In another sense, however, Streisand is often a kind of bellwether, with practically anything she chooses to produce representing a decision intuitively in keeping with popular tastes.

Perhaps in *Yentl* Streisand has picked a story that goes beyond what the contemporary audience is prepared for, despite the fact that in comparison to some earlier works by male stars her treatment of role reversals seems relatively tame. Most of the critics writing for popular magazines note in some fashion the unusualness of the film. Richard Corliss writes in *Time,* "The Jews have a word for what it took to make this movie: chutzpah."[52] *Newsweek's* Jack Kroll comments that studio chiefs had rejected the project because "they were worried because, although Streisand is very 'bankable,' she is, after all, a woman; they thought that the movie was 'not commercial' because it was 'too ethnic'";[53] and David Denby writes in *New York:* "Unlike the bumptious yet ingratiating *Fiddler on the Roof,* this movie risks giving offense with its strangeness."[54]

Despite these critics' comments that Streisand's film tackles a daring subject, *Yentl* would seem to be a sort of throwback, for the story itself takes place in a time and cultural milieu in which women are allowed virtually none of the masculine privileges of education, mobility, or intellectual freedom. Set in a nineteenth-century East European village, the film opens rather slowly, showing the traditional life of the marketplace, where men can buy religious or philosophical books and discuss ideas while the women are restricted to "light" reading, gossip, and shopping for fish. Yentl stands out immediately as a nonconformist, for she has no interest in fish, and her widower father has secretly taught her to study the Talmud.

Upon his death, she faces the grim prospect of abandoning her studies, being taken in by one of the families of the community, and learning the skills necessary to become someone's wife. Instead, she disguises herself as a boy named Anshel and goes to a yeshiva, where she finds herself falling in love with Avigdor, her unsuspecting study guide, played by popular Broadway tenor Mandy Patinkin. Avigdor is courting Hadass, demurely played by Amy Irving, and their imminent marriage seems assured until the family discovers that Avigdor's brother has committed suicide, an unclean act that condemns the surviving family to be cursed outcasts.

Both Avigdor and the family see Anshel as a perfect alternative, and in order to make Avigdor happy, the perplexed masquerader agrees to marry Hadass. Anshel makes it through the wedding night by explaining to the naive bride that it would be a sin to force sexual relations on a woman who is unwilling. In some of the most effective scenes of the film, Streisand works through the Talmud with Irving, until the Pygmalion scenario backfires, and the wife takes it on herself to initiate sexual activity, quoting lines from the Talmud as justification for her boldness.

The scene in which we see the obligatory revelation of true gender does not seem to differ significantly from a number of other cross-dressing films. The impersonator is at first punished and then gradually accepted, if not completely, at least partially. When Anshel goes on a trip alone with Avigdor, she finally decides to confess that she is a woman. Avigdor's response is one of bitter revulsion, followed by a confession of the love he had felt for the girl he believed to be a boy. He proposes marriage, but as Yentl realizes that this would mean abandonment of her life as a scholar, she makes the difficult decision to send Avigdor back to Hadass. Yentl later writes to the couple, both of whom have been altered by their encounter with the androgynous figure. Avigdor is ready to have a wife with a brain, and Hadass is ready to use her brain; she is independent enough to ignore her family's rejection of Avigdor. In an echo of the closing scene from *Funny Girl,* the final musical number finds Barbra singing on a boat. Her destination is a new country and perhaps a new future, in which she need not disguise her gender to pursue the knowledge she loves.

The ending is one of the most blatant deviations from Singer's original story, and the nature of this change points to the main problem with the film: Streisand's insistence on putting herself at the center of every scene and every song. In Singer's version, the ending finds Anshel on his/her way to a faraway yeshiva, and Hadass and Avigdor naming their firstborn son Anshel. This conclusion places emphasis on hope for the distant future rather than on a new world just over the horizon, and one cannot help but speculate that Singer's bittersweet solution might have been more moving than Streisand's choice. The use of the musical score might also have been more effective if the listeners had been able to hear Mandy Patinkin's soaring tenor as a counterbalance to Streisand's powerful soprano. Less focus on Streisand would enable the viewer to identify more fully with other characters and care more about their eventual fate.

However, the same intense emotional involvement that makes Streisand want to occupy the center stage almost exclusively in this piece is, no doubt, also the source of the film's energy and the reason for its existence. As with a number of other role reversal films, such as *Tootsie,* this one needed the passionate commitment of a determined individual to bring the project to fruition. In love with the story from the first time she read Singer's work in 1968, Streisand explains that she views the film as a way of expressing her love for her own father: "It was as if through Yentl I could tell him. Maybe I could create a father, the father I never had."[55]

The basic plot hardly makes revolutionary comments about women's rights; indeed, one wonders about the necessity for voicing the statement that it does make, at a time in which the education of women is readily accepted. Nevertheless, the response of popular critics suggests that the film's subject is less dated than it might appear to the wishful feminist. It is not so much a film about women's right to an education as it is a personal statement by Streisand about her own determination to exert influence in a world still dominated by male power structures. It is an allegory. The film makes no claims to realism, since it is, after all, a musical; believing that Streisand passes as a boy requires almost as much suspension of disbelief as it does to accept that the characters surrounding Victor/Victoria believe her to be a man. Streisand doesn't lower her voice, and although she hasn't the delicate features of Julie Andrews, she nevertheless appears decidedly female, partly because she makes no apparent attempt to imitate the mannerisms of a male.

Pauline Kael argues that the scenes that deal with sexuality are different from similar scenes directed by males, and that "the whole movie has a modulated emotionality that seems distinctively feminine."[56] It does seem true that many sexually ambiguous moments that could be played for laughs are instead treated with delicate poignancy, a rarity in role reversal films. The times when Anshel has to reject Hadass or to repress her own desire for Avigdor are tinged with a gentle sadness. Several scenes touch on the notion of homosexuality in the couple combinations: Streisand gazing perplexedly into the bosom of Amy Irving as she seductively serves tea and cookies, Streisand and Patinkin getting into a wrestling match that ends with him lying on top of her and staring with hinted arousal into his supposedly male companion's eyes. These segments create the slight humor and sense of tension typical of situations of sexual deception, but Streisand avoids the slapstick treatment. The film is designed to offend no one and to enlighten as many as possible.

The question of how many members of the audience are in need of the moderate feminist message of Streisand's film brings forth speculation on how much this impersonation of the male may indicate a trend. Since the decades of the depression, male impersonation has been rare, perhaps owing to a sense that the status of women has improved. What, then, does it indicate if once again females are returning to male disguise? *Victor/Victoria* and *Yentl* could be viewed as isolated incidents, but the trend toward male impersonation seems to be growing. A 1984 television movie entitled *Her Life as a Man* tells the story of a woman who must disguise herself as a man in order to get a job as a sportswriter. As with the Andrews and Streisand vehicles, a woman gains status and mobility by taking on a man's role, but unlike these earlier works, *Her Life as a Man* calls on the woman to perform a remarkably authentic impersonation, complete with padding to add body bulk, binding of the breasts, lowering of the voice, application of false beard and moustache, and minimization of gesture and facial expression. Douglass observes: "When Dustin Hoffman played 'Tootsie' all he had to do to be a woman was add. But in playing a man you have to take away, to bring it down."[57] This drift toward greater realism, absent from *Victor/Victoria* and only slightly more in evidence in *Yentl,* may indicate that what happened with female impersonation is now occurring with male impersonation.

One explanation is the notion that people are sensing the necessity for a kind of retrenchment. After what appeared to be giant strides forward for women's rights, many have come to realize that change is slow in coming. Indeed, with a more conservative trend in the nation as a whole, the prospects for women's rights may appear so limited as to encourage the kind of fantastic solutions we see in films in which women become men, as completely as they can manage. The popularity of androgynous entertainment figures like Michael Jackson, Grace Jones, Boy George of Culture Club, or Annie Lennox of the Eurythmics may not be so much a reflection of a unisex drive in the society as it is an indication that sex roles are returning to more rigid patterns. It has become fashionable to abandon liberal attitudes in a number of political and economic areas, but it seems that one pocket of resistance to neoconservatism lies in people's attitudes toward sex roles. Many individuals may feel themselves constrained to follow fairly rigid role models in their public behavior, but in their choice of music and movies they seek fantasy outlets in which they can identify with characters who defy gender roles.

Film Androgyny Over the Decades

A significant number of actors, actresses, and films of earlier decades that continue to interest critics and film aficionados seem to be more than reflections of the Zeitgeist. In retrospect, we may see that they captured a glimpse of the future. They may well have contributed to the creation of new images of men and women by popularizing alternative ways of behaving. In spite of the censorship of deviation from the norm, certain cross-dressing films seem to have provided a mode of expression for a segment of society otherwise repressed. Like actors, actresses, and directors who were forced to lead double lives, a handful of Hollywood films have a dual function and carry a double message—one for the heterosexual majority and a covert message for the homosexual or lesbian in-group.

The film industry has always been more eager to censor its own work than the general public or legislatures have been to censor film content. This survey of transvestism and cross-dressing implies that censorship of sexual content is never totally successful. The expression of female sexuality, when censored, seems to pop out in rather kinky places—the little girl in a tuxedo, the woman in a severe army or business uniform, the sadomasochistic dominatrix or martyred religious saint. All these images satisfy hidden urges, but they do so in a covert way that manages to slip through the cracks of standard censorship guidelines. There are several patterns in the occurrence of male and female impersonation. Through the period of censorship, female impersonation was almost invariably farcical, whereas male impersonation took a variety of forms, from serious drama to buffoonery. With the breakdown of censorship and the simultaneous rise in the status of women in the labor market, male impersonation diminished drastically, whereas female impersonation blossomed into the same kind of variety that male impersonation had demonstrated in an earlier era. If male impersonation showed a desire on the part of women to "be men" in an age when men seemed to have the advantage, the prevalence of female impersonation in the last twenty years indicates a similar desire on the part of men to "be women" in an age when women have seemed to be gaining prestige and power at the expense of the formerly dominant male. This schema may seem to be quite an overstatement when it is compared to actual statistics on comparative wages, the number of women in executive positions, the number of men who perform "househusband" duties, etc. Films do not reflect statistical reality, but they do reveal filmmakers' impressions of trends in society.

The contrast between films of the last fifteen or twenty years and the films of earlier decades points to changing concepts of what constitutes masculinity and femininity. Popular versions of masculine heroines have changed in the last twenty years. The woman may or may not end in the security of a male/female relationship. The possibility of the independent woman is gradually being accepted by filmmakers and their audiences. The vast majority of films seem to mirror contemporary anxieties and values. At the same time, the private concerns of individual actors, actresses, and filmmakers do influence audiences, and the images of men and women presented in innovative films have an effect on movie viewers. When a film presents a strong, aggressive female or a sympathetically portrayed "feminine" male, these characters become alternative role models. Imitation of these models erodes the ironclad standards of tradition, at times to the point of modifying the standards. The issue of how much films reflect or affect society is a complex one, and no simple formula applies in every case.

Why has male impersonation faded from vogue in the last twenty years, while female impersonation continues to appear in more and more lavish variety? Molly Haskell offers an observation on the general scarcity of female characters in recent years:

> When "female qualities"—softness, sensitivity, passivity—were exalted in the post-Brando hero and in the rock/anti-war ethic of the counter-culture, it did not bring about a corresponding exaltation of woman, but, on the contrary, a diminution of her role as the new movie hero appropriated her qualities without losing his place at the center of the stage.[58]

Haskell is correct in her observation that male characters have taken over "female qualities," but perhaps this has not diminished the importance of female characters in any irretrievable sense. The pattern may be a short-lived trend. Films have focused on male characters because men have undergone a dramatic change in status over the last several decades. Directors who have become wary of treading on feminist toes have chosen to focus on the "tragic fall" of male characters rather than on the triumphant rise of female Horatio Algers, perhaps, in part, because they see more dramatic potential in the image of the fallen figure. At the same time, a great deal of the hostility and anxiety concerning the emergence of the "liberated" woman and the concomitant decline in male status, as it is perceived by some, is siphoned into the horror genre. *Variety* reports that 37 percent of the box office sales of 1980 were for horror films, and a large number take thematic revenge on the independent woman by featuring intimidation, mutilation, and murder of female characters who dare to assert themselves or act independently.

The patterns of male and female impersonation are explainable in terms of trends in society and also in terms of the differences in the processes of cross-dressing transformations. When men imitate women, they add to themselves with longer hair, makeup, jewelry, dresses, elaborate underwear, and false breasts. If the transformation is complete, they also open themselves up, revealing a panoply of facial and vocal expressions, graceful body movements, and emotional displays. Male impersonation, on the other hand, relies on concealment of the breasts, inhibition of extremes in facial and vocal expression, hiding or cutting off long hair, and wearing bulky clothes that conceal the outlines of the body. During the first half-century of film, male imitation seemed a worthwhile exchange, for what the woman lost in expressiveness, she gained in mobility and freedom to enter the forbidden male realm. When the masculine world opened up to women, male impersonation came to be a bad bargain, whereas imitation of the increasingly prestigious female became more and more appealing, particularly in an art form which exalts the virtues of visual and emotional display. If films of the last twenty years are any indication, male characters will continue to imitate women for as long as this adds to their expressive range.

Film itself has created a tendency to identify with members of both sexes, and there is probably much more audience identification with both sexes than is generally assumed. The camera's ability to focus on particular parts of the body draws the viewers into an identification with both females and males. Who is to say which gender we identify with in a love scene that features close-ups of hands gliding over waists, shoulders, and backs? To what extent does the individual male or female viewer see himself or herself as the one who caresses or the one being caressed? In recent years, there seems to be a shift even in the styles of caressing and lovemaking. For example, in earlier films we often see a male character grasp the woman's shoulders rather brusquely as he draws the passive female into an embrace, whereas in more recent films this same gesture would be considered overly forceful and it might be greeted by rejection. We also see many more females in recent films taking an active role in initiating lovemaking.

Film throughout the decades has altered our perceptions of sexual appeal by featuring a number of androgynous figures as glamorous models. During the silent era, Rudolph Valentino became an idol for women attracted to his exotic, almost feminine qualities. Greta Garbo was advertised as the female Valentino, and her husky voice became the archetypal siren song. Katharine Hepburn was remarkable for her willingness to do physically demanding roles. Part of her appeal resides in the fact that we see her (not a stand-in) exerting herself, tensing her muscles, and being active in a way that many movie heroines were not. Dietrich's immobility was similarly unfeminine in contrast to the fluidity of many heroines; she is often impassive, moving very little, yet her motionless quality on screen suggests not passivity but stoic mastery over her emotions. Clifton Webb could remain urbanely oblivious to the sexual charms of women, while his sophistication and wit placed him on top of every situation. Actors like Montgomery Clift, Marlon Brando, and James Dean popularized the image of the sensitive, almost feminine male, while Doris Day and Debbie Reynolds lent star status to the tomboy. More recently, sexual role reversal and a concomitant symbolic transvestism have entered the field of major motion pictures, signaling filmmakers' attempts to keep pace with changes in the society. During the last decade, the sexually ambiguous character in film has become the emblem for positive traits, from tact to tough outspokenness, from delightful foolishness to fundamental wisdom.[59] The androgynous figure gives audiences a sense of hidden possibilities, of the potential for change and renewal. Films allow us to enter into forbidden worlds of the imagination, and when we find ourselves identifying with the other sex, we learn more of what it is simply to be human.

CHAPTER SIX

FIN DE SIÈCLE ANXIETIES
COMING OUT

THE QUINCENTENNIAL and the upcoming end of the century called on American society of the eighties and nineties to define their identity as a culture, reassess their past, and predict their future. The fact that the end of the nineties would also mark the end of a millennium added import to considerations of sexual identity, accepted roles, and boundaries. Mainstream culture became more aware of alternative sexual orientation through a growing public alarm over the AIDS epidemic. Economic changes affected families and career choices, and the increasing number of women in the work force altered the way people defined career roles for women and men. The feminist movement was influential in opening up wider possibilities for both genders, but it also encountered a strong backlash movement. At the same time that films like *Tootsie* were capitalizing on actor and audience fantasies of men being better men by becoming women, mainstream America was also gearing up for a new version of the old macho.

The rising popularity of what many critics have called fascist heroes began with Schwarzenegger's *Conan the Barbarian* (1982), which grossed more than $21 million. Susan Sontag points out in a 1974 essay on Nazi director Leni Riefenstahl that fascist films portray "the rebirth of the body and of community,"[1] a point further elaborated in Fred Glass' analysis of bodily perfection in "Totally Recalling Arnold."[2] The invincible quality of heroes played by Arnold Schwarzenegger, Sylvester Stallone, and Steven Seagal in such films as *Rocky* (1976), *The Terminator* (1984), *Under Siege* (1992), and the *Die Hard* (1988, 1990) and *Rambo* (1982, 1985, 1988) series appeals to the audience's need for certainty, the recapturing of lost power. Faced with undefined economic and cultural threats, many viewers long for revenge against a nebulous enemy. American society in these macho films is variously seen as victimized, powerless, soft, decadent, corrupt, and even in need of punishment to shock people out of their apathy. The heroes are angry, abused, and superhuman in their strength and exaggerated physical perfection.

At first glance, the highly muscled, sculpted forms of Sylvester Stallone, Chuck Norris, Steven Seagal, and Arnold Schwarzenegger appear as the antithesis of androgynous types, with their emphasis on masculine bulk and strength. A closer analysis of their appeal reveals the striking oppositions held in tension within the gleaming images of their bodies. Shots and publicity stills of these figures often highlight the chest of the hero—smooth, hairless, with bulging pectorals, key lit in such a way that it emphasizes a cleavage some women would envy. Backlighting or high spotlighting of the head adds a reddish, golden shimmer to the hair and features. Standing postures reveal the forward-thrust pelvis, a pose that is typical of female runway models. Like the stereotypical female, these heroes are loners, operating on instinct, intuition, and emotion rather than on reason. Their dress may be stock military, but more often it has out-of-the-ordinary fashion touches—black leather, snakeskin buckles, tasseled headbands, a pony tail, or imitation American-flag cloth—all items one would ordinarily associate with the feminized use of costume as more symbolic than merely functional.[3] The nearly hairless male body became fashionable in the eighties, a trend that continued into the nineties, with designers such as Calvin Klein using naturally smooth or shaven male models to sell products. This trend toward conflating male and female sexual cues speaks not only of a subtext created by a significant gay population in the fashion industry but also of a taste preference of mainstream consumers, a group conditioned by positive, powerful images of androgyny.

One of the appeals of such androgynous males may be their self-sufficiency. Bodybuilder stars have their own austere beauty, and their characters' lack of need for women fits the image of invulnerability. More often than not, females are killed, peripheral, or missing, as in Milius' *Conan the Barbarian,* or threatening and androgynous in their own right, as with Grace Jones in *Conan the Destroyer* (1984), *A View to a Kill* (1985), and *Boomerang* (1992). Sexual surrender in the macho films signifies loss of self, and female beauty often weakens, maims, kills, or causes the trcuble in the first place, when it enters the picture at all. In the era of AIDS, sexual intercourse has become literally and figuratively a battleground, with life-and-death stakes, but the figure of the sexually pure hero or heroine goes all the way back to ancient Greek tradition in the Spartan isolation of males from females. American society has always been conflicted about human sexuality, but the AIDS epidemic has drastically altered the way people view sexual behavior, with celibacy and isolation looking more and more appealing to a number of people. In addition, the isolated and self-contained hero is fundamental to the schizophrenic fantasy life of a culture in which individuals dream of independence while they actually depend upon thousands of unseen hands for almost every facet of survival.[4]

The fantasy of self-sufficiency seems to be the prevailing myth of the decade of the eighties—not a surprising phenomenon, considering the breakdown of government, social, and cultural support networks. With divorce rates reaching an all-time high, even children learned to fantasize their way to total independence from adults and avenge themselves in Chris Columbus' blockbuster films *Home Alone* (1990) and *Home Alone 2* (the former grossed more than any other film in 1990).[5] Much of the appeal of androgyny in the late eighties and early nineties resides in the comfort of not having to deal with or rely on the opposite gender. This is a common motif for both male and female cross-dressers and participants in the game of gender-bending.

The asexuality of the androgynous male has its counterpart in the constructed figures of amazon women in films. They may have metallic-looking bodies—the shiny gray and mauve of Grace Jones in *A View to a Kill*—or the black and silver leather and metal studs of Madonna in *Truth or Dare* and numerous short videos. One of the most aggressive women to appear on screen is Jones' character in *Boomerang,* wearing a provocative blend of male and female clothing designed to threaten rather than entice. Muscles born of intense bodybuilding complement exaggerated breastplates, codpieces, and other artificial molded forms that simultaneously accentuate and falsify sexual characteristics. In their shape and intent, these women's "tits are weapons," (to paraphrase the female gang leader in John Waters' 1990 parody, *Cry Baby*), with little of the soft erotic appeal usually associated with female breasts. Raymond Durgnat argues that Grace Jones' role in *A View to a Kill* "makes her a spectacular refutation of Lacanian-feminist theory, which thinks that the gaze, the camera, most forms of discourse, and the right to speak, are all male, phallic, voyeuristic, and judgmental, with women merely passive, suffering victims of men's desire."[6]

The dangerous, sexually threatening female is a popular icon among adolescent girls, eager to establish their own autonomy and right to express their sexuality brazenly and without fear of reciprocation. A more underground version of the threatening woman appears in Anne Parillaud's portrayal of a criminal-turned-spy in Luc Besson's French-Italian production *La Femme Nikita* (1990). (Bridget Fonda's portrayal in the 1993 American remake, *Point of No Return,* softens the character somewhat, but the film maintains the character's independence at the end.) This character is chosen for her ruthlessness, coordination, and amazing physical talent to become a top spy. She is eventually weakened by romantic involvement, but unlike her predecessor spies in earlier films—*Ninotchka* (1939) and its remake, *Silk Stockings* (1957), and *Modesty Blaise* (1966)—she soon regains her resolve and defeats the spy system that has trained and enslaved her.

A strain of sexless androgyny occurs in the almost monkish appearance of such figures as Sigourney Weaver in *Alien*[3]. The three *Alien* films progress from the original *Alien*'s sexually appealing but not sexually active female, through romantic heroine/mother versus machine mother, to the bereaved mother, finally raped by the alien invader. This triad provides an interesting parallel to the cultural fears and fantasies operating over the decade spanning their releases. Sequels invariably attempt to capture whatever drew audiences to the film in the first place and at the same time to update the material in a way that continues to fit moviegoers' wishes. The giant loading machine that Weaver straps on in *Aliens* is an exaggeration of the super mom image of the late eighties, and she wins in a battle of two mothers, each seeking to assure the survival of her offspring and her species. Weaver's caretaking behavior with the orphaned child Newt appeals to a society in the throes of controversy of day care, working mothers versus stay-at-home mothers, and supposed choices between career and children. In keeping with the strong heroine, which producers sensed would still appeal to audiences, Weaver's character rescues not just babies but men and robots as well. This figure also parallels the popular Rambo character, as pointed out in one review:

> One of the last summer's big blockbusters, this followup to Ridley Scott's instant classic proves that sequels can work—in the right hands. In this case, the hands belong to James *(Terminator)* Cameron, who is fast emerging as Hollywood's primo director of thrillers. Sigourney Weaver's reprise of her original role, with a Mama Rambo twist, pushed her over the top into major stardom. Don't miss it.[7]

Weaver herself stated her reservations about the part:

> If I see my role as a Chinese warrior, a Valkyrie, or as the Henry V-who-I'll-never-get-to-play, then I'm interested in it. It's a chance to do a classic male part. If I see it as gun play, I'm not interested. . . . In making *Aliens* I think I underestimated the degree to which Cameron would pay attention to guns—though, because he's so skilled, the film does transcend the violence.[8]

Another feature of *Aliens* that disturbed Weaver was Fox's decision to cut a crucial scene, in which she learns that her daughter had grown old and died back on earth while Ripley traveled through space:

> It was a little scene after I woke up. I'm sitting in this fake patio, and Paul Reiser comes in and says, "I didn't want to tell you before, but your daughter died two years ago, and this is all I have left of her."[9]

Reiser's character shows Ripley a picture that is supposed to be her daughter back on earth, actually a photo of Weaver's own mother. Weaver explains, "I based her whole trauma on the fact that she'd lost her family. She'd paid horribly for her success in surviving the alien." [10] This elimination of character detail fit in with the studio's decision to promote *Aliens* as pure adventure, a bitter disappointment to Weaver in its emphasis on guns and action over characters and emotions.

The third in the sequel brought a new set of images to the screen, to an audience that had experienced a different kind of alien invasion in the specter of AIDS. Although the supposed rationale for having Weaver shave her head is to prevent lice infestation, the power of the look comes from a number of other associations and connotations. Viewers had become familiar with the faces of real AIDS patients, many of whom have the close-cropped hair and bony face reminiscent of a concentration camp victim. Homosexuality no longer had the stereotyped faceless quality of the long-haired, effeminate "Nelly." In setting an atmosphere conducive to horror, the filmmakers called on every available fear lurking in the back of viewers' minds. Because of the decidedly sexual nature of the alien, the association with AIDS is a natural one, and Weaver's gaunt, shaven-headed appearance fits her role as the alien's victim. Shortly before the climax, the scientist Bishop brings up another concern of many women, when he tells her, 'You could still have a life. You could have children.' In the end, of course, she doesn't. Instead, she is the new religious heroine, and her final demise—falling, arms outspread in imitation of Christ—shows that only spiritual, asexual purity and self-sacrifice will suffice to conquer the alien force that invades her body. Marjorie Garber explains that the desire to see such figures as Christ or the saints "as somehow beyond gender—'neither boy nor girl'—reflects not only a contemporary religious fantasy, but also a peculiar modern anxiety about the entrapment of gender and gender roles." [11]

Other entertainment figures play on the saintly or androgynous appearance to convey a serious ideological message, using the power of close-cropped hair to increase the strength of their image. Singer Sinead O'Connor's tortured, serious manner during performance and her almost religious antipapal zeal calls forth scenes of Dryer's *Jeanne d'Arc*. Annie Lennox's appearance is at once "butch" and nunlike in its severity, a self-conscious crossing of categories. The rock video "Sisters Are Doin' It for Themselves," featuring Lennox and Aretha Franklin, further bends boundaries, with shots of Lennox in black jacket, pants, and boots, and Franklin in a red dress weaving in and out of clips, video images, and stage performances. E. Ann Kaplan notes that even the positioning and editing reinforce a postmodern feminist refusal to fulfill the stereotyped role of woman as object of the gaze:

> There is an interesting attempt in the video to avoid making Franklin and Lennox direct objects of the camera's gaze. While there are inevitably some close-ups of their faces, for much of the time the camera catches them at oblique angles, so that their gazes do not directly meet the camera's. At times, this creates an unfortunate sense of their not relating to each other, but this is in the service of avoiding, as much as possible, an objectifying camera gaze.[12]

Kaplan's observation points to one of the difficulties of trying to avoid filmic structures, which, while they may "objectify" the woman, also create in the viewer a stronger sense of the actors' relationship to each other, which in turn increases viewer identification with the actors.

The asexual clothing of *The Handmaid's Tale* (1990) again makes the link between religion and sexuality, suggesting the danger of trying to create ideology from biology or vice versa. Margerie Garber observes that "the use of Western religious costume as part of a lexicon of gender-bending, whether intended as serious social commentary or as a pop throwaway, is a striking manifestation of cultural anxiety."[13] Part of the anxiety comes from the society's suspicion of "exceptional" categories that threaten social cohesion. Military and religious dress requires uniform, supposedly gender-neutral clothing (although the military and the church still wrestle with this paradox) as a means of creating a separate category. Garber points out how the

> male nun, the female monk, feminized Jewish man are recurrent figures of fantasy as well as of history and propaganda. . . . Moreover, since ecstatic religion depends to a certain extent upon

the existence of exceptions, chosen persons who explicitly violate the very tenets that faith and custom ordain for the ordinary practitioner, the presence of transvestite figures, or of the phantom of the transvestite in the representation of holy personages (saints, virgin martyrs, rabbinical leaders) is in a way, oddly, to be expected: these are the exception that prove the rule.[14]

Slapstick versions of commingling religion and sexuality appear in *Nuns on the Run* and *Sister Act,* in which viewers are invited to take pleasure in the fantasy of naughty nuns in traditional anticlerical satires. One reason these appeal to popular audiences is because of the clear heterosexuality of the nun impersonators (male or female).[15]

Films like *A Handmaid's Tale* or the *Alien* series are not just about sexual anxieties; they also concern the issue of offspring. If androgyny offers comforting images of self-sufficiency, it also calls up anxieties over abandonment, isolation, and loneliness. The flip side of the independence fantasy occurs in role reversals on the domestic scene, with the popularity of films such as *Mr. Mom* (1983), *Baby Boom* (1987), *Three Men and a Baby* (1987), *Three Men and a Little Lady* (1990), *Curly Sue* (1991), *Sidekick* (1993), *Jack the Bear* (1993), and *One and a Half Cops* (1993). These films posit the most unlikely caretakers in situations of patent absurdity, but for popular audiences, the fantasy works, as attested by box office returns ranging from $12,079,000 to $81,313,000 in 1987.[16] Such films as *Baby Boom* and *Working Girl* (1988) initially present career women, in Diane Keaton's J. C. Wiatt and Sigourney Weaver's Katharine Parker, both nervous, cold, and driven caricatures of female executives, dressing mannishly for success and behaving neurotically to let audiences know that female careerism is a bad idea. In most popular films, these women are either conquered or transmogrified into softer women who need men, love babies, and sacrifice or somehow limit their careers in favor of domestic bliss. As in Bob Rafelson's *Black Widow* (1987), Adrian Lynn's *Fatal Attraction* (1987), Shroeder's *Single White Female* (1992), or Paul Verhoeven's *Basic Instinct* (1992), a single woman is often not just unappealing but downright sick. These films clearly present black-and-white alternatives (in characters and in the color schemes of sets and costumes), with the domesticated female triumphing in the end. Even if a woman violates her traditional role, by killing the intruder or rescuing her man, these actions ultimately support the status quo. Limited reversals of stereotypical feminine traits appear primarily in aggressive behavior, a questionable gain in the view of some feminist critics.

The issue of female aggression created an uproar in critical and viewer response when it failed to support traditional domesticity in the ground-breaking female buddy film *Thelma and Louise* (1991). Thelma and Louise are played with skill and subtlety by Geena Davis and Susan Sarandon, both actresses who carry with them a screen persona of strength and independence, bolstered by their roles in such films as Lawrence Kasdan's *The Accidental Tourist* (1988) and Luis Mandoki's *White Palace* (1990). Gloria Steinem admires the image presented by the characters, commenting that "thinking about *Thelma and Louise* draws out of us the strength of Thelma and Louise and that's what brings tears to our eyes." [17] Screenwriter Callie Khouri began with the simple idea, "Two women go on a crime spree," but *Thelma and Louise* ended up creating more controversy than the film industry had seen since Martin Scorcese's *The Last Temptation of Christ* (1988) (a film that combined the sensitive issue of religion with another, even more threatening, version of image-construction). One of the main questions was whether *Thelma and Louise* was a feminist film or merely a male-bashing, violence-endorsing rehash of *Butch Cassidy and the Sundance Kid* (1969). Sheila Benson of the *Los Angeles Times* attacks the film, commenting, "As I understand it, feminism has to do with responsibility, equality, sensitivity, understanding—not revenge, retribution, or sadistic behavior." [18] *Time* magazine's Richard Schickel, on the other hand, defends the film. He quotes Susan Sarandon's response to charges of violence as proving

"what a straight, white male world movies traditionally occupy. This kind of scrutiny does not happen to *Raiders of the Lost Ark* or that Schwarzenegger thing [*Total Recall*] where he shoots a woman in the head and says, 'Consider that a divorce.' " Sarandon insists that all concerned with the production spent a lot of time making sure *Thelma & Louise* didn't turn into "a bloodlust-revenge film." Certainly, compared with the typical male-action film, the violence here is spare and rather chastely staged. [19]

Sarandon and Schickel's hypothetical reversals demonstrate how critics like Benson have been conditioned to view violence differently, according to which gender performs it. Male characters behaving like *Thelma and Louise* would look like pacifists.

Other critics focus less on the film's violence and point to the structure, which, as Brooklyn Law School Professor Elizabeth Schneider argues, sends the message that "self-assertion and awakening lead to death."[20] This observation about the film's ultimate message is an important one, but it also reveals Schneider's own biased assumption that female death cannot be mythical, assertive, or redemptive; rather, it must be punishment for self-assertion. As a fable or fairy tale, the film ends in a way fairly typical of mythical stories, with the two principal protagonists entering a symbolic realm of the eternal, immortalized in the white burnout of the closing freeze frame. Critics did not concern themselves with the outcome of *Butch Cassidy and the Sundance Kid/Easy Rider* (1969), because a male death in the conclusion is sacrificial, symbolic, and Christ-like. A female death at the end of the story rarely receives such a heroic interpretation, from feminists or nonfeminists. In any case, the particular details are not the real issue in most controversies surrounding *Thelma and Louise*. Viewers respond not so much to the specific behavior or plot details as to the fact that it is women and not men who act in these roles.

The very fact of reversal rests at the center of many critical arguments about Ridley Scott's film. As with most of his work, dazzling visual cues provide the strongest, yet most subtle announcement of the "masculinizing" of his female characters. Thelma and Louise's shift in behavior and clothing from the beginning to the end of the film is dramatic. Geena Davis begins in a white, off-the-shoulder, puff-sleeved, wide-skirted peasant-style sundress, indicative not only of her innocence and childlike status but also of her social class, as a servant to her husband and as a member of the "peasant" class of stay-at-home lower middle-class wives. Louise, in her waitress uniform, may even have a slight sartorial edge on Thelma, since her clothing represents work in the outside world, albeit not exactly a status occupation, but one in which she at least receives payment for serving. The western-style shirt she wears for their departure still casts her in the dominant role. In the first half of the film, her character is always the more masculine in action, clothing, and emotional "command" of the situation, and it is therefore fitting that she be the one who invites Thelma on a trip, who defends Thelma's honor by shooting her attacker, and who drives the car most of the time.

Unlike the typical male buddy film, however, the roles of this single-sex couple are fluid, and by the end of the film, Thelma, a quick study, has learned by imitation to take on masculine clothing, attitudes, and behavior. These characters wash away and throw out makeup in significant scenes. The first occurs after Thelma and Louise realize what they have done in shooting the would-be rapist. They cry, vomit, and wipe the residue of makeup and mess from their faces, at the same time trying to wipe away their own guilt, responsibility, and remorse. Later on, during their flight to Mexico, Louise looks in the window of a run-down restaurant at an old woman, the mirror of what Louise might have become with time. Louise then looks at her own dust-streaked face in the car mirror, begins to apply lipstick, and, on reflection, tosses the lipstick out on the ground. Instead of the feminine makeup of earlier scenes, she wears the flat man's hat she trades with an ancient, wrinkled Indian man for her watch (another indication that she is escaping the time-bound state of ordinary reality). Wrapping a red bandana around her neck, vaquero style, she sets off on a road to nowhere.

Thelma's own clothing has come to reflect her transformation in its increasing practicality and masculinity—a cut-off sleeveless workshirt, worn blue jeans, and boots. Her actions match her clothing shift, and she learns from her one-night stand (Brad Pitt) a take-charge effective method for robbing convenience stores that she eventually uses. As he demonstrates his technique, there is something androgynous in the appeal of the slim, muscled, smooth-chested Pitt, holding a hair dryer as imitation gun, showing Thelma how to rob stores with wit and politeness rather than macho fierceness. Even his ability to please Thelma sexually is more an indication of his androgynous nature, in knowing and understanding what a woman wants, than it is of his "manliness." Thelma's football-watching husband Darryl, who never satisfied her sexually or emotionally, is the stereotype of a masculine male. He contrasts with the policemen in his home, all of whom watch an archetypal woman's weepy movie, *Dark Victory*, misty-eyed, objecting vehemently when Darryl tries to switch channels to watch the football game. Another defiance of standard gender role expectations occurs when a policeman cries, as Thelma holds a gun to him and tells him, "Well you be sweet to your wife. My husband wasn't sweet to me and look how I turned out." After the women leave the policeman locked in his trunk, a black, joint-smoking Rastafarian bicyclist stops, hears screams coming from the trunk of the police car, and blows marijuana smoke into the hole in the trunk. Such scenes satisfy a desire for revenge against authority, and the slippage among categories of gender, race, and culture deepens and expands the fantasy of role reversal, from powerful to powerless, victimizer to victimized, controlling to controlled.

Thelma and Louise does not purport to be realistic, in character or setting. Often the lighting takes on a surreal quality, confusing day and night, dawn and dusk, with the soundtrack meandering in and out of diegetic and nondiegetic music, some of which comes from the car radio, and some of which comes from that great atmospheric film device in the sky, Hans Zimmer's evocative score. In the final chase scene, the helicopter birdseye shot that reveals dozens of police cars chasing two relatively harmless criminals toward the Grand Canyon underscores the broad strokes Scott uses in painting this larger-than-life dreamscape. Exaggeration does not diminish the authenticity of emotion in these scenes, nor the realism of the relationships portrayed. Ridley Scott, who often shoots in sequence, had reserved shooting of this final scene for the end, and when the characters have tears in their eyes, they mark the genuine feelings of the actresses, who are about to say goodbye to each other and to a unique filmmaking experience. After shooting the film, the actresses expressed the exhilaration they felt in being able to bond with another woman, to perform the adventurous, dangerous scenes usually reserved for male actors, and to have this personal growth as actresses parallel the opening up of possibilities for the characters within the film. Critics who harp on such details as the fact that the characters should have switched cars clearly do not see the film in its allegorical and symbolic dimensions. The turquoise blue Thunderbird is Louise's expression of freedom and independence, and when it sails into the sky in a freeze-frame burnout to white, it joins the ranks of other symbolic objects, like the phoenix that never really dies. At that point, according to Gloria Steinem, "They went straight into our imaginations and into mythology."[21] The film garnered an Academy Award for best screenplay, and six nominations in other categories, with box office grosses of over $42 million in 1991.[22]

A popular film like *Thelma and Louise* enters the gray area between films designed to appeal to mainstream audiences and those geared to art-cinema crowds. Other films focusing on female couples or single-gender groups aimed at a more marginal audiences (translate, women and/or lesbians and homosexuals), as well as popular venues, include such films as *Beaches* (1988), which grossed $24,882,000 in 1988,[23] *Fried Green Tomatoes* (which made $37,402,827 in rentals in 1992),[24] and *A League of Their Own* (1992), again capitalizing on the strong, slightly quirky appeal of the wholesome Geena Davis and the rebellious Madonna. These movies were at pains to establish the heterosexuality of the women characters, even in the case of *Fried Green Tomatoes*, when the literary source presented the main relationship as lesbian. *A League of Their Own* director Penny Marshall was as eager to market her product as the managers of the real-life women's baseball league were to market theirs. Managers made their women wear skirts to play baseball, thus emphasizing the "ladylike" qualities of their characters (they didn't acknowledge the other ladylike features that would be displayed when these women slid into base). Marshall, ever sensitive to the demands of commercial productions, inserted a manufactured conflict between two sisters, thereby following the standard notion that women cannot get along with each other, particularly in a professional setting. Although it was minimal, Madonna's presence in the film was widely touted in the advertising campaign. Also, preview audiences were treated to the astonishing sight of Geena Davis—simultaneously sliding into base, catching a ball and doing the splits—contradictory cues of masculine competence and feminine ability to spread her legs, even beyond the usual range. This film tried to offer something for everyone, and box office returns of 110 million placed it in the top ten grossing films of 1992.[25] *Entertainment Weekly* writers note the popularity of such films and the industry's apparent reluctance to acknowledge this trend:

> One would have thought that after the unexpected success of *Fried Green Tomatoes* ($8.1 million), Hollywood would have guessed that there is a female audience hungry for movies by, for, and about women. And one would have thought that after the numbers racked up by *Sister Act* ($139.6 million), *A League of Their Own* ($107.4 million), and even *Single White Female* ($48 million), the lesson would have sunk in.[26]

While film producers have not exactly jumped en masse onto the women's picture bandwagon, some critics believe that the popularity of women's films has even influenced films for men. Peter Rainer identifies films in a postyuppie era genre he calls male weepies or "meepies." Films he considers viable candidates often illustrate a hard-edged successful male who meets an untimely "implosion of sensitivity": *Regarding Henry, The Doctor, Doc Hollywood, Dying Young, City Slickers, Terminator 2: Judgment Day, Awakenings, Dances with Wolves, Big.*[27] Another encouraging indicator is the comparatively greater representation of women in television, a more sensitive barometer for future trends than the more male-dominated features industry, where production and investment works on a slower schedule and a longer production time-frame. Linda Bloodworth-Thomason, creator of television's tough heroine in *Hearts Afire,* comments that "women in features are strong in an almost cartoonish way."[28] A number of films from the eighties would tend to substantiate this accusation, but at least movies do not have to cater to the rigorous censorship demands of prime-time television.[29] Both media have a tendency to favor binary oppositions, however, with one or the other gender being flat, villainous, absent, or dead.

When Moms Are Dads and Dads Are Rats, or Better Yet, Dead

Films featuring women as the head of the household do not necessarily have to kill off the husband literally. They may simply make him a cardboard or weak figure. *Heartland* (1979) (based on the diaries of Elinore Randall Stewart), *Terms of Endearment* (1983), *Places in the Heart* (1984), *Country* (1984), and *The River* (1984) hearken back to the mother of all popular tales of strong moms, *The Grapes of Wrath* (1940). In these films, women provide the backbone for the family and men generally provide the conflict in their battles with agribusiness, economic hard times, or their own disintegrating pride. They stand out as a few of the scarce commercial successes that feature strong, independent women, where the female lead has to take on the role of mother and father in order to save the family. *Terms of Endearment* (1983) doesn't quite count, since Debra Winger's character conveniently dies (out of sight and out of mind), and Shirley MacLaine's character is somewhat upstaged by Jack Nicholson's aging astronaut, who looks to be a permanent figure on the romantic horizon for the cantankerous Aurora Greenaway. Sally Field plays a widowed character who achieves success, with the help of a black hired hand and her children, in *Places in the Heart*. This triumph stretches but does not violate the demands of verisimilitude, but the plot veers quite unexpectedly into the supernatural, when both living and dead characters, including her husband, join her in the local church. This fantasy conclusion undercuts the strength of the message of female independence, but it may have been exactly the arty, sentimental touch audiences needed to place the film alongside other Oscar material. *Used People* is another female-focused film, starring Shirley MacLaine, Jessica Tandy, Kathy Bates, and Marcia Gay Hardin in a work that uses sentimentality and draws on the actresses' screen personae as strong females. The commercial success of such films often relies on who backs its production and vagaries of the market.

Jessica Lange pushed for years to have William Wittliff's screenplay come to movie theaters in *Country,* another ideal vehicle for a powerful woman. This film features a strong, beautiful, and steely heroine to counter the rather wishy-washy roles Lange found herself playing in *Tootsie* and/or the suffering masochist she portrayed in Graham Clifford's *Francis* (1982). Drawing on her own background as a midwestern farm girl, Jessica Lange is convincing in pants and little or no makeup, urging a

crowd of farmers to resist domination by banking and big farm-
ing interests. This role provides an inspiring model for women
as hero, but this labor of love did not enjoy great commercial
success, with grosses of $5,656,000. One of the reasons for its
lack of success may have been an accident of marketing, with
three farm movies appearing within two months and *Country*
appearing second in the batch. Another, more important cause
for the film's lukewarm reception may have been the discomfort
some male and female viewers alike might have experienced
watching men fall apart and give up hope in the face of financial
ruin. The situation may have come a bit too close to real economic and emotional distress to satisfy the American audience's
demand for fantasy solutions, regardless of the attempts to provide an ending with the community pulling together to rescue
the little guy, in echoes of *It's a Wonderful Life.*

A number of films featuring women in traditional "men's"
roles quietly slipped into oblivion during the late eighties and
early nineties. Tom Holland's *Fatal Beauty* (1987) grossed
$4,756,000,[30] with Whoopi Goldberg as an unorthodox Dirty
Harry-style cop. *Feds* (1988), a female buddy vehicle with Rebecca DeMornay and Mary Gross competing against a male FBI
training class, tried to demonstrate that women could be as
macho as men. Female gangs battle on a hair salon set in Spike
Lee's *School Daze* (1988), an attempt to highlight the destruc-
tiveness of self-imposed social, class, and color boundaries among
blacks. Other films including strong women in dangerous or
challenging occupations are Abel Ferrara's *Ms. 45* (1981), Clint
Eastwood's *Sudden Impact* (1983), Kathryn Bigelow's *Blue Steel*
(1990). Other women-as-cop films were much more popular,
such as Jonathan Demme's *Silence of the Lambs* (1991) and *Lethal
Weapon 3* (1992).

Jodie Foster's role, as Clarice Starling, in *Silence of the Lambs*
was notable for its portrayal of a tough, competent police inves-
tigator trainee, but it was hardly a case in which she just
happened to be a woman working in a role usually designated
for men. Rather, her female status and her sexuality are the
reasons for selecting her to investigate serial murders involving
the skinning of the victims. Her boss makes it clear that he
chose her for this job because he felt she would be able to use her

sexuality to enlist the aid of famous criminal Hannibal the Cannibal Lecter (Anthony Hopkins), in prison for killing and eating parts of his victims. Clarice is successful in getting Lecter to open up and give her clues about possible motivations of the at-large killer. At the same time, she is harrassed in various ways, by Lecter's probings into her own background and by the flying white liquids that whiz through the air when she passes other prisoners' cells. She sustains these assaults with admirable aplomb, and the film ends with Clarice tracking down the killer. This would be a happy ending were it not for the fact that Lecter escapes and contacts her by phone at her graduation ceremony, the suggestion being that he will let her live so that she can attempt to track him down, as he kills other victims. Rather than enhance the possibility of women being strong and independent, this peculiar symbiotic relationship between woman detective and killer actually undermines the notion. Foster's character is an exception rather than a representative model. Moreover, her success in this case, as well as her continued survival, depend on the mercy of a homicidal maniac, a situation that is hardly a model for female independence.[31]

Other films, less likely to reach mainstream audiences, look at independent women in more ordinary occupations, and they deal with their emotional ups and downs with greater realism than the sensationalized treatments of action/adventure films. *Men Don't Leave* (1990), *Gas, Food and Lodging* (1992) (winning best independent film of 1992 at L.A. Film Critics Award), *Little Man Tate* (1992), and *Leaving Normal* (1992) gave greater leeway in portraying women in masculine roles not as covertly dependent or as reversed caricatures of men, but as melanges of various traits on a continuum, from "femme" to "butch," "sissy" to "macho," and every shade of polysemous expression in between. Films that feature lone women or single mothers are a relative rarity, even though the situation is common in daily life. In Paul Brickman's *Men Don't Leave*, Jessica Lange plays a widow who has a light uncommitted relationship with an avant-garde musician. She also suffers, quite understandably, from depression after her husband's death, and the romance in her life is not presented as the usual panacea for women's troubles. Allison Anders' *Gas, Food and Lodging* features Brooke Adams as a single mother, trying to act as a positive role model for two daughters, neither of whom accepts her status. Jodie Foster directs and stars in *Little Man Tate*, a story dealing with the challenge of raising a gifted child.[32] Edward Zwick's *Leaving Normal* is a more complex and less sensational depiction than *Thelma and Louise* of two women's adventures on the road. No one is raped, and the film ends not in car chases and death but in the formation of a family of sorts. The two women teach each other about love and commitment, and this road picture, unlike many of its predecessors, concludes with a message of the value of staying put, not in marriage but in female-female friendship.

Percy Adlon's *Bagdad Cafe* (1988) shows an unconventional female couple forming, as the burly Marianne Sagebrecht turns for work and shelter to CCH Pounder, a tough black woman with sole responsibility for her family. Sagebrecht, whose screen presence in the opening scenes is reminiscent of Shirley Stoler's Nazi guard Lina Wertmuller's *Seven Beauties* (1976), busily sets to work cleaning up the chaos and filth of the Bagdad Cafe, while Pounder's character begrudgingly accepts her ministrations. Although their relationship develops after they walk out on their men, the presence of Jack Palance, playing a retired Hollywood set decorator who is obsessed with painting increasingly exposed versions of Marianne's ample body, provides an ongoing open possibility for kinky friendliness between the sexes. Adlon reinforces the theme of crossing nationality, race, and traditional gender roles in the form of the film as well, with canted framing in the opening scenes and a mid-film switch from a fairly serious tone to almost a musical comedy genre. The film itself even provided the basis for a short-lived television series that presented itself as semiserious, semicomic, a nongenre too difficult to pigeonhole for commercial success. Other films worthy of notice for providing positive models of female bonding include *Strangers in Good Company* (Canada, 1992; older women banding together) and *Housekeeping* (1987), based on Marilynne Robinson's book about two orphaned teenage girls bonding with a free-spirit aunt. Although few of these situations would seem like role reversals in real life, the film image of women getting along together, without males, is such a relative rarity in American movies that it looks like an imitation of male behavior when it occurs.

Lesbian themes are likely to receive watered-down treatment in works like *Fried Green Tomatoes,* or the toned-down lesbianism of *Silkwood* or *The Color Purple.* When women are acknowledged lesbians, or even if they demonstrate too much attachment to another female, they are likely to be killers in mainstream films. Even when lesbians or single women are not portrayed as evil, as in most mainstream films, they often appear as a threat to traditional males in alternative films as well. For example, in Stephen Frears and Hanif Kureishi's *Sammy and Rosie Get Laid* (1987), the lesbian friends of Rosie act as a catalyst in ruining Rafi, a Pakistani ruler who hopes to retire to England and watch his son, Sammy, and Rosie settle down and have children. The politically savvy lesbians warn Rosie that she should check up on the torture and civil rights abuses Rafi was responsible for before the couple accepts any money from Rafi. One of the scenes that serves as the proverbial last straw involves Rafi coming home to discover his son and wife gone (each with their own separate love interests), and the two lesbians in bed together. He runs for his life, out into the street, as the two women throw objects and Pakistani epithets at him. These two women highlight the conflicts of the film, both political and sexual. In one scene, they describe a common problem of heterosexual relations, "You know, when the man can never keep from coming too soon and the woman never comes." While these women could be seen as troublemakers for the men of the film, they also represent the moral center of film, in their commitment to personal and political honesty.

This pattern of the lesbian (or woman who may have these tendencies) creating domestic discord appears in popular movies, but in mainstream work, she is evil and/or psychotic, hardly the ethical barometer of *Sammy and Rosie Get Laid. Basic Instinct, Black Widow, Single White Female,* and *Fatal Attraction,* all feature women who kill. Considering the number of psychotic killer lesbians of recent films, one would imagine this was a national crime wave of epidemic proportions. (In fact, the number of women who actually commit violent crimes is estimated at about 5 percent of the total committed in the United States.) Positive images of lesbian relationships or even of nonsexual female friendships are a rarity, but a tradition of such films does exist. One of the most obvious reasons for the lack of such images is the fact that men have dominated the movie industry, as well as other modes of mass communication. Even with the supposed gains for women, between 1980 and 1985, of 986 directing assignments for major studies, only thirty-two went to women.[33] Many of the alternative, nonmasculine visions focusing on women and their relationships have come from nonmainstream cinema, but even there, the work of women directors has reflected the inevitable intertextuality of film images, often including allusions to mainstream works and performers. Lina Wertmuller's *Sotto, Sotto* (1984) has characters referring to Hitchcock's *Notorious* (1946). Ulriche Ottinger's *The Mirror-Image of Dorian Gray in the Yellow Press* (1984) calls on Wilde's literary figure and the film image of Dr. Mabuse. Laurie Anderson's *Home of the Brave* (1986) features Anderson wearing a white silk suit and tie, moving like Charlie Chaplin, and then switching to a silver glitter dress that could have been designed for Dorothy Lamour. Probably the most rigorous attempt to avoid replicating popular male-directed films is Yvonne's Rainer's *The Man Who Envied Women* (1985), but by making this sort of "anti" film, the director of course calls up the conventions it tries to avoid. Even the title brings to mind François Truffaut's and Blake Edwards' *The Man Who Loved Women* (1977/1983). Rainer's work does not include the face of the woman from whose point of view the audience sees the film, and one hears a voiceover narration that recalls Max Ophuls' *Letter from an Unknown Woman* (1948). The usual demands of narrative plot are not followed, and the narrator concludes, "I can't live without men, but I can live without a man."[34]

The alteration of female experiences of romance and heterosexual encounters occurs strikingly in other alternative films. Maria Luisa Bemberg's *Camila* (Argentina, 1984) frames the narrative in conventional romantic terms, and yet it features a romance between an aristocratic female lead and a priest, a topic that violates the expectations of viewers, particularly in its country of origin. Lizzie Borden's *Working Girls* (1987) presents the day-to-day life of a group of prostitutes, including a lesbian who does not reveal to her live-in lover where she goes to work. The matter-of-factness of these women offers a striking contrast to a film like Garry Marshall's Cinderella-as-a-Prostitute movie, *Pretty*

Woman (1990) or even to the gritty, sensationalized Ken Russell exposé, *Whore* (1991) (based on David Hines' British play). The ground was broken for positive images of lesbians in John Sayles' *Lianna* (1983), the sympathetically told story of a married woman who has a lesbian affair with her professor, divorces her husband, and then loses the woman she fell in love with. She is comforted in the end by a female friend who had earlier rejected her because of her lesbian affair. Another work that showed effectively the nuances of female friendship is French filmmaker Diane Kurys' *Entre Nous* (1983, based on experiences of Kurys' mother), a wistful tale of two women who leave their husbands and run off to Paris together to seek liberation. Donna Dietch's *Desert Hearts* tells the story about a woman coming to Reno for a divorce and finding love with another woman. Helen Shaver plays a some-what prissy easterner, complete with proper woman's suit and hat, while Patricia Charbonneau is the free-spirited western woman, looking fetching in cut-off shorts and cowboy boots. While one might level criticisms of sentimentality or soft-core pornography at this film, it nevertheless provides a refreshing alternative to the usual portrayals of tragedy and sickness associ-ated with earlier treatments of lesbian characters. *American Film*'s description captures the film's light-hearted, saucy quality:

> The love that dared not speak its name finds a bold new voice in this promising debut feature by documentary filmmaker Donna Deitch. East (uptight Columbia University professor, played by Helen Shaver) meets West (full-time free spirit, played by Patri-cia Charbonneau) and the stage is set for a woman's liberation. And all of this on a dude ranch in 1959 Nevada![35]

These treatments contrast with that of a similar situation in Lina Wertmuller's *Sotto, Sotto,* a film that unsuccessfully attempts to satirize lesbian desire and male violence against women, both touchy subjects for comedic treatment. In the end, her work returns its female characters to a conventional position, going back to the men who once abused them.

Even in films about relatively independent real-life women, the happy ending of heterosexual domesticity often undermines the image of a woman as capable of happiness on her own. For example in Jarvis Lapine's *Impromptu* (1991), the film opens with

George Sand (played with a neurotic edge by Judy Davis) saying "I used to think I'd die of suffocation when I was married. Now it's my freedom that's killing me." The sartorial cues are appropriately masculine, with Davis in authentic frock coat, vest, and stock throughout most of the film, occasionally appearing in red Chinese-style mandarin robe and pantaloons for variety or a dress for seduction. Sand's writing seems peripheral throughout the film, with the main conflict being her obsessive battle to seduce Frederick Chopin. The friendship between Sand and Franz Schubert's mistress, played with pouty male malevolence by Bernadette Peters, provides numerous scenes of betrayal, but it also gives Peters these lines: "You won't get him with a dress. He's not a man; he's a woman. Win him as a man wins a woman. A woman will always bend towards a strong man."

In the end, Sand does get her man, by a combination of supposedly masculine aggressiveness and stereotypically "feminine" sniveling declarations that she is his "slave." The final blow to her character is delivered by the juxtaposition of Peters' character screaming, "She'll kill him," as Sand and Chopin ride off in a carriage. Sand's insistence on keeping the window open, against the wishes of the hen-pecked Chopin, leaves the audience with the message that indeed this statement may be true. The implicit dual message of the benefits for women and the disadvantages for men of marriage (or similar arrangements) goes against research over the last forty years about the relative benefits of marriage for males and females. As Ronald C. Kessler, of the University of Michigan's Institute for Social Research, notes: "All this business about how hard it is to be a single woman doesn't make much sense when you look at what's really going on. It's single men who have the worst of it. When men marry, their mental health massively increases."[36] What is truly remarkable about *Impromptu* is how effectively the film slanders both traditional womanly wiles, as represented by Peters' character, and the masculine female character (albeit peppered with hints of female guile and submissiveness), as represented by images of George Sand.

International films are more likely to present truly unconventional women in a variety of roles. For example, Zhang Zimou's Chinese production, *Red Sorghum* (1987) contrasts with Hollywood-style commercial products in its portrayal of the past, politics, gender, and economic class. Nine (Gong Li), prepared to marry into her class, violates matrimonial custom by rejecting planned marriage, and then transgresses class and gender boundaries by falling for a porter named Yu (Jiang Wen), by beating him when he comes in drunk, and finally by becoming boss of the sorghum plantation until the Japanese invade. *American Film* magazine describes another open-ended film, *Vagabond* (1986), "Agnes Varda's detailed-but-detached painterly view of an unknowable heroine wandering through the frozen French landscape defies the audience's urge to identify by asking questions rather than providing answers: unsettling, but definitely provocative."[37] Like Parillaud's character of *La Femme Nikita,* one of the Varda heroine's most unsettling features is that this "vagabond" has a number of unattractive qualities more often associated with males than with females. She eats crudely, she seems to have no particular drive to improve her appearance, she gets obnoxiously drunk and throws up in public, and she does not make much effort to be ingratiating to others. In a male character, her behavior might seem unappealing, but in a female character, it is amazingly shocking and repellent for many viewers. What is even more disturbing is that neither the other characters in the film nor the audience outside the film feels any particular regret when she dies a violent death. If she were an outright villain, viewers would be comfortable with this response, but since she is merely unappealing, the viewer is forced to examine what constitutes a worthy human life as opposed to an unworthy one.

A similarly disorienting work that reverses the usual movie roles for men and women is *Variety* (1985), an avant-garde film that calls into question the notion of spectatorship and objectification of human beings. In *Variety,* a female ticket seller watches a male patron at a pornography theater in what *American Film* calls a "feminist subversion of male voyeurism . . . marred by uneven narrative, but nevertheless an absorbing avantgarde study of the human tendency to objectify the other sex."[38] Not all European films succeed in avoiding the objectification of women, as reviewers point out, in discussing Robert van Ackerman's *Woman in Flames* (1982): "Although we assume a greater sophistication, i.e., decadence, the Europeans can really run afoul of their Marxist agenda. Robert van Ackerman's *Woman in Flames* has a dominatrix defeated by her boyfriend, also a prostitute, in an ending disastrously more literal than 'hearts afire,' when he discovers she doesn't just do her job—she is her job."

While females participating in conventionally male activities (such as domination or aggression) occur regularly in popular and art films, actual female impersonation of males is relatively rare, and it appears in settings where women's freedom would ordinarily be limited. For example, in *Ishtar* (1987), Isabelle Adjani disguises herself as a male in a burnoose to move freely in the north African countryside, revealing her breast to Dustin Hoffman's character to prove herself female. She uses this exposure, an obviously effective recruiting device, to entice his character to side with her. In a later scene with Warren Beatty, he wrestles her to the ground, after she kisses him. He thinks she is a boy, but he notices the softness of her body—especially her breasts. This kiss is one of those confusing moments for characters and viewers, a concept that Chris Saayer explores in discussing "the paradoxical bivalent kiss," in which "narrative point of view and nonnarrative spectacle collaborate through their contradictions to create a double-entendre of simultaneous homosexual and heterosexual readings, identifications and experiences in film viewers—viewers trapped within narrative and nonnarrative interpretations with a bi-sexed figure." [39] In *Ishtar*, Beatty tells a him/her that she shouldn't go around kissing men, a piece of dialogue that carries a certain irony, coming from Warren Beatty, who has just kissed a supposed man. In a similar way, the casting against type of Hoffman as ladies' man and Beatty as a loser with women calls on viewers to contradict information given by characters within the film with their own real-life information about actors and actresses. Despite the play given to gender, genre, and type, Elaine May's handling of Adjani's character is far from revolutionary, and the character eventually ends up in female dress, triumphing only with masculine assistance.

Bertolucci's *Sheltering Sky*, based on the Paul Bowles' book, while it comes from the entirely different category of nonmainstream art film, treats the disguise and sexuality of Debra Winger's androgynously named character, Kit, in a somewhat similar fashion. After the death of her husband, Kit wanders the desert, wearing a burnoose as the prisoner of a sheik, becoming a virtual sex slave, imprisoned in a tower. The abrupt ending, showing her two years later entering the bar of the opening scene, dressed once again as a woman, leaves viewers to question the meaning of her odyssey into the desert. The open-endedness of the film challenges Hollywood conventions, but the image of woman in this film breaks new ground only in the extent to which it explores female victimization.

Nine 1/2 Weeks (1986) is another example of the female object of the gaze becoming more sexually appealing by donning male clothing. The forced cross-dressing in *9 1/2 Weeks* is a means of humiliating her, and it supposedly increases her sexual appeal. The film's ultimate example of debasement is when Mickey Rourke's character forces Basinger's character to have a lesbian menage à trois. This supposed humiliation is the last straw that convinces her to leave. While her departure might be viewed as a statement of liberation, the film so obviously exploits everything else that leads up to this point that it can hardly be viewed as a feminist tract.

Reversals on the sado-masochistic relationship, with the woman in control, are hardly ever as one-sided. In Ken Russell's *Crimes of Passion* (1984), the scene in which the prostitute China Blue sodomizes the police officer with his own night stick was deleted from theater versions, reappearing only in certain restored video versions. Even as early as 1972, Bernardo Bertolucci's anal intercourse scene in *Last Tango in Paris,* with Marlon Brando's character performing forcible anal intercourse on Maria Scheider, remained uncensored in most theater versions. One could attribute this to a change in the times, and yet a more recent example of anal rape, performed by a male on both male and female victims, occurs uncensored in Edward James Olmos' *American Me* (1992). One must go all the way back to *Myra Breckenridge* (1970) to discover a relatively popular film featuring a female as the rapist, and, after all, Myra was not really a true biological female. While fears of NC-17 ratings power the censorship of such scenes, the filmmakers also believe, probably with good reason, that the public is much readier to view males rather than females in the role of anal rapist.

American film's determination to avoid female domination goes beyond scenes of anal rape, usually by making the villainous woman suffer and die. Uli Edel's *Body of Evidence,* while casting Madonna as a dominatrix, nevertheless counters her image of the androgynous female, as established in earlier work. Her hair is pulled back in a subdued forties-style roll, and her makeup is subtly drawn, with light mascara and lipstick, traditional female attire, and rather old-fashioned underwear. Madonna's character, Rebecca (a name that carries shades of the 1940's Hitchcock film featuring another evil woman), is literally and figuratively on top through much of the film. The infamous scenes in which Rebecca ties up her lawyer and drips hot wax on his chest and genitals or when she forces him to have sex lying on a car hood covered with broken glass demonstrate her character's dominance. However, when she interferes with his domestic tranquillity by calling his wife, the lawyer takes retribution by handcuffing her and raping her, an action that Rebecca perversely enjoys. Like a host of would-be dominant women, Rebecca loses in the end, and after being shot and crashing through the window, a high-angle shot captures a closeup of her dead body, floating face-up in the water outside her houseboat. The defense and prosecuting attorneys leave, if not hand in hand physically, at least psychologically bound to each other in defeating this female embodiment of evil. The shot of Madonna submerged in water is a visual homage to *Fatal Attraction*'s penultimate shot of Glen Close's face submerged in a blood-filled tub—not just stabbed, but shot as well by a wife defending her domestic territory, the kind of overdetermination that reveals the anxiety surrounding her figure. Dominatrix characters, lesbians (either in or out of the closet), and single career women are usually portrayed as cold or self-righteous, at best; at their worst, such women are psychotically obsessed with heterosexuals (male or female), determined to have them as lovers and/or destroy them. These villainous women are almost always destroyed in mainstream movies, increasingly by the traditional wives whose positions they allegedly threaten.

When unconventional women do not receive retribution within the plot of the story, the film itself may experience difficulties with censors. For example, one need only look at the case of David Burton Morris' *Patti Rocks* (1988), an echo of Victoria Wozniak's *Loose Ends* (1975). Susan Faludi remarks on the difficulties this picture had, in contrast to other more conventional works:

> *Patti Rocks* received its share of good reviews from the critics, but generated nothing but animosity and rejection from the guardians of Hollywood. [Producer Gwen] Field was turned away by one studio after another and always for the same reason; they told her the film's message was "irresponsible" because it showed a single woman indulging in sex with whomever she pleased. (This same moral concern never surfaced over *Three Men and a Baby,* where the randy bachelors randomly scatter their seed.) The industry's rating board tried to assign the film an X rating, even though it featured no violence and no more sex than the average R movie. Field recalls that the board members disapproved not of the visual display but "the language"—the same offense that brought down Mae West a half century earlier. As Field observes, "It was very ironic that we had received an X rating for a film that is against what pornography depicts—the degradation of women." It took three formal appeals before the board members finally approved an R rating. Ultimately *Patti Rocks*'s chances for commercial success were slim anyway; as an independently produced film with out-of-the-mainstream content; it would get distributed to only a handful of theaters.[40]

The film ends with the pregnant Patti rejecting the male offer of financial assistance, and refusing to accept the label of "whore" or "slut," not a shocking decision in real life, but a strikingly rare conclusion in films.

A more ambiguous portrait of unconventional choices and sexual obsession appears in Jean-Jacques Annaud's *The Lover* (1992), based on the Marguerite Duras tale. This film presents an eccentric heroine in the figure of a sixteen-year-old girl (Jane March), whose "man's hat" no woman, native or European, would wear. In a voiceover narration by Jeanne Moreau, the heroine explains how the hat reifies the girl's distinctiveness and deliberate defiance, becoming both symbol and self-professed source of her bravery. Her story begins with her miserable family life, which is dominated by the presence of her opium addict brother, who is the favorite of her widowed mother, a white school teacher in French Indochina. On her way back to school in Saigon after a vacation, the girl decides to accept a ride from and eventually have an affair with a Chinese man. Their torrid affair is hardly conventional, for she considers herself above a Chinese man, and he, as the son of a wealthy man, would never consider any marriage other than the wealthy match his father has arranged for him. The dynamics of power in this relationship are skewed, with his wealth, class, and age counterbalanced by her race, racism, and the callow insensitivity of her youth. It is only after she is forced to leave Indochina, on a boat with her family, that she realizes she loved him. Years later the narrator speaks of hearing from him by telephone in Paris, where he tells her that he always loved her and loves her still. The scenes of watching and being watched do not follow the typical models of having woman be the only object of the gaze. Instead, the camera often rests rather lovingly on the exquisitely muscled buttocks of David Leung. The authenticity of the film's graphic sex scenes has created some controversy over whether they were enactments or the real thing.

David Lynch's kinky work *Blue Velvet* also stirred up controversy over its sexual dynamics, with much of the discussion focusing on objectification of women and portrayal of men as perverted beasts. Beginning with the opening shots, Lynch makes viewers uncomfortably aware of body parts, from symbolic connections between a garden hose and a vein in the neck of a stroke victim to Kyle MacLachlan's character, Jeffrey Beaumont, finding a severed ear in the grass. Lynch plays with looking and being looked at throughout this film, and his characters are keenly aware of the power of the gaze. When Isabella Rosellini's character, Dorothy Valens, catches Jeffrey peeping at her through a closet door, she holds an enormous butcher knife to him, makes him kneel, and tells him not to look at her, and then has steamy sex with the petrified young man. The phrase "Don't fucking look at me," is echoed by Frank, played with maniacal intensity by Dennis Hopper, when he insists that she look away as he comes to orgasm, holding the blue velvet of her dressing gown stuffed in his mouth. The kinky sadomasochism becomes even more explicit when Dorothy asks Jeff if he has been a bad boy, if he would like to do bad things, like hurt her. When she taunts him into hitting her, a roaring sound bridges from an extreme closeup of her open mouth to a shot of a flame, symbolizing the intensity of his own desire. Later, Frank tells him they are alike, during a scene at Ben's "Pussy Heaven," a name whose irony is understood by the presence of overweight prostitutes who look like someone's grandmother in a tightfitting dress. Ben (Dean Stockwell) is implacable in the face of Frank's bursts of fury, and Frank admires his appearance—glazed eyes, eyeliner, red lipstick, earring, long cigarette holder, and heavy pancake makeup complementing a ruffled tuxedo and brocade jacket—calling him "one suave fuck."

After a shocking jump cut, in which Frank screams, "Let's fuck," and then literally disappears through the magic of editing, they leave Ben's "party." Frank takes Jeffrey, Dorothy, and his buddies on a joy ride. When they stop, Frank tries to get Dorothy to show him her breasts, whimpering "Give, mommy, baby wants to kiss them," a reenactment of primal Oedipal scenes that Jeffrey cannot tolerate. When Jeffrey defends "Mommy," and tells Frank to leave her alone, Frank hits him, takes him out of the car, puts lipstick on him, kisses him, wipes the lipstick off Jeffrey's lips with the fetishized blue velvet, asks him to feel his muscles, and finally beats him up.[41] All of this action is accompanied by the car radio playing Roy Orbison singing, "In dreams I walk with you," a reference to the kind of dream work accomplished through Frank's ritualized actions. Lynch's symbols never work out neatly, but the film explores powerfully the connection between victimization and sexuality, suggesting a complex, subtle process which melds victim and torturer and male and female identities. The evocative power of Lynch's images pulls at and threatens most viewers, leaving no one's fantasies untainted by something that may seem perverse to them. Images of female domination slip into masochism, with a woman being struck in the face and enjoying it; scenes of masculine dominance over "Mommy" end in male-male kissing and hints at homosexual sadism. Only viewers comfortable with exploring the dark side of human sexuality can actually enjoy viewing *Blue Velvet,* but it provides any viewer with a rich body of material for analysis because of the byzantine complexity of its many gender role reversals.

Fantasy Fathers and Absent Mothers

In a reversal of a real-life nine-to-one ratio of single mothers to single fathers, films follow about a five-to-one frequency ratio of single fathers to single mothers. The Hollywood dream factory has created popular hit versions of this fantasy of the loving father and the dead or absent mother in *Star Trek III: The Search for Spock* (1989), *Field of Dreams* (1989), *Indiana Jones and the Last Crusade* (1989), and *Dad* (1989). Susan Faludi comments on the disappearance of women's roles in 1990: "When Screen Actors Guild conducted a count of female roles in 1990, the organization discovered that women's numbers had sharply dropped in the last two years. Men, the guild reported, were now receiving more than twice as many roles as women."[42] While this signals bad news for women actors of the nineties (just as Dustin Hoffman's appropriation of a woman's role in *Tootsie* did in the 80s), another view of motherly fathers is that their emergence may signal or even encourage a shift in men's roles. The very existence of such a plethora of supportive film fathers represents a fantasy need created by something actually missing in society, but one must not underestimate the power of media to produce real-life imitators of reel-life behavior. On the other hand, the salutary effects of imitating such sterling models may be counterbalanced by people's tendency to opt for comforting fantasies at the expense of real solutions. How much easier and more convenient it is to believe that fathers are as warm and loving as they are in movies than to wrestle with real issues of support payments or child care. And how much more pleasant it is for men to laugh at the humorous scatalogical scenes of *Three Men and a Baby* than to change the dirty diapers of their own babies.

Fantasy families in mainstream films have their underground correlative, as documented in Jennie Livingston's *Paris Is Burning* (1992). This film, which won best documentary at the Sundance Festival in 1992, details the gay world of Harlem, as represented by the ball entitled Paris Is Burning. Even this name, an overturning of the popular World War II novel and film, *Is Paris Burning?* reveals the participants' awareness of mirror images and reversals discussed throughout the film. Livingston's documentary style is to let the subjects speak for and describe themselves, without ever letting the viewer see the camera operator or filmmaker.[43]

Paris Is Burning offers a fascinating example of form imitating its subject. What appears at first to be a "real" slice of gay life in New York, with little manipulation by the filmmaker, is actually an artfully crafted construct, just as the "real" appearance of the transvestite is a carefully and self-consciously engineered product. The film poses a series of dialectics, beginning with a contrast between youth and age and gay and straight. Statements from a thirteen-year-old and his fifteen-year-old companion, just entering the gay subculture, counterpoint an interview with one of the older members of the group, Pepper Labeija, "legendary mother, not founder" of the House of Labeija, one of the many homosexual "families" in the community. With shots of Harlem's gay nightlife, Pepper's voiceover describes how a black gay has three strikes against him—he's black, he's male in a culture that offers a harder life for males, and he's gay in a society that does not accept homosexuality. Pepper then goes on to explain how there are so many "little kids" who need his protection and mothering, which he has offered during his two-decade reign. The two young gay boys, who speak at the opening and closing and at key moments throughout the film, offer touching descriptions of how gay elders provide the love and acceptance young homosexuals do not receive from their own biological parents, if they even see them.

One of the central social functions of the self-constructed families is preparation for walking in shows called "balls," competitions which serve as initiation into houses, along with establishing and maintaining the reputation of individuals and houses. In order to explain this complex network of actions and relationships, Livingston provides the only readily apparent intrusion of structure for the film, a series of vocabulary words, flashed on screen as various members of the subculture describe the meaning of each term: Legends, Houses, Voguing, Reading, Shade, Realness, etc.

Two of the most important institutions represented here are the houses and legends. Houses are constructed families of gay black men, led by the "mother," a legend who has established her power by successfully competing and winning an impersonation at one of the many balls.[44] Balls provide opportunities for these men to have their fifteen minutes of fame, impersonating anything from a famous movie star to an army general. Legendary Mother Dorian Corey describes the shift from the old days (preseventies), when transvestite gays tried to look like "Las Vegas showgirls, "coming down" to the seventies, when people tried to look like movie stars, to the early seventies, when people tried to look like models such as Christie Brinkley, and finally to the countless "categories" of late eighties balls: school girl, military man, executive realness, bangee girl, opulence, etc.[45] Corey explains this move toward a more egalitarian approach, without apparent resentment (or perhaps with resentment cloaked in the almost invisible irony termed as "shade") as "something for everyone," an example of "nature—I'm such a nature-lover— the young ones bucking to move older ones out of the way." Both older and younger participants are aware of the history and standing of their houses, and they provide insightful analyses of the social functions of their activities. Corey observes that the balls are "addictive," but that it is a "good high" that "won't hurt you. If everybody went to balls and did less drugs it'd be a fun world." A number of men and boys who do not have starring roles in balls or the important roles of "mother," "father" or "first daughter" of a house speak of the joy and sense of belonging provided by houses and their participation in balls: "You feel 100% right," with balls offering the same sense of bonding as football or basketball for heterosexual males. Several speakers mention parallels with black heterosexual street gangs. These gangs represent immature femaleless families of a sort, and while they may serve similar functions as the gay houses, behavior and social codes differ drastically. Instead of fighting for one's brothers as a means of establishing group solidarity, members of gay houses support fellow members by such traditionally "feminine" modes as ironing clothes or providing pep talks before competitions. It is difficult to say what category has more influence on the flavor of activities of the houses—the primacy of the "female" role or the respect for "legends," who by their very nature represent age and wisdom. The youths who talk about the importance of family clearly understand the function of families in a way that many middle-class people have never even considered. While the emphasis on competition and wealth in this subculture may be typical of mainstream American society, the understanding of the actual nature of social structure appears to be much more sophisticated than that of participants in the larger social structure.

The microcategories of the ball reflect delineations within their own neighborhoods as well as the larger society. Judgment of walkers is based on the ability to capture what they call "realness," a concept that immediately calls into question its own validity. The fact that participants act these roles makes them aware of the play-acting quality of what they call the "real world." To quote Roger Ebert, "What I saw was a successful attempt by the outsiders to dramatize how success and status in the world often depends on props you can buy or steal almost anywhere—assuming you have the style to know how to use them."[46] In a similar vein, Dorian Corey observes that most black homosexuals would not be executives because of the lack of "education, opportunity, or social standing in life." Corey adds that the few blacks who make it into such positions "are usually straight," and that winning a prize for "executive realness" offers comfort to people by demonstrating "I could be one because I can look like it." While an initial middle-class response to such a statement may be that there is more to being an executive than merely looking like one, it is also apparent that there is more involved in looking like an executive than one would suppose, particularly if one comes from a culture that does not train members for such roles. Individuals able to capture the nuances of psychology, behavior, costume, and performance inherent in creating this image might very well have potential for executive leadership, given other circumstances and training.

While *Paris Is Burning* demonstrates ball-walkers' awareness of the constructedness of such images, this knowledge does not make their imitations parodies or satires. They are quite serious about the importance of "passing" as a particular category, since failure to pass may have life-and-death consequences. As one man notes, if female impersonators can walk out of a ball into daylight and "still get home with all their clothes on and no blood running off their bodies," they are "real fem queens." Another observes, "When you're a man or woman you can do anything you want. When you're gay you monitor everything you say and do." As one gay male points out, blacks in general offer "the greatest example of behavior modification in the history of humanity," with the ability to adopt protective coloration or behavior, a kind of new self, as a key to survival. This self-consciousness heightens attention to detail, and it calls attention to the notion of categories. At balls, the emcee announces categories, often explaining the meaning of these terms at the same time. For example, the schoolboy or schoolgirl contestant imitates the person "going to school or college—*not* here," the emcee emphasizes. In the "luscious body" category, it's "not enough to look good; you have to be sexy," he explains, as the camera captures transsexuals, preop or postop, with developed breasts bared and groins covered by tiny G-strings. Persons competing under the category of opulence "own everything," explains the emcee.

Linguistic and semiological sophistication shines through in various speakers' analysis of what it means to "read." A read appears to partake of the complex African American (and African) tradition of dozens, what Henry Louis Gates analyzes as "signifying" in *The Signifying Monkey*.[47] One speaker explains how "difference," in the form of invidious distinction, is essential to a good read, giving the example of how two members of the same group—two queens—would not be "reading" if they called each other queens, since that would be "just a fact." Pointing out a sartorial faux pas such as polyester fabric, or lapses in "realness" or taste such as overly heavy makeup, on the other hand, would constitute a "read." This keen understanding of clothing as text and language as weapon is further developed in the concept of "shade," which is cited by one speaker as the origin of "voguing." Another speaker argues that this dance form is actually a way of streetfighting or expressing hostility without weapons. The term first entered popular parlance when Madonna featured it in her video, "Vogue." Shade is described as a read that takes place before the other person understands or realizes what has happened—an expression of hostility or put-down so subtle and ironic that it is only in retrospect, perhaps in reconstructing the text of conversation, that the listener will fully understand its meaning. The sophistication of this community goes beyond attention to visual, sartorial cues into gestural and linguistic realms.

At times during the film, one might imagine one has dropped into the filming of a carnivalized Modern Language Association meeting on Postmodern Deconstruction. Various speakers' explanations of terms demonstrate how thoroughly a group outside mainstream society can understand the cultural concepts that constitute the in-group's "reality." While the film appears at first to be a fairly random collection of comments, the themes of family, power, position, and status appear throughout. The "stars" of the film appear interwoven around these themes, sometimes contrasting with each other but more often than not rephrasing and reinforcing the vision of others (both transvestite and "real" women) who fulfill their functions. The "mothers" of houses describe with wisdom, self-assurance, and matter-of-factness the challenges of their position as caretaker, role model, and substitute mother. Young and delicate transvestites speak with longing about becoming "real" women, pursuing modeling careers, becoming wealthy, and marrying and adopting children of their own. *Paris Is Burning* presents a number of dialectics, juxtaposing the New York of 1987 with 1989 toward the end of the film. An excerpt from a news broadcast explains to its mainstream audience that voguing is "attitude, style, institutionalized showing off," as the reporter covers a vogue ball that brought in over $350,000 for the New York Foundation for AIDS. Clips of the modeling and dance work of Willie Ninja demonstrate the fulfillment of his dream, images of success that sharply contrast with descriptions of the death of the delicate young blond transvestite, Venus Xtravaganza. Livingston counterpoints earlier scenes of a carefree and laughing Venus with Angie Xtravaganza's explanation that Venus, "the main daughter of my house," was reckless, going with many men. Angie states matter-of-factly that she mourns yet accepts her death as "part of being transsexual in New York City." Venus was unable to fulfill her dream: "All I ever wanted was to be a spoiled rich white girl."

It is ironic and fitting that it took a rich white girl, the self-constructed blond icon, Madonna, to bring voguing to national attention. Comparing *Paris Is Burning* with Alex Keshishian's documentary film about Madonna, *Truth or Dare,* reveals how much Madonna owes to the gay world documented in Livingston's film. The fascination with her image and her work marks a popular culture and high culture nexus, with the Madonna Phenomenon receiving attention from tabloids and Lacanian critics, some seeing her as simply exploiting the sensationalism of sex in order to make money and others seeing her as a self-reflexive and self-conscious manipulator of images, determined to challenge people's notions of propriety, morality, sexuality, and identity itself. Some critics argue that Madonna manages to operate independently, as the ultimate manipulator, first shocking and disappointing her fans' expectations by advertising for Pepsi, and then even able to outwit this major company by creating an ad they would not be able to use, because of its allusions to a subsequent controversial music video featuring miscegenation and rape. If one looked only at Madonna's videos, Susan Seidelman's *Desperately Seeking Susan, Truth or Dare,* or her book *Sex* (with an initial $25 million gross for Warner Books),[48] one might well come to the conclusion that she exemplifies woman as boss.

> In some sense, then, Madonna represents the post-feminist heroine in that she combines unabashed seductiveness with a gutsy kind of independence. She is neither particularly male nor female identified, and seems mainly to be out for herself. This post-feminism is part of a larger postmodernist phenomenon which her video also embodies in its blurring of hitherto sacrosanct boundaries and polarities of the various kinds discussed. The usual bi-polar categories—male/female, high art/pop art, film/television, fiction/reality, private/public, interior/exterior—no longer apply to many rock videos, including "Material Girl."[49]

The self-conscious constructedness of Madonna's image brings up the question of what substance resides behind her image. As Warren Beatty asks ironically at one point in the film, "Why do anything if it's not on camera?"

While she is clearly the boss as she is presented in *Truth or Dare,* in the films directed and controlled by males, her image as a dominating, gender-bending woman does not triumph or even survive by the end of the film. In *Dick Tracy* (1990), Warren Beatty's use of Madonna as male villain fits with her androgynous, amazon persona, and it does what cartoon-style films do—punish evildoers. The climax of the film reveals what has been hidden behind the dark mask and black male clothing of the husky-voiced villain, none other than Madonna's pale feminine face. Before she dies, she softens a bit, asking Dick Tracy if they might not have had a romance if things had been different, but the audience knows her type never stands a chance against the "true femininity" of Tess Truehart. Uli Ebel's *Body of Evidence* (1993) uses Madonna's screen persona as a kinky, dominant female, one whose sexual appetite and "ambition" are so great that she "fornicates a man to death" for his money. In some audiences, the single action that caused the most audience response of shock and disgust was not the hot wax or the broken glass. Rather, it was Madonna's insertion of her finger in her own mouth and suggested (out of the frame) masturbation. Marjorie Garber observes similar outrage at Madonna's appropriation of the symbolic penis at a music video awards show:

> But the moment that scandalized critics was a moment of sheer quotation from Michael Jackson, when Madonna danced toward the audience and squeezed her crotch. Now, in video and in live dance performance Michael Jackson often makes this kind of theatrical gesture, and no one ever complains—quite to the contrary. But Madonna, squeezing what she hadn't got (or *had* she?), emblematized the Lacanian triad of having, being, and seeming. Squeezing the crotch of her pants became for her, onstage, the moment of the claim to empowered transvestism, to seem rather than merely to have to be—not (and this distinction is important) just a claim to empowered womanhood.[50]

Actually, Jackson's crotch-grabbing disturbed audiences as well, so much so that the initial version of his "Black and White" music video was edited to eliminate most of the offensive actions. But Garber is right in pointing to the fact that men may perform certain suggestive or threatening actions with much less recrimination than females would receive after similar behavior.

The Transformed, Deformed Body: The Beast Within and Without

In contrast to the physical perfection of a body like Madonna's, other characters find themselves trapped in hideous, aging, or disintegrating bodies, a situation that seems to serve as a metaphor for loss of self-determination. People are unwillingly thrust into bodies, or evicted from their proper bodies by circumstances beyond their control. Body-swapping is another version of the constructed fantasy self, appearing in a variety of films: *Like Father, Like Son* (1987), *Vice Versa* (1987), *18 Again* (1988), *Big* (1988), *Switch* (1991), and *Prelude to a Kiss* (1992). Angels, time travel, and returning from the afterlife often feed similar desires for immortality or invulnerability, and they stave off anxieties about deformation, death, or dismemberment, most notably in *Star Man* (1984), *Almost an Angel* (1990), *Jacob's Ladder* (1990), *Edward Scissorhands* (1990), and *Forever Young* (1992). In literature, Anne Rice's *Tale of the Body Thief,* a work ripe for film adaptation, tells the tale of someone who knows how to force himself into another's body, much as it occurs in *Prelude to a Kiss* (1992). Like the various versions of *Beauty and the Beast* (1991), the fantasy of entering another body or somehow transforming from one physical shape to another may appeal more to female and homosexual viewers than to male viewers. One explanation for this tendency is that some women and homosexuals want to have a different body, for a variety of reasons, including increase in status, power, or beauty. Some of the men who want to have a female body construct one through hormones and surgery (and deconstruct their own male bodies). The reverse phenomenon is relatively rare, in part because of the difficulty of creating a penis surgically. While male bodybuilders want to alter their bodies, many films of shape shifting do not appeal to their fantasies, because these films often feature the taming of the beast by a woman, a situation men may experience as unpleasant, since it hints at castration or rendering impotent or less powerful. Women may also be more keenly aware of alterations in body shape because they develop breasts during puberty or large abdomens during pregnancy, physical changes that are usually impossible to disguise. *Death Becomes Her* (1992) parodies the narcissism and masochistic willingness some women have to alter their bodies at any cost. The role women play in most beauty/beast or body change stories often empowers them as key actors in the drama, who use traditionally "female" traits to rescue the hero. In *Elephant Man* (1980), *Mask* (1985), and *The Fly* (1958, 1986), and *The Company of Wolves* (1985), strong women see through hideous exteriors to appreciate the male character's inner attributes, and these motherly figures often nurture and protect the male protagonist from a cruel and uncaring society.

Children also find tales of transformation appealing, partly because they are in the midst of such dramatic transformations themselves, but, more important, because such films call on characters to see through the unimpressive exterior to the powerful inner being. The commercially successful Walt Disney version of *Beauty and the Beast* (1991) emphasizes an untraditional female role, with Belle being a voracious reader, longing for adventures beyond her "provincial" home. Alan Menken's music (with lyrics written by Howard Ashman, who later died of AIDS), satirizes the stereotypical masculinity of Gaston— "No one's neck is incredibly thick as Gaston's"—"I'm especially good at expectorating," and "Every square inch of his body is covered with hair"—by focusing on male gender cues and making them seem ridiculous. Belle's independence and strength of purpose combine with an intuitive sense of the goodness (or badness) of the inner self, which does not rely on physical strength.[51]

Peter Pan offers another sort of transformation or refusal to undergo the transformation from liminal preadolescence to adult sexuality. When Robin Williams played the part of Peter Pan in *Hook,* the fascination of gender confusion that is central to the stage and previously filmed versions of J. M. Barrie's tale were diminished. The most important boundary being violated in

Hook was that of age rather than gender, with the aging Williams pretending to be boy and parent at the same time and the sex symbol Julia Roberts trying to pass as an innocent little fairy. Marjorie Garber explains the appeal of the original cross-dressing versions, both staged and filmed:

> What the middle-class children of America—and of Britain— saw, when they looked at Peter Pan, was, then, an adult woman, who was also a little boy. . . . And what I want to suggest here is that this split vision is precisely what entranced, what held spellbound: the power of transvestism in and as the cultural Imaginary. . . . The therapeutic work that *Peter Pan* is doing is not only to rewrite a relationship with boys (or children) as a story about men and women, Peter as a kind of closet Rosalind, but also to do the opposite: to recast (literally) the problematic perception of "masculinity" and dominance in women as a contest between a boyish woman hero and a feminized male villain, both of whom are crossover figures, repeatedly twinned in the text: Peter Pan and Captain Hook, a dream and a nightmare of transvestism.[52]

Despite the fact that Peter Pan toys with the nightmare version of transvestism and its consequence, the open-ended quality of the story of Peter Pan is comforting to adults and children alike. It leaves the boy forever in that liminal state as a kind of fantasy escape hatch, and it takes home lost children to the protection of boundaries in case the fantasy world becomes too threatening. Children's ability to believe in both worlds is part of their power, as this tale would have it.

This validation of intuition may empower such unlikely heroic figures as women, children, or even insects. *Charlotte's Web* (1973) features a girl who stands up to her father's authority and rescues an intelligent runt pig she names Wilbur. The role of rescuer is then taken over by Charlotte, a spider who is able to save Wilbur from the usual fate of beasts—being eaten—by being a good writer. Once Charlotte dies, Wilbur takes on the feminine role of carrying Charlotte's eggs home and caring for future generations of her offspring. In this case, the ability and willingness of two females (one human and one arachnid) to love the beast actually transforms him, if not into a handsome prince, at least into a good mother. Tales of transformation from beast to human almost invariably empower female characters and feminize male characters. The females must take an active role in discovering, protecting, and rescuing the beast. In turn, the beast must become more "civilized," pay more attention to grooming, attempt to have good table manners, etc., all behaviors associated with traditional feminine roles.

Kisses, words, and loving gazes from the female carry magical properties, a fantasy that derives its power from the comfort of the infant and maternal bond. When this situation is reversed and the rescuer is masculine, the magic does not work as well. In *Prelude to a Kiss,* Alec Baldwin's character sees and kisses the true spirit of Meg Ryan's character inside the body of Sydney Walker. This scene received such a negative response from preview audiences that they almost cut it in the final version. The studio decided to leave in this questionable scene, perhaps because it was pivotal to the entire plot, but when has that ever been a consideration that stopped a profit-conscious producer from relegating a clip to the cutting room floor? In fact, *Premiere* magazine states that "in response to negative reaction from some preview audiences, it did test a version of this movie that omitted the climactic, non-sexual, only-the-entire-plot-revolves-around-this-moment kiss between Alec Baldwin and Sydney Walker."[53]

A Freudian interpretation of the Beauty and the Beast motif would have it that the female's desire actually summons the beast, and that her acceptance tames and transforms both her own sexual desire as well as the masculine violent expression of desire, an interpretation that fits Neil Jordan's *The Company of Wolves,* John Woods and Ted Hughes' television dramatization, and the CBS television series based on the tale.[54] The ability to see through external physical form appears in various films, but it is usually women who are most ready to do this. In *Ghost* (1990), the empathic and psychic ability of Whoopie Goldberg's character enables Demi Moore's character to join again physically with Patrick Swayze's luscious body. But a strange visual pun occurs, as we witness Goldberg's body speaking to Moore, then Swayze's body dancing with her, then the interruption of the fantasy humorously jolted back to the shot of a black woman embracing a white woman. As Marjorie Garber points out, the violation of standard gender boundaries often intersects with the abrogation of class and race, a pattern clearly demonstrated in this film, which was the top-grossing movie of 1990.[55]

Another popular fantasy along similar lines is embodied, as it were, in *The Bodyguard* (1992), a film that features Whitney Houston commanding the body of Kevin Costner. Critics account for its appeal in various ways, including the concept of viewer identification:

> When Kevin Costner and Whitney Houston's romantic thriller, *The Bodyguard,* overcame withering reviews to become a smash ($95.8 million and still going) everybody seemed surprised. They still didn't get it, but *The Bodyguard* was one of the few holiday movies with genuine appeal to women. "Young black girls identify with Whitney," explains Warner distribution chief Barry Reardon. "Fortunately, women bring men to movies." Ditto Mel Gibson's *Forever Young* (currently at $39.9 million).[56]

Relationships counselor Kevin Grold argues that "we all have a need to become protected—in fact, the protection fantasy is a powerful aphrodisiac."[57] An adequate explanation of the appeal of such films is probably a bit more complex, involving much more mental body exchange than these writers imagine. First of all, the vast majority of viewers of *The Bodyguard* are white women, whose own bodies probably resemble Kevin Costner's at least as much as they do Whitney Houston's. Therefore, one of the primary cross-identifications for most female viewers is racial. Another sort of crossover occurs where male bodies intervene between a vulnerable female and the threat of a hostile world, death, or old age. In a sense, the woman in *Bodyguard* "wears" this male body between herself and the outside world, much as Sigourney Weaver wears a mechanical body, the "loading unit," to protect, extend, and enlarge her own body in her battle with the alien mother in *Aliens.* The notion of having a strong male body at one's command provides the thrill of a kind of psychic transvestism, in which the inner woman commands and the outer male body obeys.

Reversals of inner and outer essence provide a recurrent theme for a number of women filmmakers. The notion of one's true nature appears in most Susan Seidelman films—first in 1982, with Susan Berman in *Smithereens* becoming a female wrestler. In

Desperately Seeking Susan (1985), Seidelman again explores the notion of identity, and it becomes apparent through a number of devices that the central character, Roberta, played with goofy charm by Roseanna Arquette, has no sense of her own identity. Her husband Gary (Mark Blum) has not the faintest idea of the interior being of his wife. Madonna, who literally got down on her knees before producers (Sarah Pillsbury and Midge Sanford) and begged for the part of Susan, brings an interesting set of gender twists to the character. As she helps Gary look for his missing wife, in a scene featuring Madonna/Susan in boxer shorts, a man's tee shirt and shirt, and a garter belt and hose, Susan explains to him that Roberta's diary depicts such an empty life that it had to be a cover—no one's real life could be that boring. Susan takes charge and marches out to track down Roberta, with Gary meekly following her aggressive lead. After a series of mistaken identities and near misses, Roberta and Susan end up capturing a thief, making the cover of the local paper for their heroism, and finding true love.

Seidelman's *Making Mr. Right* (1987) plays on the notion that one would have to build a man from scratch to get a good one, in a film about Frankie Stone's (Ann Magnuson) creation of a human personality for the android Ulysses, built by Dr. Jeff Peters (both of whom are played by John Malkovich). Having the woman be the creator of this personality reverses gender on the usual Pygmalion/Galatea. Even though Dr. Peters is the original maker of the android, Ulysses, the significantly named Frankie Stone is the one who carves this raw material into a feminist male who can love and be loved by Frankie. This is yet another configuration of the beauty/beast/machine question of just what constitutes worthwhile humanity.

In a more sinister version of the beast, the vampire film often reveals a similar empowering and at times masculinizing of women. Pat Dowell, critic for *In These Times,* argues that the early literary form of *Dracula* offered a combined nightmare and "dream come true. . . . And if the vampire's religious blasphemies had lost some of the power to thrill and chill by 1897, what Dracula did to and for women—commanding them to unholy pleasures outside the control of their husbands and fathers—struck to the heart of Stoker's Victorian readers, who had

already encountered the first wave of militant English feminists."[58] In Francis Ford Coppola's *Bram Stoker's Dracula,* the
happy ending has a female lunging a stake into the male vampire's heart and surviving, an improvement on the fate of females
over the literary source and most of the subsequent film versions,
in which females had to be sacrificed at the end. Even in John
Badham's version of *Dracula* (1979), viewers witness a sexually
ambiguous scene when Dracula (Frank Langella) cuts his breast
and has Mina (Kate Nelligan) drink from it, in a sensuous
reversal/version of nursing. Not everyone agrees that Coppola's
Dracula acknowledges the power of women. Dowell argues that
it is a step backward:

> While other vampire movies over the years have increasingly
> taken up that question with more ambitious and more powerful
> heroines, Coppola's Lucy and Mina are merely horny. He must
> not have noticed that even among the Undead it's the year of the
> woman. *Buffy the Vampire Slayer* (1992) revealed what power
> lurks within the teenage airhead. *Innocent Blood* found a Ms.
> Dracula capable of cleaning up the town like any John Wayne.
> (Of course, she has to be a monster to do it.)[59]

One might also argue that James V. Hart's screenplay of *Bram
Stoker's Dracula,* while generally faithful to its source, adds elements to Stoker's tale that make it more mysogynist. Hart has
his original Vlad turn against the church after it refuses to bury
his wife (a victim of suicide) in consecrated ground, and he is
then cursed with vampirism. As in the tales of Pandora's box
and Adam and Eve, it is originally the fault of woman that evil
is loosed upon the world.

Sometimes It's Hard to Be a Woman: The Crying Game

The nature of man and woman and the concept of "nature"
itself are explored in Neil Jordan's *The Crying Game,* one of the
most successful and shocking reversal films of the nineties. The
film attained commercial and artistic success, with Miramax's
production grossing over 6.3 million in forty-seven days, on
only 130 screens. It also made more than one hundred critics'

top ten lists for films of 1992, more than any other film of the year. At first, Miramax was unable to afford the usual free copies of preview videos for members of the academy, one of the usual necessities for having a chance at an Academy Award.[60] It nevertheless won an Academy Award for best original screenplay. *The Crying Game* is structured to overturn expectations and call into question such categories as "nature," "gender," and "love." What appears at the opening to be a romantic situation between a black Britisher named Jody (Forest Whitaker) and an Irish woman named Jude (Miranda Richardson) quickly turns into a surprise kidnapping. Fergus (Stephen Rea), a character whose worried, boyish face belies his role as ruthless terrorist, begins by guarding Jody, an apparently vicious prisoner.[61] At the first opportunity, Jody lunges at Jude and seems for a moment to be the black British answer to Hannibal Lecter. Within the space of a few more minutes' dialogue, however, Fergus and Jody have established a rapport, even though Fergus still stands guard over his hooded, bound prisoner. Jody tells Fergus the story of a scorpion who promises a frog not to sting him if he gives him a ride across the river. When the scorpion stings the frog and thereby kills them both, the scorpion explains that he couldn't help himself, because stinging was in his nature. Fergus asks him, "What's that supposed to mean?" a key question repeated throughout the film. Contradicting his earlier statement that it was against the nature of Fergus' people to let him go, Jody tells him it is Fergus' nature to be kind-hearted. Fergus replies that he shouldn't be so sure, a warning not just to Jody but to the audience as well. When Jody convinces Fergus to take off the hood so that he can breathe, the unveiling confirms what Jody had suspected—that it is in Fergus' nature to be soft-hearted, regardless of the "nature" of his people.

Different types of hiddenness and unveiling serve as motif throughout the film: from Jody's early comment about the novelty of pissing behind a curtain while holding a woman's hand, to the parallel comic scene of Fergus taking out and reinserting Jody's penis to urinate while holding Jody's handcuffed hands, to the climactic unveiling of Dil's nude body before Fergus' astonished gaze. The relatively sparse dialogue takes on added richness as the various "natures" of characters are revealed, reconsidered, and reconstructed, with almost every line demonstrating multiple layers of meaning and ambiguity. Jody explains to Fergus that Jude wasn't his type, whereas his beautiful "girl," Dil, is, as Fergus puts it, "Anybody's type." Once Jody has died and Fergus seeks out Dil, the audience learns just how unusual Dil is. After proceeding from a haircut at the salon where Dil works, to an engineered meeting in a bar, to receiving fallatio from Dil, Fergus finally learns the physical "nature" of Dil, as the camera tilts down from Dil's lovely sculpted face to reveal the flat chest and genitalia of a man. Fergus promptly loses his evening's drinks, an uncomfortably humorous moment that is heightened by the surprise of most audience members. Viewers who have read about the film or who are particularly attuned to such cues of gender as large hand size or cleft chin shape may realize that Dil is no ordinary girl, but Jaye Davidson's voice, appearance, and manner provide a striking example of "passing." As the audience learns of Dil's biological gender, viewers find themselves mentally reconstructing dialogue and rereading such lines as "not my type" or "anyone's type" or "women are trouble." As Marjorie Garber argues in her analysis of cross-dressing, the territory of the transvestite marks "not just a category crisis of male and female, but the crisis of category itself."[62] Neil Jordan's cleverly crafted film exemplifies this principle in various ways, with such binary categories as political idealist/terrorist, black/white, heterosexual/homosexual, romantic love/platonic friendship, comedy/tragedy, and even the category of category itself being stretched and revealed as layers of possible meaning rather than fixed boundaries. The constant transgression of boundaries in *The Crying Game* points to a destabilization of the concept of nature—a paradigm shift that educates the audience to tolerate ambiguity and thereby lose their reliance on stereotypes.

The structure of *The Crying Game* reinforces this education by encouraging a recursive, cyclical understanding of plot and character. Rather than the usual formula of repeated cross-cutting and creation of suspense through delay of the final wished-for outcome, Jordan ends scenes with surprising revelations. In the next scene, the camera follows the same characters to a new location, just as events have carried them to a new mental location. This egalitarian refusal to privilege or create omniscience in the camera's point of view signals the director's desire not to manipulate audience response. In a well-constructed Hollywood-style film, reaction shots of characters within the film yet outside the action frequently cue the viewer's sympathetic (or comic or shocked, etc.) response. Cal, the bartender, serves this function visually, with a number of shots of his back and the two characters, or a side angle of one character and a deep-focus straight-on shot of the other principal, while Cal busies himself in the background, repeating what one or the other has said. This set-up provides more than comic relief; it highlights the significance of the sparse communication in the film.

Repeated phrases, stories, and shots emphasize the significance of framing, perspective, and point of view to meaning itself. Shots occur through hanging layers of gauze, wooden frames, windows, and the frames around the bar or stage, thus pointing to the artificiality of our perceptions about boundaries and presentation of "real" identity. The kind of cross-cutting common in Hollywood adventure movies often sets up binary oppositions of good guy/bad buy, pursuer/pursued, male/female, plot/subplot, in a story that dictates what viewers want to see and how they will feel about it. Consequently, there is little question of how an audience will respond to the revealing of true gender in *Tootsie* or *Victor/Victoria*. The audience's inside knowledge of the secret encourages the laughter of superiority, a response reinforced by the series of shocked reactions of "naive" characters within the film. The only time Jordan allows *The Crying Game* this kind of manipulation of viewer response through omniscient perspective is in the penultimate scenes, cross-cutting between shots of Jude preparing to meet Fergus, while Fergus finds himself tied up, literally, unable to rendezvous for the assassination. The denouement leads full circle to a camera crane up and away (repeating in reverse the crane down and into the opening scene) from a shot of Dil visiting Fergus in prison, while the prisoner Fergus tells Dil the scorpion/frog story he had once heard from his prisoner. On the soundtrack, Lyle Lovett sings, "Sometimes it's hard to be a woman," a line that has multiple resonances as we consider the case of Jude, who has died, and Dil, who finds it hard to be a woman in more ways than one.

While *The Crying Game* makes an affirmative statement for androgyny, homosexuality, transvestism, and self-sacrifice, neither Irish Republican Army nor women's groups will be using this as a propaganda film any time soon. The only biological woman in the film, Jude, played with strong-jawed nastiness by Richardson, comes across with all the worst characteristics of two opposing types of women. She is willing to prostitute herself (within limits) for the men in charge of IRA operations, and, in this respect, she fulfills the stereotype of the passive woman. At the same time, she exhibits the aggressiveness and cold-heartedness of the woman warrior when it comes to killing people. When she wants sex with her old boyfriend, Fergus, she plants her hand on his crotch and says, "Let's fuck," in the style of a supposedly liberated woman, and yet she exhibits all of the jealousy and possessiveness of a traditional wife when she learns that Fergus has another "girl." The "girl," Dil, is, for the most part, a fantasy of womanhood—devoted, suffering, and ready to stand by her man.

Setting all this aside (or perhaps only realizing it in retrospect), the viewer is drawn inexorably into a truly touching romance that clouds the usual boundaries of gender, sexuality, and political ethics. *The Crying Game* requires viewers to reexamine how they have constructed the meaning of familiar phrases and concepts, within the film and, probably, outside the film as well. If *Tootsie* demonstrates the constructedness of gender, from its very opening shots of makeup and false moustaches to the leg-shaving and eyebrow plucking of later transvestite scenes, *The Crying Game* represents the deconstruction of gender, with its repetition of scenes that offer surprising revelations and repeated images and phrases within new contexts. Categories such as nationality, race, and personal identity shift and crumble, with shifts and evenhanded jabs for everyone. As Julie Wheelwright asks, "Would you rather find out your boyfriend is an IRA killer or your girlfriend is a man?"[63] Fergus questions Jody's nationality, which turns out to be mixed. Fergus becomes Jimmy (Pat to his new boss), his Irish background becomes

Scottish, the tantalizingly mulatta Dil "becomes" a man, the androgynously named Jody becomes less of a man, at least in the conventional sense. Even the eponymous "Crying Game" theme song comes in different versions, sung successively by Kate Robbins (as Dil lip synchs), Dave Berry, and, most appropriately in the closing credits, by Boy George and the Pet Shop Boys.[64] Lyle Lovett's male rendition of Tammy Wynette's "Stand By Your Man" takes on even more layers of irony in the final scene, when a woman who's not a woman visits a man who's not "her man" doing a prison sentence for a crime he didn't commit. The list goes on, with the most important ambiguity being the way an audience is to respond to this bittersweet, neither comic nor tragic nonending. In the tradition of *Some Like It Hot,* this open vehicle offers no predictions for the future of the odd couple but an acceptance of alternative ways of being.

Old Stereotypes and New Queer Cinema

Serious considerations of sexual responsibility (portraying characters who may risk contracting AIDS) and financial considerations of losing offended market subgroups (as serious as life or death to producers) began to power decisions about how to depict women, homosexuals, lesbians, and ethnic groups. Susan Lehman, of *Premiere* magazine, notes:

> Making money with very un-PC lesbian-bashing got uneasy Hollywood insiders worrying about how much is too much. Words like "responsibility" became part of the industry lexicon for the first time in many a year—so much so that Basic [*Basic Instinct*] writer Joe Eszterhas claimed he had his consciousness raised by the controversy and wrote a script sympathetic to gays, while Jonathan Demme, auteur of last year's gay-is-weird movie, *The Silence of the Lambs,* embarked on Hollywood's first AIDS feature.[65]

Despite this alleged consciousness raising, a host of films present apparently unprotected sex (both gay and straight) and gay or lesbian characters as negative caricatures, usually emphasizing features of dress or mannerism to identify them as "aberrant." Sandra Bernhard's sadomasochistic nurse in *Track 29* (1988) offers one example. *Mannequin* (1987) and *Mannequin Two: On the Move* (1991) presented Meshach Taylor's flamboyant gay designer, one of the most offensive stereotypes in recent years; *Mascara* (U.S.-Netherlands-France, 1989) features a transvestite death; *Law of Desire* (Spain, 1987) features a homosexual film director who is out of control; *Miller's Crossing* has a homosexual gang leader; *Less Than Zero* and *Last Exit to Brooklyn* feature the abuse of homosexuals, showing gangs smearing lipstick on them to humiliate them; Gary Busey appears in a drag scene in *Under Siege,* not as a specifically homosexual character, but in female disguise as he uses a machine gun to kill. Masculine activities also continued to be the subject for masculine voyeurism and specularization in such female wrestling pictures as *Smithereens* (1983), *All the Marbles* (1981), and *Thunder and Mud* (1992).

Other films, often produced or written by gays, featured a variety of stronger images. Openly gay characters appear in *Edward II* (1992) and *Poison* (1991), *Salome's Last Dance* (1988), Ken Russell's treatment of the life of Oscar Wilde, complete with a campy drag scene; *Torch Song Trilogy* (1988) and *Too Outrageous* (1987) (a sequel to the cult favorite *Outrageous*) both present sympathetic, by turns touching and bitingly humorous portraits of gay drag queens. The follow-up films *La Cage aux folles II* and *III* also provide basically positive (if somewhat stereotyped), lighthearted images of the drag queen. *Wonderland* (Great Britain, 1988) is a homosexual *Some Like It Hot,* featuring two gay youths in London who witness a crime and have to run for their lives. *Matinee* (1986) is a Mexican experimental film in which gay gangsters disguise themselves as priests and are subsequently shot down during the assault on the basilica of Guadalupe. Jorge, the central character, loses his father in a truck hijacking, then gets involved in stopping the gangsters' plot to rob the basilica. Finally, Jorge heads home, where he is welcomed as a hero, and Aaron hops a train to an open-ended future. The gangster and religious connection linked with homosexuality calls to mind *Trouble in Mind* (1985), notable for Divine (who usually acts in campy women's parts) in a straight role as a gang leader, with no references to his ordinary transvestite role.

Mainstream films usually handle comedy less successfully than *Outrageous* or *La Cage aux folles* do. For example, in James Burrows' *Partners* (1982), gay and straight cops pretend to be a couple to solve a murder case in Los Angeles, a situation that has limited potential, almost none of which is fulfilled. Ryan O'Neal and John Hurt's play on the predictable stereotypes, in an occasionally amusing but more often offensive parody of *Cruising*. The screenplay was written by Francis Veber, who also did *La Cage aux folles,* with much more wit. Another odd duo appears in *Too Much Sun* (1991), with a son and daughter— lesbian and gay—trying to produce an heir in order to get their inheritance, as stipulated in their father's will. Great Britain, with its more lighthearted tradition of transvestism, produced a number of good-humored productions. *Nuns on the Run* (1990) once again creates the well-worn combination of transvestism and crime, putting crooks in the nunnery to escape capture. Bob Hoskin's black comic touch in *Raggedy Rawny* (1990/1988) deftly presents a deserter who hides disguised as a woman. *Shadey* (1985) is an obscure comedy about a man named Shadey (Antony Sher) who can read minds and then project thoughts as film images. He wants to save up the money he makes performing to have a sex change operation. Some of these films may have been designed to become cult films, but none of them have the necessary combination of wit, edge, or campiness.

A number of other serious films tell the story of gradual acceptance of gay or effeminate characters by the straight world, with the revelations of the homosexual characters creating trans- formations in the heterosexual world around them. In the made for television movie *Consenting Adults* (1985) (based on Laura Z. Hobson's novel), a son tells parents he is homosexual and even- tually gains their acceptance. Marco Risi presents Michele Pla- cido as a teacher in a reform school for boys, in *Forever Mary* (1991). The teacher manages to teach the boys to accept a transvestite prostitute who has been placed in the school. *The Time of Harvey Milk* (1984), an account of real-life gays earning public recognition, is a moving documentary about Harvey Milk (the first gay supervisor elected in San Francisco), Mayor George Moscone, and Dan White, who killed Milk and Moscone. Di- rected by Robert Epstein and narrated by Harvey Fierstein, this gripping film won an Academy Award for Best Documentary of 1984. In a reversal of the usual pattern of straights discovering hidden homosexual tendencies in others or themselves, *A Different Story* (1978) portrays a gay and a lesbian who are thrown together, eventually fall in love, marry, and have a baby—a dual conversion fantasy. *Frankie and Johnny* (1992) shows Frankie's (Michelle Pfeiffer) gay neighbor acting as a friend to the heroine, commenting that he needs to borrow her clothes, helping her get ready for her dates, with his character integrated into the plot in an unobtrusive, sympathetic way. The homosexual friend in *Single White Female* offers another sympathetic sidekick for a heroine. Unfortunately he meets the sharp end of a stiletto high heel when he attempts to rescue his friend from her psychotic female roommate. Jaime Humberto Hermosillo's *Doña Herlinda and Her Son* (Mexico, 1986) is the "first totally out-of-the-closet movie from south of the border."[66] It is self-reflexive, in that its main character is a man from a provincial town who accepts a part as a homosexual in a pornographic film. The mother helps to shelter her son and his homosexual love from scandal, and eventually the household expands to five people: herself, her son, his wife, their child, and the male lover of her son. In this film, according to Elliott Stein, "stereotypes are subverted and hypocrisy becomes a moral choice."[67]

William Hurt's portrayal of a homosexual in *Kiss of the Spider Woman* (1985), one of the most widely publicized films featuring a gay character, is problematic. Elliott Stein comments, "Puig would not have awarded any Oscars to the film version of his novel *Kiss of the Spider Woman*."[68] Hurt won an Academy Award for his role, but his depiction serves to reinforce many stereotypes about homosexuals. Hurt takes some risks as he applies makeup, wraps his hair in a towel, simpers and bats his eyelashes in imitation of his favorite movie star (played by Sonia Braga). The two characters, Luis Molina and Valentin Arregui, the first a declared homosexual and the other a political prisoner, move from a conflict of opposites to an eventual reversal of roles. What begins as enmity eventually develops into affection, with Molina trying to woo Valentin, both to spy on him in exchange for his own early release and because he genuinely likes him. By the end of the film, they share an effective on-screen kiss and implied off-screen sex in a powerful scene, a turning point for the character of Molina, who decides to help Valentin contact his outside political allies. Molina and Valentin undergo an interesting exchange of personalities, with Molina becoming more masculine and Valentin softening, as they develop their relationship. Throughout the film, Babenco returns repeatedly to black and white scenes that capture Molina's "telling" of his movies. His favorite one is about a love affair between a beautiful woman and a handsome Nazi, thus highlighting the connection between art, sexuality, and politics.[69]

Dream Boys Revue (1987) also treats sex and bisexuality in a positive light. *Edward II* plays on the Shakespearean transvestite tradition, with campy, nineties metal costuming and references to gay bashing. *Torch Song Trilogy* (1988) features a gay drag queen and *Land and Blood* (France, 1987) shows the deepening relationship between a doctor and his bullfighter friends, along with their mutual acceptance of the two very different worlds they occupy. Other kinds of acceptance—of aging, separation, and dying—are the subjects of *We Think the World of You* (1988), in which an older homosexual gives love to a dog while his younger lover is in jail, and *To Forget Venice* (1979), featuring a homosexual couple reflecting on the process of growing older. *Polyester* and *Hairspray* (1988) feature the late Divine, one of the most famous and long-lived transvestites in film, acting in the part of a woman, in marginally mainstream films. The restored version of *Spartacus* (1991) includes reinsertion of the legendary oysters and snails scene, which had been censored from the 1960 version because of its symbolic reference to male and female anatomy and the suggestion of bisexuality. In this scene at the Roman baths, Laurence Olivier's Crassus asks a slave (Tony Curtis), "Do you prefer oyster or snails?" Tony Curtis replies that he prefers oysters, but Olivier says he prefers both.

Psychotic male transvestites continue to appear as standard figures of horror and suspense in such films as *The Silence of the Lambs* (1991), *Psycho II* (1983), *Psycho III* (1986), *Psycho IV: The Beginning* (1990), *Sonny Boy* (1987), and other features, from blockbusters to cult films. *Blue Velvet* hints at homosexuality and transvestite behavior, all as indicators of the depraved world lurking behind the blue skies, green lawns, and picket fences of small town Lumberton. The fetishization of the blue velvet, the various scenes of voyeurism, and the controversial depiction of women and sadomasochism are all designed to suggest decadence almost verging on the supernatural. A similar surreal quality appears in *The Silence of the Lambs*, with scenes that could only occur in nightmares and movies. The psychotic killer who wants to make a coat out of a woman's skin is embellished from a real-life case, but the exaggerated film portrayal sensationalizes the transvestite, making the fixation on women's body parts almost erotic. These mainstream films are not the only works to portray transvestite and/or homosexual characters as sick and twisted. In *Querelle* (1983), adapted from Jean Genet's novel, Rainer Werner Fassbinder (homosexual himself) offers surreal atmosphere in the drama of a psychotic homosexual sailor. His negative portrayal is not limited to gay characters, though. Karen Jaehne comments

> It's hard to find someone in a Fassbinder film who is not prostituted at some level of interpretation, so thorough was his perception of the social application of the tricks of the trade. His transvestite in *A Year of 13 Moons* [the story of a transexual] anticipated Bertrand Blier's *Menage* by ten years with its assumption: To become a woman is to be forced into prostitution.[70]

Another Country (Great Britain, 1984) presents the story of real-life spy and homosexual Guy Burgess. *Colonel Renl* (Hungary, with Germany-Austria, 1985) is another fiction film based on the real-life incident of a Jewish homosexual suicide. Another gay filmmaker who does not shy away from troubled or psychotic characters is Tom Kalin. As director of *Swoon* (1992), Kalin wished to reprise Alfred Hitchcock's *Rope* (1948) and Richard Fleischer's *Compulsion* (1959)—two versions of the true case of Nathan Leopold and Richard Loeb, two young homosexuals who kidnapped and killed a fourteen-year-old, Bobby Franks. According to Amy Taubin (commenting on Tom Kalin's 1992 *Swoon*), "this queer cinema has much more in common with the current crop of male violence films (Quentin Tarantino's *Reservoir Dogs* or Nick Gomez's *Laws of Gravity*, for example) than it does with any feminist cinema."[71] Some note that, with the greater violence, sensationalism, and misogynist messages of some gay male films, financial backing and publicity among homosexual and lesbian filmmakers still favors men.

While a number of critics bemoan the negative portrayals of women and gays, in the form of killer lesbians, psychotic heterosexually obsessed women, or gay killers, the self-named New Queer Cinema movement has diverse opinions on the "positive image" argument. Jonathan Demme was attacked for negative gay stereotyping in *The Silence of the Lambs* (1991) and Gus Van Sant's *My Own Private Idaho* "was attacked by some of the same critics for its lack of positive images of gay life."[72] Tom Kalin responds to these objections by observing, "We're in a sorry state if we can't afford to look at 'unwholesome' lesbian or gay people. . . . I think the solution is to make more images rather than less."[73] Clarke Taylor discusses how films have changed in their treatment of homosexual and lesbian characters: "The first wave [*Making Love* (1982), *Personal Best* (1982)] treated gays like Problems. The new wave [*My Beautiful Laundrette* (1985), *Prick Up Your Ears* (1987), *Waiting for the Moon* (1987)] treats them like people with problems. Is this progress, or just another way of closing the closet door?"[74] Hanif Kureishi's work (including *My Beautiful Laundrette, Prick Up Your Ears,* the screenplay for *Sammy and Rosie Get Laid,* and *London Is Killing Me*) all follow the doctrine of making homosexuality simply "an attribute of specific characters," regardless of whether the portrayals are positive or not.[75]

Offensive images are more likely to be accepted if they are created by homosexual directors than by heterosexuals. For example, a filmmaker at the Sundance festival called for "a campaign to demand that Oliver Stone not direct his announced biopic of Harvey Milk."[76] Eventually, Gus Van Sant took over as director, with Oliver Stone as co-producer. Apparently, Stone's depiction of Clay Shaw in drag at a private party in *JFK* put his work in a category with offensive stereotypes. Stone certainly makes a villain of Tommy Lee Jones' character, using his sexuality as a primary way to portray Clay Shaw's decadence and folly, with Joe Peschi, Jones, and Kevin Bacon in drag, S/M clothing, gold lamé, and painted skin. In the director's rerelease, other scenes were added that revealed how cuts were made in the original theater version to eliminate some of the worst cases of homophobia. Steve Daly, of *Entertainment Weekly* describes one such clip:

On his way back to Louisiana, Garrison is then set up by cops in an airport men's room and nearly arrested for soliciting sex. This unpleasant scene (based on unsubstantiated claims by Garrison) makes even more explicit the movie's knee-jerk, homophobic equation of gayness with crime, corruption, and sleaze. It's also wildly overplayed, like a fever dream. And finally, as Garrison arrives home to find his case against alleged conspirator Clay Shaw (Tommy Lee Jones) is in shambles, he announces to his staff and family that Bobby Kennedy will be shot because he wants to "stop th' wo-ah"—and that very night RFK is murdered.[77]

The inclusion of gay and lesbian characters has come to be a marketing device in itself, regardless of whether they represent positive or negative images. Amy Taubin points out that "gay-themed films have garnered the kind of attention that makes Hollywood want a slice of the action." Much of the attention came as a result of media focus on the AIDS epidemic, which crept into the consciousness of heterosexual America in the mid-eighties.

AIDS Alters the American Conversation About Sexual Orientation

I suppose there are two themes: there's sex and dying and between the two very little.[78]

A growing awareness of the AIDS epidemic forced mainstream culture to acknowledge openly the existence of homosexuals in the United States. Norman Rene's *Longtime Companion* follows one set of gay friends who learn of the AIDS epidemic in a relatively light-hearted way. Their growing awareness of the disease begins as a backdrop and eventually becomes the central focus of the film. The film has a number of touching moments, but it is leavened throughout by humor. For example, one character tells the story of being caught in his sister's wedding gown. Before the ceremony, he tried it on, fell down the stairs, and was discovered at the landing by guests and family. This is both an amusing anecdote and a rich comment on the multiple functions of ritual, costume, and convention. In putting on a wedding dress, the gay character is "putting on" the role of bride, both in the sense of imitation and mockery. Marjorie Garber comments, "It might indeed be argued that in a way all marriages, even heterosexual marriages, are 'mock marriages' in their dependence upon certain aspects of sartorial tradition and ceremony."[79] A funeral scene in *Longtime Companion* provides a similar sense of wistful melancholy and humor, as characters stand up, Quaker-style, and simply talk about things they remember about the person who died. The final segment, in which characters walk along the beach and begin to see all characters who died during the course of the film, is particularly effective (in contrast, I would argue, to the disorienting and sentimental use of a similar device in *Places in the Heart*).

In another AIDS-related work, the opening cross-dressing scene of *Peter's Friends* (1992) exemplifies the use of gender-bending clothing as a means of calling attention to central conflicts. The title, based on a character named "Peter," hints that the penis and its uses will figure in the progress of the film. In opening shots of a group of men and women in dinner jackets and top hats dancing and singing, the camera pulls back to long shots that show them from the waist down, in their petticoats, garter belts, and high heels. This mildly startling visual surprise prefigures the overall movement of the film, in its gradual revelation, first of Peter's homosexuality/bisexuality, and then of his reason for calling his friends together in a reunion—the fact that he has HIV positive. In yet another twist, the film ends not with melancholy, but with the group of friends singing together and laughing, a tribute to the notion of living for the moment rather than in fear of the future.

The AIDS epidemic created a new urgency in the filmmaking of a number of gay and lesbian artists, who no longer (if they ever did) advocate an "art for art's sake" approach to film. B. Ruby Rich observes that the 1992 film

> *R.S.V.P.* suggests that the tragedy and trauma of AIDS have led to a new kind of film and video practice, one which takes up the aesthetic strategies that directors have already learned and applies them to a greater need than art for its own sake. This time it's art for our sake, and it's powerful: no one can stay dry-eyed through this witty elegy.[80]

While such films as *Stories from the Quilt* and *Longtime Companion* offer touching testimony to the urgency and painful struggle of AIDS patients and their friends and families, they also include incidents of humor and touches of mundane domesticity, thus making them, as Kureishi recommends, simply stories about people who have problems, not about people who are problems. Another work that accomplishes this is *Parting Glances* (1986), directed by Bill Sherwood. This independent film tells the story of a man who struggles with the departure of a current lover and the gradual dying process of an ex-lover, in an understated, nonsensationalized way. Michael Lindsay-Hogg's *As Is* (1986), a television movie adapted from William Hoffman's stage play, recounts the decision of a photographer to stay with his lover— a newly published author—when he discovers he has AIDS. These films and others, in a spate of made-for-television movies, television programs, and fundraisers, were important conscious- ness-raisers, but they also led to overblown panic among seg- ments of the population. In an underground protest against popular attitudes, Todd Haynes' *Poison* features a trio of tales, one of which is called "Horror," the story of a contagious fiend called the "Leper Sex Killer." David Ansen comments, "Compli- cated camp, this section functions as a metaphor for AIDS—but it's also a commentary on the way in which AIDS has been sensationalized by the media."[81]

A growing acceptance of AIDS sufferers, and of gay and lesbian lifestyles in general, coincided with the increase in films on the topic. Filmmakers tried to respond to the issue by por- traying the tragic consequences of AIDS, with one of the most effective and well publicized being *Common Threads: Stories From the Quilt,* which won the 1989 Academy Award for best docu- mentary. This film's proceeds go to the NAMES Project Foun- dation, and it features interviews with survivors who loved and cared for some of the victims commemorated in the AIDS Me- morial Quilt. The film includes several homosexual cases, and it also shows the parents of a hemophiliac boy who died, the wife of a reformed intravenous drug user, and a lesbian woman who married and had a child with a homosexual Olympic athlete. It is one of the most moving testaments on film to nurturing, regardless of age, gender, race, or class. The stories of *Common Threads* undermine the stereotypes and misconceptions connected with AIDS, and all the people in this film, including the victims, epitomize the nongendered ideal of steadfast love.

Future Directions in Sex Role Reversals

While the eighties and nineties witnessed swings in the pendulum from liberation movements to conservative reactions, the general trend seemed to be toward greater tolerance for difference. If clothing styles may be interpreted as barometers of acceptance for alternative roles, the variety in hair and dress styles for males and females indicates a shift from earlier periods in which a standard "uniform," was de rigeur in most social circles. Athletes began wearing earrings and ponytails, women wore pants in any social situation with impunity, and casual wear for adults broke the age barrier by imitating the playful sports clothing of children. Bipolarity weakened in the political sphere, when the United States witnessed for the first time in over a century the possibility of a viable three-candidate race. In the world of scholarship, similar barrier violation occurred, with the rise in multidisciplinary and multicultural studies, and the lines between popular culture and high culture blurring and dissolving. Reversals in gender roles ceased to be reversals, per se, as males and females, homosexuals and heterosexuals, minorities and majorities all began to see themselves as partaking of a common human experience. In a sense, all human beings play the role of the transvestite, creating a persona for public view that may contradict or correspond to only a small portion of the inner being. We all put on a role—go out into the world in a kind of psychic drag—and for many of us, this public presentation actually contradicts our own sense of our inner selves. Grownups may look mature, in an effort to conceal the inner child, and children may look young and innocent, yet conceal desires, experiences, and needs that we assume are reserved for adults. Most films imitate and cement the gender and social categories established over many years of practice, and analysis of what these works represent helps us understand ourselves as a culture. The films that merit greater individual study are those works that present new versions of personal identity—possibilities that take us outside the limits created by our culture.

Susan Sarandon (left) and Geena Davis created controversy as a female buddy team who became outlaws in Ridley Scott's *Thelma and Louise* (1991). (Courtesy of MGM/United Artists)

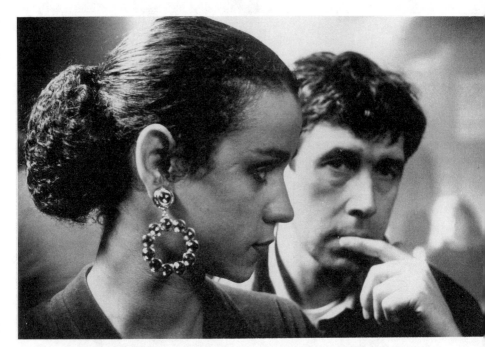

Stephen Rea (right) plays an offbeat hero, and Jaye Davidson (left) was nominated for best supporting actor for his role as Dil in *The Crying Game* (1992), which won Neil Jordan the Academy Award for best original screenplay. (Courtesy of Miramax Films)

In a reprise of Merle Oberon's performance in *A Song to Remember* (1945), Judy Davis (top left) plays cross-dressing novelist George Sand, in James Lapine's *Impromptu* (1992), with Julian Sands (middle, standing), Bernadette Peters (right, standing), Mandy Patinkin (seated, left), and Hugh Grant. (Courtesy of Jerry Ohlinger's Movie Store)

Leonard Nimoy's *Three Men and a Baby* (1988), one of the top-grossing films of the eighties, features (left to right) Steve Guttenberg, Tom Selleck, and Ted Danson as three bachelors who care for a baby abandoned by an ambitious actress. (Courtesy of Touchstone Pictures)

Kurt Russell plays a plainclothes policeman who puts on women's clothes in order to capture criminals in Andre Koncholovesky's *Tango and Cash* (1990). (Courtesy of Warner Brothers)

Isabelle Rossellini's character gets to be on top of Kyle MacLachlan's youthful hero in David Lynch's kinky *Blue Velvet* (1986). (Courtesy of Dino De Larentis Productions)

Sigourney Weaver's Ripley becomes increasingly masculinized in the *Alien* trilogy, with her most exaggerated version calling for a penal camp–style shorn head in David Fancher's *Alien 3* (1992). (Twentieth Century Fox)

Elaine May's *Ishtar* (1987) features a fetching revolutionary, played by Isabelle Adjani, whose bedouin disguise temporarily fools Dustin Hoffman and Warren Beatty. (Courtesy of Columbia Pictures)

Jennie Livingston uses real-life cross-dressers in her documentary, *Paris is Burning* (1991). (Courtesy of Miramax)

Debra Winger plays a prisoner, wearing traditional North African male attire, in BernardoBertolucci's *The Sheltering Sky* (1991), based on Paul Bowles' novel. (Courtesy of Warner Brothers)

James Ivory's *Maurice* (1987) brings to the screen E. M. Forster's novel about homosexuality, with James Wilby (left) and Hugh Grant playing leading roles. (Courtesy of Cinecom)

Imitating James Bond's classic pose, this publicity still of Grace Jones demonstrates the androgynous appeal she brings to every role she plays. (*A View to a Kill*, 1985, Courtesy of United Artists)

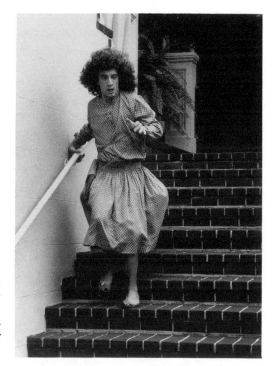

In a traditional plot device, Martin Short dons women's clothes in order to escape danger in Francis Veber's *Three Fugitives* (1989). (Courtesy of Touchstone Pictures)

Female impersonator Craig Russell imitates Mae West and Judy Garland in Richard Benner's *Too Outrageous* (1987), a sequel to the underground cult classic, *Outrageous.*

One of the most famous impersonators is the late Divine, pictured here in a still for John Water's first "mainstream" film, *Hairspray* (1988). (Courtesy of Newline Films)

Eric Idle assists his partner, Robbie Coltrane, in putting on a brassiere, in Jonathan Lynn's *Nuns on the Run* (1990), a slapstick chase movie. (Courtesy of Twentieth Century Fox)

In Zalman King's *Wild Orchids* (1990), Jacqueline Bisset (left) and Carrie Otis don moustaches (similar to Jamie Lee Curtis' look in *A Fish Called Wanda*) to achieve masculine impersonation. (Courtesy of Vision Films, Columbia)

Jamie Leigh Curtis uses a moustache and glasses to pass as a male in Charles Creighton's *A Fish Called Wanda* (1988). (Courtesy of MGM/United Artists)

In Mike Nichol's *Working Girl* (1988), Sigourney Weaver (right) plays the "boss from hell," providing a foil to Melanie Griffith's "feminine" version of the career woman. (Courtesy of Twentieth Century Fox)

Madonna, like her predecessors, Marlene Dietrich and Greta Garbo, uses masculine clothing to increase her power and sexuality. (Courtesy of Jerry Ohlinger's Movie Store)

Anne Parillaud plays a criminal-turned-assassin in Luc Besson's *La Femme Nikita* (1990), a much harsher version of the lead character than Bridget Fonda's portrayal in the American remake, John Badham's *Point of No Return* (1993).

Sylvester Stallone, in Peter Macdonald's *Rambo 3*, sports the long hair, smooth body, and sculptured look that is, ironically, often associated with female characters. (Courtesy of Carolco Productions)

Amy Madigan and Richard Pare play modern-day mercenaries in Walter Hill's *Streets of Fire* (1984). (Courtesy of MCA/Universal Pictures)

John Lithgow, playing a transsexual football player, Roberta Muldoon, embracing lead character Garp (Robin Williams) in George Roy Hill's 1982 adaptation of John Irving's *The World According to Garp*. (Courtesy of Warner Brothers)

Notes

Chapter 1. An Overview

1. According to the Indiana University Institute for Sex Research, the term "cross-dressing" applies to any case in which a male wears female clothing or vice versa, for whatever purposes. Transvestism usually refers to heterosexual, fetishistic use of clothing of the opposite sex. Dressing "in drag" is an expression usually appied to homosexuals who wear clothing of the opposite sex, but within the homosexual subculture being "in drag" may mean wearing any sort of uniform that suggests self-conscious role-playing. In this book I have occasionally used the terms interchangeably in order to highlight the intent, style, or flavor of an impersonation. For example, I may refer to Bob Hope being "in drag" (even though he presents himself as a heterosexual, non-fetishistic cross-dresser) in order to emphasize the "camp" appeal of his exaggerated, self-reflexive impersonation.

2. Esther Newton, *Mother Camp: Female Impersonators in America* (Chicago: University of Chicago Press, 1979), p. 51.

3. Newton, *Mother Camp*, p. 52.

4. Leslie Fiedler, Rutgers University 1965 lecture in Godfrey Hodgson, *America in Our Time* (New York: Doubleday, 1976), p. 312.

5. Raymond Durgnat, *Durgnat on Film* (London: Faber and Faber, 1976), p. 231.

6. Durgnat, *On Film*, p. 28.

7. Erving Goffman, *Gender Advertisements* (New York: Harper Colophon, 1976), p. 27.

8. Naomi Weisstein, "Why We Aren't Laughing Any More," *Ms.,* February 1963, p. 49.

9. Goffman, *Gender Advertisements*, p. 29.

10. Peter Farb, *Word Play* (New York: Knopf, 1974), p. 53.

11. Farb, *Word Play*. p. 56.

12. Goffman, *Gender Advertisements*. p. 49.

13. Harold Garfinkle, "Gender Identification," in Herant Katchadourian, ed., *Human Sexuality* (Berkeley: University of California Press, 1979), p. 9.

14. Anne Hollander, *Seeing Through Clothes* (New York: Viking Press, 1978), p. 344.

15. Joseph Degler, "The Changing Place of Women in America," in Robert Jay Lifton, ed., *The Woman in America* (Boston: Houghton Mifflin, 1965), p. 42.

16. Newton, *Mother Camp,* p. 56.

17. Chuck Waters, "Cult Initiates 'Virgins' in Bizarre Midnight Ritual," *Encore Arizona Daily,* September 19, 1979, p. 9.

8. "French Comedy Sets U.S. Record for Film in Other Language," *Wall Street Journal,* December 29, 1980, p. 3.

19. Norman Holland, *Journal of the Society of Cinematologists* (1963), 3:18.

20. Paul Rotha, *The Film Till Now* (London: Spring Books, 1967), p. 109.

21. "Let Them Eat Cake, But Not at Their Desks," *Newsweek,* February 9, 1981, p. 40.

22. Max Gluckman, *Essays on the Ritual of Social Relations* (Manchester: University of Manchester Press, 1962), pp. 22–28.

Chapter 2. Female Impersonators Before 1960

1. I am referring here to the schema established by Leo Braudy in *The World in a Frame* (Garden City, N.Y.: Anchor, Doubleday, 1977), a model that has much in common with Alan Friedman's analysis of open and closed narrative forms in *The Turn of the Novel: The Transition to Modern Fiction* (London: Oxford University Press, 1966).

2. Braudy, *The World in a Frame,* p. 51.

3. Judith Crist, *The Private Eye, the Cowboy and the Very Naked Girl* (Chicago: Holt, Rinehart, and Winston, 1967), pp. 96–97.

4. Parker Tyler, *Screening the Sexes* (New York: Holt, Rinehart and Winston, 1972).

5. Rev. of *Charley's Aunt* (1941), *Time,* August 18, 1941, p. 71.

6. Philip Hartung, Rev. of *Charley's Aunt* (1941), *Commonweal,* August 29, 1941, p. 448.

7. Robin Wood, "Return of the Repressed," *Film Comment* (July–August, 1978), 14:30.

8. Crist, *Private Eye,* p. 268.

9. Robert Sklar, *Movie-Made America* (New York: Random House, 1975), pp. 81–82.

10. Ibid., p. 175.

11. Ibid., p. 267.

12. *Variety,* September 13, 1949, p. 14.

13. Sklar, *Movie-Made America,* p. 287.

14. Joseph Degler, "The Changing Place of Women in America," in Robert Jay Lifton, ed., *The Woman in America* (Boston: Houghton Mifflin, 1965), p. 46.

15. Jay Wilson, "The Artful Bride," *Saturday Evening Post,* August 27, 1949, p. 20.

16. Advertisement in *Variety,* December 15, 1948, p. 17.

17. Robert M. Yoder, "What *Do* Women Want, Anyway?" *Saturday Evening Post*. September 17, 1949, p. 34.

18. Godfrey Hodgson, *America in Our Time* (New York: Doubleday, 1976), p. 37.

19. Ibid., p. 41.

20. Ibid., p. 41.

21. Ibid., p. 42.

22. Degler, "Changing Place," p. 25.

23. Joseph Goulden, *The Best Years: 1945–1950* (New York: Atheneum Press, 1976), p. 132.

24. Ibid., p. 141.

25. Degler, "Changing Place," p. 71.

26. Goulden, *Best Years,* p. 141.

27. Ibid., p. 55.

28. Ibid., p. 203.

29. Ibid., p. 204.

30. Jon Tuska, *Closeup: The Contract Director* (Metuchen, N.J.: Scarecrow Press, 1976), p. 398.

31. Naomi Wise, "Working with Hawks," *Take One* (1972), 6:195.

32. Ibid., p. 195.

33. Barbara Bernstein, "That's Not Brave, That's Just Stupid," *Focus: Chicago Film Journal* (Autumn 1972), no. 8, p. 32.

34. Joan Mellen, *Big Bad Wolves* (New York: Pantheon, 1977), p. 242.

35. Ibid., p. 242.

36. Brandon French, *On the Verge of Revolt* (New York: Frederick Unger Press, 1978), p. 148.

37. Ibid., p. 148.

38. Douglas Brode, *Films of the Fifties* (Secaucus, N.J.: Citadel Press, 1976), p. 284.

39. Tom Wood, *The Bright Side of Billy Wilder, Primarily* (New York: Doubleday, 1970), p. 42.

40. Ibid., p. 19.

41. Gerald Mast, *The Comic Mind* (Indianapolis and New York: Bobbs-Merrill, 1973), p. 258.

42. "Movie of the Week," *Life,* September 19, 1949, p. 70.

43. Rev. of *I Was a Male War Bride* (1949), *Newsweek,* September 5, 1949, p. 67.

44. Bosley Crowther, Rev. of *I Was a Male War Bride* (1949), *New York Times,* August 27, 1949, p. 2355.

45. Philip Hartung, Rev. of *Some Like It Hot* (1959), *Commonweal,* March 20, 1959, p. 652.

46. A. H. Weiler, Rev. of *Some Like It Hot* (1959), *New York Times,* March 30, 1959, p. 23.

47. Moira Walsh, Rev. of *Some Like It Hot* (1959), *America,* April 25, 1959, p. 25.

Chapter 3. Male Impersonation Before 1960

1. Molly Haskell, *From Reverence to Rape* (New York: Holt, Rinehart, and Winston, 1973), p. 61.

2. Kalton Lahue, *Continued Next Week: A History of the Motion Picture Serial* (Norman: University of Oklahoma Press, 1964), p. 36.

3. Raymond William Stedman, *The Serials* (Norman, Okla.: University of Oklahoma Press, 1971).

4. Rev. of *Tugboat Annie* (1930), *Newsweek*, August 19, 1930, p. 28.

5. Rev. of *Anna Christie* (1930), *Commonweal*, March 26, 1930, p. 590.

6. Haskell, *From Reverence to Rape*, p. 129.

7. Charles Affron, *Star Acting: Gish, Garbo, Davis* (New York: Dutton, 1977), p. 180.

8. David White and Richard Averson, *Sight, Sound, and Society* (Boston: Beacon Press, 1968), p. 99.

9. Affron, *Star Acting*, p. 179.

10. Haskell, *From Reverence to Rape*, p. 132.

11. Ruth A. Inglis, *Freedom of the Movies* (Chicago: University of Chicago Press, 1947), pp. 122–23.

12. Rev. of *A Song to Remember* (1945), *Commonweal*, February 16, 1945, p. 449.

13. Rev. of *Joan of Arc* (1948), *Time*, November 15, 1948. p. 102.

14. Mr. Harper, rev. of *Joan of Arc* (1948), *Harper's*, January 1949, p. 111.

15. Will Wright, *Six Guns and Society* (Berkeley: University of California Press, 1975), p. 152.

16. Haskell, *From Reverence to Rape*, p. 91.

17. Robert Warshow, "Movie Chronicle: The Westerner," in *The Immediate Experience* (New York: Doubleday, 1962), p. 139.

18. Rev. of *River of No Return* (1953), *Time*, November 23, 1953, p. 114.

19. Rev. of *Annie Get Your Gun* (1950), *Life*, April 17, 1950, p. 174.

20. Ibid.

21. Rev. of *Calamity Jane* (1953), *Time*, November 23, 1953, p. 120.

22. Wright, *Six Guns*, p. 172.

23. Ibid., p. 166.

24. Rev. of *Yellow Sky* (1949), *Life*, January 10, 1949, p. 46.

25. Philip Hartung, rev. of *Johnny Guitar* (1954), *Commonweal*, June 18, 1954, p. 270.

26. Wright, *Six Guns*, p. 172.

27. Rev. of *Cat Ballou* (1965), *Time*, May 21, 1965, p. 107.

28. Jim Kitses, *Horizons West* (Bloomington: Indiana University Press, 1970), p. 158.

29. Manny Farber, Rev. of *Pat and Mike* (1952), *Nation*, August 9, 1952, p. 117.

30. Haskell, *From Reverence to Rape*, p. 92.

31. Raymond Durgnat, *Durgnat on Film* (London: Faber and Faber, 1976), p. 231.

32. Rev. of *Silk Stockings* (1957), *Time*, July 15, 1957, p. 104.

33. Haskell, *From Reverence to Rape*, p. 133.

34. Josef von Sternberg, *Fun in a Chinese Laundry* (New York: Collier, Macmillan, 1965), p. 228.

35. Ibid., p. 246.

36. Ibid., p. 247.

37. Ibid., p. 247.

38. Peter Bogdanovich, *Pieces of Time* (New York: Arbor House, 1973), p. 117.

39. Leo Handel and J. P. Mayer, *Hollywood Looks at Its Audience* (Urbana: University of Illinois Press, 1950), p. 153.

40. Haskell, *From Reverence to Rape*, p. 107.

41. Bogdanovich, *Pieces of Time*, p. 120.

42. Andrew Sarris, *The Films of Josef von Sternberg* (New York: Doubleday, 1966), p. 39.

43. Herman G. Weinberg, *Josef von Sternberg* (New York: Arno Press, 1978), pp. 216–17.

44. Sarris, *Films of Sternberg*, p. 54.

45. Alexander Walker, *Sex in the Movies* (London: Michael Joseph, 1966), p. 94.

46. Rev. of *Sylvia Scarlett* (1935), *Newsweek*, January 4, 1936, p. 25.

47. Rev. of *Sylvia Scarlett* (1935), *Time*, January 13, 1936, p. 43.

48. Haskell, *From Reverence to Rape*, p. 61.

49. Rev. of *First a Girl* (1935), *Time*, January 13, 1936, p. 43.

Chapter 4. 1960–1985: New Directions

1. Susan Sontag, "A Feast for Open Eyes," *Nation*, April 13, 1964, p. 374.

2. Gavin Lambert, *On Cukor* (New York: Putnam, 1972), pp. 154–55.

3. I. C. Jarvie, *Movies as Social Criticism* (Metuchen, N.J.: Scarecrow Press, 1978), p. 128.

4. David White and Richard Averson, *Sight, Sound, and Society* (Boston: Beacon Press, 1968), pp. 204–5.

5. Rev. of *Chelsea Girls*, *Time*, December 30, 1966, p. 37.

6. Jack Kroll, Rev. of *Chelsea Girls*, *Newsweek*, November 14, 1966, p. 109.

7. Richard Schickel, Rev. of *Lonesome Cowboys*, *Life*, June 13, 1969, p. 15.

8. Andrew Sarris, *Confessions of a Cultist* (New York: Simon and Schuster, 1970), p. 276.

9. Robert Sklar, *Movie-Made America* (New York: Random House, 1975), p. 185.

10. Raymond Durgnat, *Durgnat on Film* (London: Faber and Faber, 1976), p. 140.

11. François Truffaut, *Hitchcock*, trans. Helen G. Scott (New York: Simon and Schuster, 1967), p. 205.

12. Ibid., p. 208.

13. Ibid., p. 208.

14. Ibid., p. 211.

15. Ibid., p. 214.

16. James Naremore, *Filmguide to Psycho* (Bloomington: Indiana University Press, 1973), p. 18.

17. Truffaut, *Hitchcock*, p. 214.

18. Leo Braudy, *World in a Frame* (New York: Anchor, Doubleday, 1977), p. 49.

19. "What Ever Happened to the Family Film?" *Life*, February 23, 1962, p. 92.

20. Renata Adler, Rev. of *No Way to Treat a Lady*, *New York Times*, March 21, 1976, p. 56.

21. Rev. of *No Way to Treat a Lady*, *Time*, March 29, 1968, p. 98.

22. John Simon, *Movies into Film* (New York: Dial Press, 1971), p. 194.

23. Pauline Kael, Rev. of *The Damned*, *New Yorker*, January 3, 1970, p. 61.

24. Simon, *Movies into Film*, p. 159.

25. "Adult Subjects Draw Youths," *Variety*, March 20, 1968, p. 78.

26. Dan Wakefield, Rev. of *Lonesome Cowboys*, *Atlantic Monthly*, April 1969, p. 141.

27. Richard Schickel, Rev. of *Performance*, *Life*, October 2, 1970, p. 6.

28. Simon, *Movies into Film*, p. 364.

29. Anne Hollander, *Seeing Through Clothes* (New York: Viking Press, 1978), p. 346.

30. Esther Newton, *Mother Camp* (Chicago: University of Chicago Press, 1972, 1979), pp. 101–2.

31. Naremore, *Filmguide to Psycho*, pp. 30–31.

32. "Vidal Looks for Myra," *Variety*, April 3, 1968, p. 6.

33. Rev. of *Myra Breckenridge*, *Time*, July 6, 1970, p. 70.

34. Joseph Morgenstern, Rev. of *Myra Breckenridge*, *Newsweek*, July 6, 1970, p. 85.

35. Jay Cocks, Rev. of *200 Motels*, *Time*, November 29, 1971, p. 55.

36. Rev. of *Freebie and the Bean*, *Newsweek*, January 13, 1975, p. 71.

37. Janet Maslin, Rev. of *The Tenant*, *Newsweek*, June 28, 1976, p. 78.

38. Jay Cocks, Rev. of *The Tenant*, *Time*, July 26, 1976, p. 68.

39. Colin Westerbeck, Rev. of *The Tenant*, *Commonweal*, August 27, 1976, p. 563.

40. Penelope Gilliat, Rev. of *The Tenant*, *New Yorker*, July 5, 1976, p. 62.

41. "French Comedy Sets U.S. Record for Film in Other Language," *Wall Street Journal*, December 29, 1980, p. 3.

42. David Ansen, Rev. of *La Cage aux folles*, *Newsweek*, August 13, 1979, p. 77.

43. Richard Schickel, Rev. of *La Cage aux folles*, *Time*, August 26, 1979, p. 57.

44. "50 Top Grossing Films," *Variety*, March 4, 1981, p. 11.

45. Bill Henkin, *The Rocky Horror Picture Show Book* (New York: Hawthorn Books, 1979), p. 16.

46. Leo Handel and J. P. Mayer, *Hollywood Looks at Its Audience* (Urbana: Univ. of Illinois Press, 1950), p. 153.

47. David Thompson, *America in the Dark* (New York: William Morrow, 1977), p. 97.

48. Henkin, *Rocky Horror Book*, pp. 106–7.

49. Ibid., p. 23.

50. Henkin, *Rocky Horror Book*, p. 123.

51. Rudolph Karl Bultmann, *Primitive Christianity in Its Contemporary Setting*, trans. R. H. Fuller (New York: Meridian, 1956).

52. Henkin, *Rocky Horror Book*, p. 123.

53. Angela Bonavoglia, "Protesting Chic Porn," *Ms.*, December 1980, p. 26.

Chapter 5. 1960–1985: Other Screens, Other Voices

1. Charlie Eckert, "Capitalism and the Movies," Lecture, Indiana University, Bloomington, Indiana, November 17, 1978.

2. John T. Harzog, Rev. of *The World According to Garp, Film Quarterly,* Winter 1982, p. 44.

3. David Ansen, Rev. of *The World According to Garp, Newsweek,* July 26, 1982, p. 77.

4. Marilyn French, Rev. of *The World According to Garp, Ms.,* September 1982, p. 54.

5. John Lithgow, "My Life as a Woman," *Mademoiselle,* September 1982, pp. 46–47.

6. Ibid., p. 48.

7. Michael Sragow, Rev. of *The World According to Garp, Rolling Stone,* August 19, 1983, p. 34.

8. Ansen, Rev. of *Garp,* p. 79.

9. Richard Grenier, Rev. of *The World According to Garp, Commentary,* September 1982, p. 64.

10. David Ansen, Rev. of *Come Back to the 5 & Dime, Jimmy Dean, Jimmy Dean, Newsweek,* December 20, 1982, p. 90.

11. Lawrence O'Toole, Rev. of *Come Back to the 5 & Dime, Jimmy Dean, Jimmy Dean, Macleans,* January 17, 1983, p. 52.

12. Pauline Kael, Rev. of *Come Back to the 5 & Dime, Jimmy Dean, Jimmy Dean, New Yorker,* November 15, 1982, p. 183.

13. Pauline Kael, Rev. of *Tootsie, New Yorker,* December 27, 1982, p. 71.

14. Richard Schickel, Rev. of *Tootsie, Time,* December 20, 1982, p. 77.

15. Colin Westerbeck, Rev. of *Tootsie, Commonweal,* January 28, 1983, p. 50.

16. Stanley Kauffmann, Rev. of *Tootsie, New Republic,* January 24, 1983, p. 25.

17. John Simon, Rev. of *Tootsie, National Review,* February 4, 1983, p. 132.

18. Westerbeck, Rev. of *Tootsie,* p. 53.

19. Kauffmann, Rev. of *Tootsie*, p. 26.

20. *National Review*, Rev. of *Alien*, July 6, 1979, p. 870.

21. Stanley Kauffmann, Rev. of *Alien*, *New Yorker*, June 11, 1979, p. 154.

22. *New York*, Rev. of *Alien*, June 4, 1979, p. 71.

23. Martin Jackson, Rev. of *Alien*, *USA Today*, September 1979, p. 64.

24. Lawrence O'Toole, Rev. of *Alien*, *Macleans*, June 4, 1979, p. 71.

25. Arthur Schlesinger, Rev. of *Alien*, *Saturday Review*, August 4, 1979, p. 71.

26. Jack Kroll, Rev. of *Alien*, *Newsweek*, May 28, 1979, p. 105.

27. Jeff Walker, "A Secret Too Good To Keep Quiet," *Rolling Stone*, May 31, 1979, p. 31.

28. The names of the various characters seem to have been chosen to indicate their places in this modern morality play on capitalism: Ripley, as in Ripley's believe it or not, a woman as hero; Lambert, the innocent lamb; Dallas, a hero as all-American and gung-ho as his name implies, etc.

29. Walker, "A Secret."

30. Judith Newton, in the "Symposium on *Alien*," *Science Fiction Studies* (1980), 7:295, notes that this is a girly magazine. The defeat of this attack is another indication that Ripley is not going to have sexist stereotypes shoved down her throat.

31. Frank Rich, Rev. of *Alien*, *Time*, June 4, 1979, p. 60.

32. Jackson, Rev. of *Alien*, p. 64.

33. Rich, Rev. of *Alien*, p. 60.

34. Charles Nicol, "The Brutalists: Mean and Ugly," *Saturday Review*, October 1980, p. 14.

35. Samuel R. Delaney, Science Fiction Symposium, "Women World-walkers," Texas Tech University, Lubbock, Texas, January 28, 1983.

36. Peter Fitting, in the "Symposium on *Alien*," *Science Fiction Studies* (1980), 7:289.

37. "Symposium on *Alien*," pp. 296–97.

38. Ibid., p. 278.

39. John Reider, "Embracing the Alien: Science Fiction in Mass Culture," *Science Fiction Studies* (1980), 7:289.

40. Ernest Larsen, Rev. of *Dawn of the Dead* and *Alien*, *Jump Cut* (1980), no. 21, p. 1.

41. Fitting in "Symposium on *Alien*," p. 289.

42. Nicol, "The Brutalists," p. 14.

43. Paul Leggatt, "Science Fiction Films: A Cast of Metaphysical Characters," *Christianity Today*, March 21, 1980, p. 33.

44. Richard Anobile, "Alien," *Publishers Weekly*, August 6, 1979, p. 48.

45. Walker, "A Secret," p. 31.

46. Ibid.

47. Lawrence O'Toole, Rev. of *Victor/Victoria*, *Macleans*, March 29, 1982, p. 59.

48. John Simon, Rev. of *Victor/Victoria*, *National Review*, June 11, 1982, pp. 708–9.

49. Carrie Rickey, "Let Yourself Go," *Film Comment,* March–April 1982, p. 44.

50. Catharine Stimpson, Rev. of *Victor/Victoria, Ms.,* April 1982, p. 38.

51. James M. Wall, Rev. of *Victor/Victoria, Christian Century,* May 5, 1982, p. 547.

52. Richard Corliss, "Toot, Toot, Tooseleh," *Time,* November 21, 1983, p. 93.

53. Jack Kroll, "Barbra, the Yeshiva Boy," *Newsweek,* November 28, 1983, p. 109.

54. David Denby, "Educating Barbra," *New York,* November 28, 1983, p. 111.

55. Jack Kroll, *Newsweek,* November 28, 1983, p. 110.

56. Pauline Kael, "The Perfectionist," *New Yorker,* November 28, 1983, p. 176.

57. Jerry Buck, "Strong Suit," *Austin American Statesman Show World,* March 11, 1984, p. 1.

58. Haskell, *From Reverence to Rape,* pp. 116–17.

59. This seems to hold true even in a film that uses a woman to play a male role without referring directly to the reversal within the context of the film. Peter Weir's *The Year of Living Dangerously* (1982) features Linda Hunt in the role of Billy, who serves as a kind of ethical and emotional bellwether for the rest of the characters.

Chapter 6. Fin de Siècle Anxieties Coming Out

1. Susan Sontag, "Responses to Speech," *Nation,* February 27, 1982, 234:231.

2. Fred Glass, "Totally Recalling Arnold: Sex and Violence in the New Bad Future," *Film Quarterly* (Fall 1990), 44(1):2–13.

3. It should be noted that neither masculine nor feminine dress is simply functional, as a general rule, but traditional female clothing in our culture carries with it more connotative range; having a wider variety, females are generally more accustomed to considering the symbolic or affective dimension of clothing choices, and they are more likely to wear a variety of ornaments in ways that accentuate the "meaning" of the chosen items, in terms of color, symbolism, mood, etc.

4. Gary Colombo, *Rereading America* (New York: St. Martin's, 1989), pp. 5–6.

5. Barbara Dafoe Whitehead writes in the *Atlantic* (April 1992), 271(4):50, that divorce rates peaked at twenty-three divorces thousand by 1979 and leveled off at twenty-one divorces per thousand by 1991. "Home Alone: Top Grosser," *Variety,* January 4, 1993, p. M86.z.

6. Raymond Durgnat, "Amazing Grace: Keeping Up with the Jones Mystique," *American Film,* January–February 1986, pp. 31–35.

7. "Fast-Forward," *American Film,* March 1987, p. 62.

8. Marcia Pally, "Sigourney Takes Control," *Film Comment,* 1986, p. 21.

9. James Kaplan, "Last in Space," *People,* May 29, 1992, pp. 20–24.

10. Kaplan, "Last in Space."

11. Marjorie Garber, *Vested Interests: Cross-Dressing and Cultural Anxiety* (New York: Routledge, 1992), p. 217.

12. E. Deidre Pribram, ed., *Female Spectators* (London: Verso, 1988), p. 152.

13. Garber, *Vested,* p. 211.

14. Ibid., p. 213.

15. In the early eighties, much more controversy surrounded homosexual nun impersonators such as Sister Boom Boom, who led the Sisters of Perpetual Indulgence and who received over twenty-three thousand votes for city supervisor in San Francisco. Garber, *Vested,* p. 214.

16. *Variety,* October 15, 1990, pp. 140–96.

17. Gloria Steinem, "When Thelma Met Louise." *Showtime* Special Presentation, written and produced by Deborah Goodwin and Mary Jo Kaplan, 1992.

18. Sheila Benson, "Thelma and Louise," in Peter Rainer, ed., *Love and Hisses* (San Francisco: Mercury House, 1992), pp. 164–65.

19. Richard Schickel, "Zeitergeist Zone," in Peter Rainer, ed., *Love and Hisses* (San Francisco: Mercury House, 1992), p. 163.

20. Ibid., p. 164.

21. Steinem, *Showtime.*

22. The annual film grosses listed in January were over $42 million, with profitability to the studio of over $20 million, as reported in *Variety,* February 22, 1993, p. A-86.

23. Ibid.

24. The rental is the distributor's share of the box office gross. It is a lower number than total ticket sales and represents more closely than actual profit what is made by the company. Ibid.

25. Profitability for the studio was over $53 million, according to *Variety.* Ibid.

26. Gregg Kilday and Anne Thompson, "The Year at the Box Office," *Entertainment Weekly,* January 22, 1993, p. 15.

27. Peter Rainer, "Male Weepies," in Peter Rainer, ed., *Love and Hisses* (San Francisco: Mercury House, 1992), pp. 170–74.

28. Lyn Elber, "Powerhouse Women Change Television," *Daily Record,* January 8, 1993, p. 14. Lynn Elber is an AP television writer.

29. Bloodworth-Thomason's sexually aggressive lead female character was forced by prime-time demands to marry in order not to offend middle-class sensibilities. The character eventually became the subject of a lawsuit, after some dispute over the use of a real-life person with similar circumstances.

30. *Variety,* October 15, 1990, p. M156.

31. The male character in *Silence of the Lambs* presents yet another issue of transvestism, dealt with in more detail in the discussion of male transvestites.

32. While this film offers a strong female lead, one could argue that the female psychiatrist who wants to adopt Foster's son represents the stereotype of the single, childless career woman as neurotic and cold. But then, such women do exist, and to avoid creating these characters in film may be an arbitrary limitation of human experience.

33. Marlaine Glicksman, "Ms. Treatment," *Film Comment* (December 1985), p. 20.

34. For a detailed analysis of these films, see Lucy Fischer's *Shot Counter-shot* (Princeton: Princeton University Press, 1989).

35. "Fast-Forward," *American Film*, December 1986, p. 55.

36. Faludi, *Backlash* (New York: Crown, 1991), p. 17.

37. "Fast-Forward," *American Film*, March 1987, p. 62.

38. Ibid.

39. Chris Straayer, "Redressing the 'Natural': The Temporary Transvestite Film," *Wide Angle* (January 1992), 14:(1):43.

40. Susan Faludi, *Backlash*, p. 135.

41. According to a number of sources, Lynch originally had a homosexual rape scene here that he eventually deleted from the final cut.

42. Faludi, *Backlash*, p. 138.

43. An interesting feature of Livingston's entry into this subculture is some of the participants' initial assumption that she was a transvestite. Some commented, "You're good," in appreciation of her supposed imitation of a real woman. Personal Interview, Clay Campbell, Albuquerque, New Mexico, May 1992.

44. Although the houses are all-male families, certain men and boys consistently identify themselves as "she," as do the other members of the house.

45. The shift from beauty and glamour to "realness" parallels the shift from conspicuous consumption of the Reagan era to the more preppy look of the Bush administration.

46. Roger Ebert, *Movie Home Companion* (Kansas City: Andrews and McNeel, 1992), p. 489.

47. Henry Louis Gates, Jr., *The Signifying Monkey* (New York: Oxford, 1988).

48. Maureen O'Brian, "Sex: Bestseller and an Apparent Sellout," *Publisher's Weekly*, November 2, 1992, pp. 9–10.

49. E. Ann Kaplan, "Whose Imaginary? The Television Apparatus, the Female Body, and Textual Strategies in Select Rock Videos on MTV," in E. Deidre Pribram, ed., *Female Spectators* (London: Verso, 1988), p. 146.

50. Garber, *Vested*, p. 127.

51. For a more detailed analysis of Beauty and the Beast see the October 1989 issue of *Sight and Sound*.

52. Garber, *Vested*, p. 175–76.

53. "The Misses," *Premiere*, February 1983, p. 80.

54. Linda Hamilton's television role in *Beauty and the Beast* may have created resonances for her well-muscled form in *Terminator 2*.

55. Garber, *Vested*, p. 133.

56. Kilday and Thompson, "The Year at the Box Office."

57. Shelley Levitt, "If You'll Be My Bodyguard," *People,* January 20, 1993, p. 46–50.

58. Pat Dowell, "Not Much Bite," *In These Times,* November 30, 1992, p. 33.

59. Ibid.

60. With the success of *The Crying Game,* Miramax recanted and sent out copies, and the film received six nominations, including best actor and supporting actor (for Rea and Davidson), best picture, director, and original screenplay, and an award for best screenplay.

61. Rea had already played a role that stretched sexual boundaries in *Loose Connections* (1983), a British film in which Rea, pretending to be gay, hooks up with a dedicated feminist and drives to Germany. It should also be noted here that the names of Fergus (the legendary Irish hero) and Jody carry significance, as does Dil, in having mythical or androgynous connotations.

62. Garber, *Vested Interests,* p. 17.

63. Julie Wheelwright, "Opening the Borders," *New Statesman Society,* October 30, 1992, p. 35.

64. The song "The Crying Game" was originally done by Dave Berry and the Cruisers, an androgynous-looking group whose costumes and elaborate hand gestures Jaye Davidson effectively imitates in his lip-synching of the song.

65. Susan Lehman, "A Boffo Year in '92," *Premiere,* February 1993, p. 84.

66. Elliott Stein, "Don Hermosillo and the Sun," *Film Comment,* pp. 53–57.

67. Ibid., pp. 53–57.

68. Ibid.

69. See also "Dialogue on Film, Hector Babenco," *American Film,* April 1986, pp. 13–15.

70. Karen Jaehne, "Two or Three Things We Know About Her/Hooker," *Film Comment,* June 1987, pp. 25–32.

71. Amy Taubin, "Beyond the Sons of Scorsese," *Sight and Sound,* September 1992, p. 37.

72. B. Ruby Rich, "New Queer Cinema," *Sight and Sound,* p. 37; Amy Taubin, "Beyond the Sons of Scorsese."

73. Seun Okewole, "New Queer Cinema: Tom Kalin," *Sight and Sound,* September 1992, p. 37.

74. Clarke Taylor, "Joe and Kenneth and Gertrude and Alice," *American Film,* May 1987, p. 44.

75. Taylor, "Joe and Kenneth," p. 45.

76. Okewole, "New Queer Cinema," p. 31.

77. Steve Daly, "Stoned to Death," *Entertainment Weekly,* January 22, 1993, pp. 58–59.

78. Marlaine Glicksman, "Irish Eyes," *Film Comment,* pp. 9–11, 68–71. Interview with Neil Jordan.

79. Garber, *Vested Interests,* p. 142.

80. Rich, "New Queer Cinema."

81. David Ansen, "Poison," in Peter Rainer, ed., *Love and Hisses* (San Francisco: Mercury House, 1992), pp. 103–4.

Index